Patricia A. Crist, PhD, OTR/.
Marjorie E. Scaffa, PhD, OT.
Editors

D0303773

Best Practices
in Occupational Therapy
Education

Best Practices in Occupational Therapy Education has been co-published simultaneously as *Occupational Therapy in Health Care*, Volume 18, Numbers 1/2 2004.

The Haworth Press, Inc.
New York

Best Practices in Occupational Therapy Education

Patricia A. Crist, PhD, OTR/L, FAOTA
Marjorie E. Scaffa, PhD, OTR, FAOTA
Editors

Best Practices in Occupational Therapy Education has been co-published simultaneously as *Occupational Therapy in Health Care*, Volume 18, Numbers 1/2 2004.

The Haworth Press, Inc.

New York • London • Victoria (AU)
www.HaworthPress.com

Best Practices in Occupational Therapy Education has been co-published simultaneously as *Occupational Therapy in Health Care*™, Volume 18, Numbers 1/2 2004.

The development, preparation, and publication of this work has been undertaken with great care. However, the publisher, employees, editors, and agents of The Haworth Press and all imprints of The Haworth Press, Inc., including The Haworth Medical Press® and Pharmaceutical Products Press®, are not responsible for any errors contained herein or for consequences that may ensue from use of materials or information contained in this work. Opinions expressed by the author(s) are not necessarily those of The Haworth Press, Inc. With regard to case studies, identities and circumstances of individuals discussed herein have been changed to protect confidentiality. Any resemblance to actual persons, living or dead, is entirely coincidental.

Cover design by Jennifer Gaska

Library of Congress Cataloging-in-Publication Data

Best practices in occupational therapy education / Patricia Crist, Marjorie E. Scaffa, editors.
    p. cm.
"Best Practices in Occupational Therapy Education has been co-published simultaneously as Occupational Therapy in Health Care, Volume 18, Numbers 1/2 2004."
Includes bibliographical references and index.
ISBN 0-7890-2175-7 (hard cover : alk. paper) – ISBN 0-7890-2176-5 (soft cover : alk. paper)
1. Occupational therapy–Study and teaching. I. Crist, Patricia A. Hickerson. II. Scaffa, Marjorie E. III. Occupational therapy in health care.
RM735.42.B47 2004
615.8'515'071–dc22

                            2004008132

Indexing, Abstracting & Website/Internet Coverage

Occupational Therapy in Health Care

This section provides you with a list of major indexing & abstracting services. That is to say, each service began covering this periodical during the year noted in the right column. Most Websites which are listed below have indicated that they will either post, disseminate, compile, archive, cite or alert their own Website users with research-based content from this work. (This list is as current as the copyright date of this publication.)

<u>Abstracting, Website/Indexing Coverage</u> . . . . <u>Year When Coverage Began</u>

- *Abstracts in Social Gerontology: Current Literature on Aging* **1989**

- *Academic Abstracts/CD-ROM* **1995**

- *Biology Digest (in print & online)* **1990**

- *Biosciences Information Service of Biological Abstracts (BIOSIS),*
  a centralized source of life science information
  <http://www.biosis.org> . . . . *

- *Brandon/Hill Selected List of Journals in Allied Health Sciences*
  <http://www.mssm.edu/library/brandon-hill > **2000**

- *Cambridge Scientific Abstracts (Health & Safety Science Abstracts)*
  <http://www.csa.com> **1985**

- *CINAHL (Cumulative Index to Nursing & Allied Health*
  Literature) <http://www.cinahl.com> **1987**

- *EMBASE/Excerpta Medica Secondary Publishing Division*
  <http://www.elsevier.nl> **1985**

(continued)

(continued)

* Exact start date to come.

Special Bibliographic Notes related to special journal issues (separates) and indexing/abstracting:

- indexing/abstracting services in this list will also cover material in any "separate" that is co-published simultaneously with Haworth's special thematic journal issue or DocuSerial. Indexing/abstracting usually covers material at the article/chapter level.
- monographic co-editions are intended for either non-subscribers or libraries which intend to purchase a second copy for their circulating collections.
- monographic co-editions are reported to all jobbers/wholesalers/approval plans. The source journal is listed as the "series" to assist the prevention of duplicate purchasing in the same manner utilized for books-in-series.
- to facilitate user/access services all indexing/abstracting services are encouraged to utilize the co-indexing entry note indicated at the bottom of the first page of each article/chapter/contribution.
- this is intended to assist a library user of any reference tool (whether print, electronic, online, or CD-ROM) to locate the monographic version if the library has purchased this version but not a subscription to the source journal.
- individual articles/chapters in any Haworth publication are also available through the Haworth Document Delivery Service (HDDS).

Best Practices in Occupational Therapy Education

CONTENTS

PREPARATION FOR COMMUNITY-BASED PRACTICE

EDITORS' INVITED COMMENTARY ON PROFESSIONAL ISSUES

ABOUT THE EDITORS

Patricia A. Crist, PhD, OTR/L, FAOTA, is Founding Chair and Professor for the Department of Occupational Therapy at Duquesne University in Pittsburgh, Pennsylvania. Dr. Crist has numerous publications including *Innovations in OT Education* (co-editor), the self-study, *Meeting the Fieldwork Challenge* (co-author), and the popular *Fieldwork Issue* column in *OT Advance*. She recently co-edited *Education for Occupational Therapy in Health Care: Strategies for the New Millennium* through The Haworth Press. Dr. Crist has completed numerous scholarly works regarding fieldwork education, mental health interventions, parents with disabilities and research. Currently, she is President of the Board of Directors of the National Board for Certification in Occupational Therapy. She is a Fellow of the American Occupational Therapy Association.

Marjorie E. Scaffa, PhD, OTR, FAOTA, is Associate Professor and Chairperson of the Department of Occupational Therapy at the University of South Alabama in Mobile, and of the OT therapy program she founded in 1993. She is the editor of the book *Occupational Therapy in Community-Based Practice Settings.* Dr. Scaffa has worked in a number of clinical and community settings, including inpatient rehabilitation, home health, long-term care, hospice, alcohol/drug prevention and treatment programs, and community mental health. She served as an editorial board menber for the *American Journal of Occupational Therapy* from 1997-1999 and is a Fellow of the American Occupational Therapy Association.

Message from the Editors

We are proud to present to you our second special volume focusing on innovation and scholarship in education.[1] We commend Anne Dickerson, OTHC editor, for her desire to further the art and science of education in occupational therapy. Also, we recognize The Haworth Press, Inc. for the publication of this resource which will contribute to the knowledge and practice of occupational therapy.

He, who dares to teach, must never cease to learn.

–Richard Henry Dana

A new set of ideas and models are presented in this volume. All authors were required to present outcomes to support their thesis or learning objectives, as time has come to move beyond the art of teaching in education. We must provide evidence to support our claims regarding our choice in teaching approaches that maximize the professional development of students for entry-level practice. Only through continuing to study teaching in the classroom and through fieldwork will we be able to substantiate the best practices in education. This is the motivation that sustains us as editors and, hopefully, will provide impetus for a third volume regarding education in the future!

We commend all authors who submitted manuscripts for competitive review. You were willing to subject your educational approaches to scrutiny. We regret that we were unable to publish more as our submissions this time were higher in number and more developed. We urge you and many other aca-

[Haworth co-indexing entry note]: "Message from the Editors." Crist, Patricia A., and Marjorie E. Scaffa. Co-published simultaneously in *Occupational Therapy in Health Care* (The Haworth Press, Inc.) Vol. 18, No. 1/2, 2004, pp. 1-3; and: *Best Practices in Occupational Therapy Education* (ed: Patricia A. Crist, and Marjorie E. Scaffa) The Haworth Press, Inc., 2004, pp. 1-3. Single or multiple copies of this article are available for a fee from The Haworth Document Delivery Service [1-800-HAWORTH, 9:00 a.m. - 5:00 p.m. (EST). E-mail address: docdelivery@haworthpress.com].

Digital Object Identifier:10.1300/J003v18n01_01

demic and fieldwork educators to engage in the challenge of studying our educational practices and converting preference into documentation of claims.

This publication has grouped information around five major headings: *Fieldwork Education; Instructional Methods; Focus on Student Professional Development; Instructional Technology;* and *Preparation for Community-Based Practice.* Scanning the table of contents, you will find full manuscripts demonstrating sufficient depth, specificity and outcomes that can be used to guide innovative application and/or best practices in recognizable educational approaches. Since we support innovation, some ideas are very new or focused; we accepted several works as "Brief or New" to encourage new insights, enrich educational practices, as well as provide impetus for future study by others.

We could not have completed this activity without the help of key individuals. First, we want to thank the invitational editorial board for this special collection. Each ended up reviewing more manuscripts than anticipated but also, provided exceptional input to evaluate each carefully and assist the editors in editing, re-reviewing and selection responsibilities. The board participants were:

Martha Branson Banks   Alfred Bracciano
Denise Chisholm   Mary Metzger-Edwards
Erika Gisel   Dyhalma Irizarry
Elizabeth Kanny   Scott McPhee
Penny Moyers   Jaime Muñoz
Ruth Schemm   Patricia Scott
Julie Shaperman   Perri Stern
Randy Strickland   Patricia Stutz-Tanenbaum
Pam Toto   Donna Whitehouse

As senior editor, I want to commend Heidi Benner, who on this edition, as well as the 2002 publication, provided exemplary organizational, tracking and communication activities for the editors and authors. We thank her for weaving this task into her multi-tasking daily activities as the department's administrative assistant at Duquesne.

To the occupational therapy students who benefit from this information through improved teaching, we remind you of the following:

> *I am not a teacher; only a fellow traveler of whom you*
> *asked the way. I pointed ahead–ahead of myself as well*
> *as you.*
>
> *–George Bernard Shaw*

We hope that you find this publication stimulating and valuable. Join us in celebrating excellence in education and all those educators, both academic and fieldwork, who share the passion with us for we all know that . . .

> *Education is not the filling of a pail*
> *But the lighting of a fire!*
>
> *–William Butler Yeats*

We dedicate this publication to our fellow educators, past, present and future, who share the desire to improve our teaching in the classroom, lab, community and fieldwork.

> *Learning is pleasurable but "doing" is the height of enjoyment.*
>
> *–Novali,* German poet

Special Volume Editors:

Patricia A. Crist, PhD, OTR/L, FAOTA
Founding Chair and Professor
Duquesne University
Pittsburgh, PA

Marjorie E. Scaffa, PhD, OTR, FAOTA
Founding Chair and Associate Professor
University of South Alabama
Mobile, AL

NOTE

1. The first special issue was published in 2001 by the editors titled: *Education for Occupational Therapy in Health Care: Strategies for the New Millennium.*

Supervisor and Student Expectations of Level II Fieldwork

Kimberly A. Vogel, BFA, MS in OT, EdD, OTR
Kimatha Oxford Grice, MOT, OTR, CHT
Stephanie Hill, MOT, OTR
James Moody, MOT, OTR

SUMMARY. *Objective:* The purpose was to learn if fieldwork supervisors have greater expectations of students beginning Level II fieldwork

Kimberly A. Vogel is Associate Professor, University of Texas Health Science Center at San Antonio, Department of Occupational Therapy, Mail Code 6245, 7703 Floyd Curl Drive, San Antonio, TX 78229-3900 (E-mail: vogel@uthscsa.edu). Kimatha Oxford Grice is Associate Professor, University of Texas Health Science Center at San Antonio, San Antonio, TX. Stephanie Hill is associated with Playworks, Pediatric Therapy Services, Dallas, TX. James Moody is associated with Christus Santa Rosa Hospital, San Antonio, TX.

The authors would like to thank the fieldwork supervisors and students who participated in this study; occupational therapy department chair and faculty members: Gale Haradon, PhD, OTR, FAOTA, Alison Beck, PhD, OTR, BCP, and Karin Barnes, PhD, OTR, for reviewing and providing feedback for the questionnaires; and Betty Hall, Administrative Assistant I, for helping with survey collection. Special thanks to John Schoolfield, Programmer Analyst III, for giving instruction and advice regarding statistical analysis.

[Haworth co-indexing entry note]: "Supervisor and Student Expectations of Level II Fieldwork." Vogel, Kimberly A. et al. Co-published simultaneously in *Occupational Therapy in Health Care* (The Haworth Press, Inc.) Vol. 18, No. 1/2, 2004, pp. 5-19; and: *Best Practices in Occupational Therapy Education* (ed: Patricia A. Crist, and Marjorie E. Scaffa) The Haworth Press, Inc., 2004, pp. 5-19. Single or multiple copies of this article are available for a fee from The Haworth Document Delivery Service [1-800-HAWORTH, 9:00 a.m. - 5:00 p.m. (EST). E-mail address: docdelivery@haworthpress.com].

http://www.haworthpress.com/web/OTHC
Digital Object Identifier:10.1300/J003v18n01_02

compared to five years ago and how these compared to student expectations. Supervision was examined.

Methods: Data were obtained through questionnaires from 81 fieldwork supervisors and 29 students doing second fieldwork rotations.

Results: Supervisors have higher expectations of students. Supervisor and student expectations agreed. Demands of health care environments and new educational requirements influenced these changes. Supervisors still use traditional supervisory techniques.

Conclusion: Findings give insight into expectations of current students and help universities develop programs that better prepare students for fieldwork. *[Article copies available for a fee from The Haworth Document Delivery Service: 1-800-HAWORTH. E-mail address: <docdelivery@ haworthpress.com> Website: <http://www.HaworthPress.com> © 2004 by The Haworth Press, Inc. All rights reserved.]*

KEYWORDS. Fieldwork, education, supervision

Traditionally, fieldwork has been the place for occupational therapy students to become proficient in their skills and build on the knowledge base they received in the academic portion of their program. However, according to feedback from recent graduates, supervisors appear to have greater expectations of beginning skill level for students entering Level II fieldwork experience as compared to five years ago. The purpose of this study was to investigate whether supervisors' expectations of students have increased, and if so, what may have contributed to this change. Additionally, supervisory style and teaching techniques were explored to see if they have changed, reflecting apparent greater expectations. Student expectations were also examined, in particular, if the knowledge and skill levels students anticipated as being expected of them prior to beginning Level II fieldwork were similar to or different from what supervisors actually expected of them during Level II fieldwork.

LITERATURE REVIEW

Level II fieldwork experience is an important component of the educational process in preparing occupational therapy students for entry into practice. The purpose of Level II fieldwork is to provide opportunities for occupational therapy students to apply theories and techniques and to develop skills (AOTA, Commission on Education, 1984, p. 1). Supervised fieldwork experience is intended to promote students' development into competent, entry-level practitioners.

Once an occupational therapist agrees to supervise students for fieldwork placements, he or she undertakes several responsibilities in training occupational therapy students to become professionals. The supervisor serves many roles during fieldwork education, such as mentor, role model, and evaluator. A study of effective/ineffective supervisor characteristics by Christie, Joyce, and Moeller (1985) emphasized the importance of the supervisor as the determining factor in a good versus poor fieldwork experience (p. 681). Although there is little formal training required to be a fieldwork supervisor, through experience, therapists develop the skills, attitudes, and values to supervise students (AOTA, Commission on Education, 1984, p. 93).

Students have a number of responsibilities in the fieldwork education process as well. They take an active role in applying classroom learning to develop practical skills and achieve competency (AOTA, Commission on Education, 1984, p. 1). Students assume patient caseloads, use appropriate assessments and treatment interventions, communicate and document information correctly, and practice interpersonal skills with patients and health care staff to develop characteristics of a professional (Cara, 1998). Through "doing," the student learns how to become independent in thinking, decision-making, and functioning as an occupational therapy practitioner. Students must be active participants in the fieldwork education process by identifying their own learning styles and goals, collaborating with their supervisor in developing strategies to meet their needs, and providing feedback to their supervisors to ensure their fieldwork experience has the best potential for success (Gaiptman & Anthony, 1989).

Although no two occupational therapy students are alike, they can share similar concerns such as issues related to the transition from the academic setting to the fieldwork environment (Frum & Opacich, 1987). Many students are both excited and apprehensive about beginning Level II fieldwork experience. In moving to the fieldwork setting, a student must adjust to a different situation in which the focus is no longer student-centered, but client-centered. The student must take on new responsibilities and become more self-reliant in thinking and behavior as he or she can no longer rely on the predictable structure and available support of faculty and peers in the academic world (Cohn, 1998). These transitions from school to fieldwork education can be quite stressful. While students are generally enthusiastic about finally putting into practice the theories and techniques learned during the didactic portion of their education, they may be anxious and concerned about shifting from the student role to entry-level practitioner role.

In order to facilitate easier transition for students, supervisors should be aware of student perceptions about the move to the fieldwork environment, help promote the use of healthy coping skills, and be sensitive to individual differences in ability to adapt to change. According to Frum and Opacich (1987), the relationship between the supervisor and student is the means through which knowledge is shared (p. 1). Often, supervisors and students have different assumptions and expectations about the supervisory process. Supervisors usually have an idea of the level of competence needed to function effectively in their setting, while students may have certain expectations based on previous interactions with individuals in authority (Cohn, 1998, p. 794). The disparity in beliefs about supervision can cause conflict, which could interfere with learning. Interpersonal difficulties between supervisors and students can be due to a lack of communication and awareness of each other's expectations (Frum & Opacich, 1987). Supervisors may anticipate a high degree of independence from the student, when students, on the other hand, may expect a high degree of structure and direction. The goals of the supervisor and student may also be different, with the supervisor focusing on guiding the student towards becoming a professional and the student concentrating on learning treatment techniques (Cara, 1998). Expectations on both sides need to be clearly identified and discussed at the onset of fieldwork placement to ensure the supervisor/student relationship is effective.

Managed care and reimbursement issues are also having a great impact on the clinical environment, and therefore on supervisory approaches and techniques for educating occupational therapy students. Cost containment changes have resulted in occupational therapy practitioners having to make major adjustments in services delivery. Today, there are greater demands for productivity in patient treatment, and therapists must develop ongoing strategies to provide more efficient services, while maintaining quality patient care. Because of decreased operating budgets, many facilities have also reduced occupational therapist positions, causing staff shortages in which the remaining few practitioners are required to take on larger patient caseloads. In order to ensure reimbursement, therapists spend more time now in documentation to meet the constant demand by managed care to justify the need for occupational therapy services (Punwar, 2000a). Higher productivity, larger caseloads, and increased documentation requirements because of managed care all have altered occupational therapy practice and have affected fieldwork education as well. Fieldwork supervisors are now faced with new challenges to cope effectively with the changing health care environment, while still devoting time and efforts toward providing meaningful learning experiences for students (Kautzmann, 1990).

Changes in the educational requirements for occupational therapy students will also influence Level II fieldwork. In 1999, the AOTA's Representative Assembly passed Resolution J, which proposed moving entry-level education for occupational therapists from a baccalaureate to a master's level by the year 2007 (Barrett, 2001). Revised educational standards were also implemented shortly before this change. The new *Standards for an Accredited Educational Program for the Occupational Therapist* (ACOTE, 1998) require students to be prepared as new graduates to take on expanded occupational therapy roles of "manager, researcher, educator, advocate, and entrepreneur" (Punwar, 2000b, p. 56). As a result, academic programs and fieldwork supervisors "must prepare students differently, with a focus on more complex curriculum objectives, advanced reasoning skills, and a readiness to practice in emerging practice areas" (Barrett, 2001, p. 17). Additionally, students will be expected to learn more independently (Barrett, 2001, p. 17).

The purpose of this study was to look at changes in the provision of Level II fieldwork. In this study, researchers explored whether supervisors' expectations of students have increased compared to five years ago, along with factors that may be contributing to fieldwork changes. Expected levels of proficiency for specific performance skills were examined, as were supervisory approaches and techniques. What students anticipated as being expected of them prior to beginning Level II fieldwork was also compared to what supervisors actually expected of them during fieldwork experience. Researchers hoped to gain insight into current fieldwork programs, which could, in turn, help academic educators better prepare occupational therapy students before they embark on their Level II fieldwork education.

METHOD

Subjects

Subjects in this study included both fieldwork supervisors and occupational therapy students involved in Level II fieldwork. Questionnaires were sent to 244 fieldwork supervisors at facilities with which the university has fieldwork contracts. These sites included inpatient, outpatient, acute, rehabilitation, long-term care, school, and private practice settings. A total of 84 questionnaires were returned by practitioners for a response rate of 34%. Three of these questionnaires were unusable because they were incomplete. Questionnaires were also sent to 32 undergraduate students from the university's occupational therapy program. These students were currently in the first two weeks of their second rotation of Level II fieldwork (June-September 2000). A total of 29 questionnaires were returned by the students for a response rate of 91%.

Instruments

A practitioner's questionnaire and a student's questionnaire were developed by two occupational therapy instructors in response to a number of students expressing anxiety about perceived lack of preparation for Level II fieldwork. The two questionnaires were designed to investigate expectations of fieldwork supervisors and students regarding Level II fieldwork experience. The practitioner's questionnaire consisted of four parts: Part I: Expectations of Student Performance; Part II: Performance Skills; Part III: Student Learning and Supervision at Fieldwork Site; and Part IV: Therapist Characteristics. In Parts I, II, and IV, the items were arranged as questions with multiple choice answer formats, where participants could check "yes" or "no" or check all choices that applied. Part II asked participants to rank their expectations of students' level of proficiency in doing 20 psychomotor skills, using a 1, 2, or 3 gradation. Clear definitions of the meaning of 1, 2, and 3 were given. An N/A choice was also available. Measurement scales were nominal and ordinal. A comments section was included to allow practitioners to discuss issues not addressed by the questionnaire. The student's questionnaire included an equivalent Performance Skills part along with two additional questions for comparison to the practitioner's responses regarding expectations of student performance. The practitioner's questionnaire was pilot tested by three other occupational therapy department faculty members who provided feedback for modifications. The faculty also reviewed and commented on the student questionnaire.

Procedure

Letters were sent to fieldwork supervisors and occupational therapy students to explain the study and to request their participation by completing the enclosed questionnaire. Envelopes were coded for anonymity and checked off upon return by the occupational therapy department administrative assistant. Researchers were blind to identification of the returned questionnaires. A follow-up letter was sent to occupational therapy students one month after the initial mailing because of slow returns.

Data Analyses

Raw data from questionnaires were analyzed using the Statistical Package for the Social Sciences (SPSS) version 10.0. Analyses involved descriptive statistics, including frequency counts, percentages, and means; tests for significant differences, including Pearson's chi-square tests, binomial tests, and

Mann-Whitney U tests; and tests for correlation, using Spearman rho. Comments from practitioners were reviewed for frequency of qualitative themes.

RESULTS

Expectations of Student Performance

By questionnaire, the practitioners were first asked to compare expectations of fieldwork students five years ago (or the earliest fieldwork student supervised if < 5yrs) with expectations of current fieldwork students, and to decide if there are now greater expectations. More than half (67.9%) of the practitioners indicated that yes, expectations of current students have increased. A binomial test of this figure showed that this observed proportion of respondents was significantly different from 50%.

The practitioners who answered yes were then asked to identify areas (performance, judgment, and/or attitude) in which greater expectations of students were required. Among the three areas, greater expectations were called for in judgment (87.3%), followed by performance (76.4%), and then attitude (65.5%).

Practitioners were next asked to indicate whether there were greater expectations of students beginning their second rotation of fieldwork as compared to expectations for students beginning their first rotation. Most of the respondents (91.3%) reported yes, that higher expectations existed for those students beginning their second rotation of Level II fieldwork.

This same question was asked of students regarding supervisors' expectations at the beginning of second rotations versus at the beginning of first rotations. Of the respondents, 51.7% signified that they felt more was expected of them, 37.9% that expectations were about the same, and 10.3% that less was expected of them by supervisors when starting second Level II fieldwork. A comparison of practitioners' and students' data on this question using chi-square showed that there is a significant relationship between the two groups' expectations of knowledge for beginning their second fieldwork rotation (p < .01). Practitioners and students agreed that expectations were greater for second rotation versus first rotation of Level II fieldwork.

Researchers were also interested in student expectations of Level II fieldwork, which was the motivation for this study. Students' concern about their preparedness for fieldwork prompted a question about comparisons of what students anticipated as being expected of them before beginning their Level II fieldwork versus what supervisors actually expected of them during the fieldwork experience. Of the student respondents, 48.3% said that actual and anticipated expectations were about the same, 27.6% said that less was actually expected of them than was anticipated, and 24.1% said that more was actually expected of them than what was anticipated.

Performance Skills

Another objective of this study was to examine expected levels of proficiency for specific performance skills. For this, practitioners were asked to review a list of 20 randomly selected psychomotor skills and tasks and to rate them according to whether they (1) had no expectations of students knowing how to do the skill or task, (2) expected students to have a general idea of how to do the skill or task, or (3) expected students to already know how to do the skill or task at the beginning of their first rotation of Level II fieldwork. Students were also asked to review the same list of psychomotor skills and tasks and to likewise rate them according to the level of proficiency their supervisors expected them to have when beginning their first rotation of Level II fieldwork. Frequency counts for practitioners' data and students' data were calculated. Levels of proficiency for specific performance skills by category of highest frequency were reported (see Table 1). A general trend emerged showing that practitioners and students agreed that students should have a general idea of how to do most of these skills or already know how to do them with some proficiency. When chi-square tests were used to compare practitioners' and students' ratings of each skill or task, they showed that there was a significant relationship ($p < .05$) only between the two group's answers on "evaluating a patient using FIMS or WEEFIMS scales" and "carrying out balancing activities on a ball with a young child with a traumatic brain injury." Both agreed that the student is expected to have a general idea of how to do these skills.

Student Learning and Supervision at Fieldwork Site

In this study, researchers also wished to explore changes in supervision and techniques fieldwork supervisors used in teaching students. When practitioners were asked to compare time spent directly teaching students five years ago with current students, 53.1% of respondents replied that they spent about the same amount of time directly teaching students, 28.4% that they spent more time now, and 18.5% that they spent less time than five years ago. A chi-square test was conducted to examine whether there was a relationship between time spent directly teaching students now and increased expectations of current students; however, no significant relationship was found.

TABLE 1. Performance Skills

Levels of Proficiency Expected	
Practitioners	**Students**
No Expectation	**No Expectation**
	Demonstrate directions for decoupage activity to psychiatric pts.
	Demonstrate procedure for pts. to do Box and Block test
General Idea	**General Idea**
Demonstrate use of reacher to THR pt.	Demonstrate use of reacher to THR pt.
Demonstrate proper lifting techniques to pts.	Demonstrate proper lifting techniques to pts.
Set up supplies for 8 pts. for an arts and crafts group	Set up supplies for 8 pts. for an arts and crafts group
Demonstrate dressing techniques for a CVA pt.	Demonstrate dressing techniques for a CVA pt.
Assist hemiplegic pt. with a 90 degree pivot transfer	Assist hemiplegic pt. with a 90 degree pivot transfer
Fabricate a simple resting splint from a thermoplastic material	Fabricate a simple resting splint from a thermoplastic material
Carry out balancing activities on a ball with a child with TBI *	Carry out balancing activities on a ball with a child with TBI *
Elicit a righting reaction in a child with hypotonic CP	Elicit a righting reaction in a child with hypotonic CP
Write a complete treatment plan, including evaluation summary, goals, and plan of action	Write a complete treatment plan, including evaluation summary, goals, and plan of action
Carry out an NDT muscle elongation technique with a child with spastic CP	Carry out an NDT muscle elongation technique with a child with spastic CP
Write a discharge summary and home education program	Write a discharge summary and home education program
Evaluate a pt. using FIMS or WEEFIMS scales *	Evaluate a pt. using FIMS or WEEFIMS scales *
Demonstrate directions for decoupage activity to psychiatric pts.	Carry out PROM on an UE joint
Demonstrate procedure for pts. to do Box and Block test	Position pt. and carry out MMT of UE
Already Know	**Already Know**
Collapse and store wheelchairs in storage area	Collapse and store wheelchairs in storage area
Use a dynamometer to measure pt.'s grip strength	Use a dynamometer to measure pt.'s grip strength
Use a goniometer to measure a pt.'s ROM	Use a goniometer to measure a pt.'s ROM
Use a pinch meter to measure tip pinch strength	Use a pinch meter to measure tip pinch strength
Position pt. and carry out MMT of UE	
Carry out PROM on an UE joint	

Practitioners were also asked if their expectations of current students to take initiative, responsibility, and to learn independently were different than their expectations of students five years ago. More than half (55.6%) of practitioners reported that they did have greater expectations of current students doing independent learning compared to students five years ago, with 44.4% saying that their expectations were about the same. None of the practitioners reported having decreased expectations of students regarding independent learning. A chi-square test was then utilized to investigate whether there was a relationship between increased expectations of independent learning and greater expectations of current students, with the results indicating that there was a significant relationship between these two variables (p < .01).

In addition, given a list of various teaching techniques, practitioners were asked to identify which they employed when supervising Level II fieldwork students. Techniques used were "student tries hands-on with parts of the procedure under direct supervision" (100%), "student gradually carries out more and more of the evaluation and treatment process with observation" and "student receives positive and negative feedback from supervisor" (98.8%), "student meets with supervisor to discuss clinical issues" and "student observes supervisor doing procedure" (97.5%), "student is challenged to verbally justify his/her critical thinking process" (95.1%), "direct in-sight supervision is gradually withdrawn as student demonstrates increased competency in patient care" (91.4%), and "student demonstrates accepted level of skill through competency testing" (48.1%). Some practitioners (13.6%) reported various additional supervisory techniques specific to the particular fieldwork setting that were not listed on the questionnaire.

Therapist Characteristics

This study also examined the work and supervisory experience of participating practitioners and inquired about their job responsibilities. Of the respondents, practitioners reported having worked an average of 13.4 years (range = 3 to 31 years) and having supervised Level II students an average of 8.9 years (range = 1 to 26 years). Mann-Whitney U tests were utilized to investigate whether there was a relationship between higher expectations of current students and practitioners' years in occupational therapy practice or practitioners' years as a supervisor. Results indicated that there was no significant relationship between higher expectations of students and practitioners' work or supervisory experience.

Researchers were also interested in changes in practitioners' job responsibilities and if and how job responsibilities affect the supervision of Level II students. When asked whether job responsibilities have increased over the last two years, most practitioners (91.1%) reported that responsibilities have increased, with 7.6% reporting that responsibilities have stayed the same, and 1.3% that responsibilities have decreased. A chi-square test was used to explore whether there was a relationship between increased job responsibilities and higher expectations of current students, however, no significant relationship was found between these variables. Increased job responsibilities were also compared to the amount of time spent teaching students on Level II fieldwork. A Spearman rho test determined there was no significant relationship between practitioners' greater job responsibilities and time practitioners spend directly teaching current students.

Practitioners who have experienced greater job responsibilities were next asked to identify in which areas of practice have responsibilities increased. Of those who responded, 77.8% indicated that more administrative duties were required, 61.1% that there were more patient care and documentation duties, 40.3% that they had more students to supervise (including volunteers, Level I and Level II students), and 11.1% of respondents reported additional areas of increased job responsibilities not listed on the questionnaire. These responsibilities included such tasks as more participation in committees, keeping up with insurance changes, and more time supervising certified occupational therapy assistants.

Additionally, practitioners were asked how greater job responsibilities have affected the supervision of Level II students. Practitioners reported the following as a result of more job responsibilities: 60.8% have more experiences to share with students, 54.1% have higher expectations of students, 37.8% have less time to spend teaching and supervising students, 17.6% are less willing to take students, 13.5% listed a variety of other influences on student supervision, and 4.1% indicated that they can no longer take students because of increased job responsibilities. While many practitioners responded that increased job responsibilities increased expectations of students and decreased time spent teaching students, statistically significant relationships were not demonstrated among these variables (as stated in the previous section).

DISCUSSION

The results of this study indicate that expectations of students beginning Level II fieldwork have increased as compared to five years ago, especially in the areas of judgment, initiative, responsibility, and independent learning. According to practitioner survey responses, a number of factors have contributed to these greater student expectations in recent years. It is appropriate that students are now expected to take on more responsibility for their own learning experiences. In light of the new educational *Standards*, academic curricula will be preparing students differently by placing more emphasis on clinical reasoning and problem-solving skills, as well as greater understanding of the multiple and emerging roles of the occupational therapist. New graduates at the post baccalaureate level will be held to higher educational standards, and therefore fieldwork experiences must change as well. Fieldwork supervisors will need to develop programs consistent with the revised curricula that require an advanced level of study for students because fieldwork is intended to be compatible with and an extension of academic education. As the educational requirements for occupational therapy students increase, so must the expectations of students to take on expanded responsibilities during fieldwork education.

Aside from the new *Standards* for occupational therapy programs, a number of additional factors have influenced changes in expectations of students. Most of the practitioners in this study reported having increased job responsibilities as compared to two years ago, due to the demands of the managed care environment, i.e., larger caseloads, more documentation, and more administrative duties. Greater job demands for fieldwork supervisors can affect the provision of Level II fieldwork for students. Fieldwork supervisors are challenged to handle escalated job responsibilities while still finding time to provide effective learning experiences for students. Given the many demands on practitioners in today's workplace, it would be reasonable to suspect that fieldwork supervisors devote less time now to student teaching. Study results, however, indicated that even though job responsibilities for practitioners have increased and more is expected of current students, fieldwork supervisors perceive that they still spend the same amount of time or more time directly teaching students. While it would seem that these responses are contradictory, researchers postulate that these findings speak to practitioners' commitments to providing fieldwork education to occupational therapy students. Despite major adjustments in occupational therapy practice because of changes in the health care system, fieldwork supervisors remain dedicated to the educational process necessary for the development of future practitioners. Another positive outcome of this study was practitioners' recognition that although their jobs are more complex, they believe their increased job responsibilities offered more experiences to share with students.

The supervisory approaches and teaching techniques utilized by the fieldwork supervisors who responded to the survey are compatible with those traditionally used to gradually progress occupational therapy students towards entry-level competency. During fieldwork experience, students are initially provided a high degree of direction and supervision as they get acclimated to practice in the fieldwork setting. Over time, students are assigned more responsibilities with guidance and feedback from their supervisors as they demonstrate greater proficiency with practice skills. The fact that most of the practitioners applied similar methods of supervision supports the idea that these traditional supervisory approaches and techniques are still effective for facilitating the growth and development of students into entry-level occupational therapy practitioners.

Students about to begin Level II fieldwork tend to be understandably anxious about transitioning from the classroom to the practice setting. The change will require adaptation to a new environment, new activities and responsibilities, and new roles. Some students may feel unprepared for this important transition to fieldwork education, as was expressed by several students from our program who were about to enter Level II fieldwork experience. The students' apprehensions about fieldwork centered on their perceptions of what would be expected of them by fieldwork supervisors. When comparing what students anticipated being expected of them with what supervisors actually expected of them during fieldwork, results from Parts I, II, and IV indicated that student and supervisor expectations were mostly in agreement. In Part II, a comparison of expected proficiency levels for a sample of specific performance skills likewise revealed similarities among student and supervisor expectations. Additionally, both students and supervisors agreed that there are greater expectations of students for second fieldwork rotations than expectations for first rotations. This seems logical since students on their second rotation will already have had the opportunity to adjust to practice, have had some experience with techniques, assessments, interactions with patients and health care staff, and have progressed toward independent functioning during their first fieldwork affiliations. Overall, the findings of matched expectations between students and fieldwork supervisors suggest that students' perceptions of fieldwork expectations are on target with that which supervisors will want them to know. Although students may feel unprepared, accurate awareness of supervisor expectations will help activate student coping skills to deal with the transition to the fieldwork environment, and in turn will help ready them to meet the new challenges of fieldwork education. Fieldwork supervisors, as well as academic faculty, can help facilitate this process by recognizing student anxiety about the transition, and then teaching and supporting healthy coping strategies that will serve to reduce students' stress.

STUDY LIMITATIONS

The participants in this study were limited to practitioners from facilities with which the university has fieldwork contracts, which are primarily in Texas, and occupational therapy students who graduated from the university's program. Because of the anonymity of the surveys, no distinction could be made between therapists working in community-based settings vs. those in medically-based settings. Therefore, it is not possible to determine whether the therapists' perceptions of the changes in their responsibilities were totally reimbursement driven. Although the findings may provide insight into fieldwork supervisor expectations and current practices, the results cannot be generalized to other practitioner or student populations. Additional research is needed to determine if the results hold true for practitioners in other areas of the country and for graduates of other educational facilities.

CONCLUSION

Student concerns regarding preparedness for Level II fieldwork education prompted this exploratory study of fieldwork expectations. The results of the study indicate that fieldwork supervisors do have higher expectations for today's students. Changes in practitioner job responsibilities and the implementation of new educational *Standards* have influenced greater student expectations. Having increased job complexity, however, has not affected supervisors' time or techniques for teaching. Although students generally do have anxiety about beginning Level II fieldwork experience, the study findings show that student perceptions of supervisor expectations are accurate. It is hoped that information learned from this study will provide a clearer understanding of supervisor expectations of students during Level II fieldwork education. This information can enable academic faculty to develop programs consistent with the current practice environment, and also strengthen the overall process for educating students for entry into the occupational therapy profession.

REFERENCES

Accreditation Council for Occupational Therapy Education (1998). Standards for an accredited educational program for the occupational therapist. *American Journal of Occupational Therapy, 53*, 575-582.

American Occupational Therapy Association (AOTA), Commission on Education (1984). *Guide to fieldwork education*. Bethesda, MD: Author.

Barrett, K. (2001). Guide for occupational therapy fieldwork supervisors. *OT Practice, 5*, 17-19.

Cara, E. (1998). Fieldwork supervision in the mental health setting. In E. Cara & A. MacRae (Eds.), *Psychosocial occupational therapy: A clinical practice* (pp. 609-640). Albany, NY: Delmar Publishers.

Christie, B. A., Joyce, P. C., & Moeller, P. L. (1985). Fieldwork experience, part II: The supervisor's dilemma. *American Journal of Occupational Therapy, 39*, 675-681.

Cohn, E. (1998). Interdisciplinary communication and supervision of personnel. In M. E. Neistadt & E. B. Crepeau (Eds.), *Willard & Spackman's occupational therapy* (9th ed., pp. 791-802). Philadelphia, PA: Lippincott-Raven Publishers.

Frum, D. C., & Opacich, K. J. (1987). *Supervision: Development of therapeutic competence.* Rockville, MD: AOTA.

Gaiptman, B., & Anthony, A. (1989). Contracting in fieldwork education: The model of self-directed learning. *Canadian Journal of Occupational Therapy, 56,* 10-14.

Kautzmann, L. N. (1990). Clinical teaching: Fieldwork supervisors' attitudes and values. *American Journal of Occupational Therapy, 44,* 835-838.

Punwar, A. J. (2000a). The art and science of practice: Adapting to managed care. In A. Punwar & S. Peloquin (Eds.), *Occupational therapy principles and practice* (3rd ed., p. 106). Baltimore, MA: Lippincott Williams & Wilkins.

Punwar, A. J. (2000b). Professional education and credentialing patterns: Occupational therapist education. In A. Punwar & S. Peloquin (Eds.), *Occupational therapy principles and practice* (3rd ed., p. 56). Baltimore, MA: Lippincott Williams & Wilkins.

An Exploratory Study of Web-Based Supports for Occupational Therapy Students During Level II Fieldwork

Donna Wooster, MS, OTR/L, BCP

SUMMARY. Occupational therapy students often experience high levels of anxiety about transitioning from the academic student role to the fieldwork student role. The separation from their classmates and the geographical relocation may isolate some students. Additionally, the quality and quantity of on-site supports available to individual students vary with each placement.

A web-based resource was designed to assist occupational therapy students from the University of South Alabama with the transition from student role in an academic environment to level II fieldwork in off-campus work environments. Participation was voluntary and no grades were assigned. Students were invited to participate as needed with their classmates for support and information sharing. Resources were provided asynchronously so students could access them whenever and wherever they could gain access to the Internet.

Quantitative and qualitative analysis of the data was conducted. Data analysis included frequency of web-based communication, analysis of emerging themes based on the communication, outcome of student

Donna Wooster is Assistant Professor at the University of South Alabama, Department of Occupational Therapy, 1504 Springhill Avenue, Room 5108, Mobile, AL 36604 (E-mail: dwooster@jaguar1.usouthal.edu).

[Haworth co-indexing entry note]: "An Exploratory Study of Web-Based Supports for Occupational Therapy Students During Level II Fieldwork." Wooster, Donna. Co-published simultaneously in *Occupational Therapy in Health Care* (The Haworth Press, Inc.) Vol. 18, No. 1/2, 2004, pp. 21-29; and: *Best Practices in Occupational Therapy Education* (ed: Patricia A. Crist, and Marjorie E. Scaffa) The Haworth Press, Inc., 2004, pp. 21-29. Single or multiple copies of this article are available for a fee from The Haworth Document Delivery Service [1-800-HAWORTH, 9:00 a.m. - 5:00 p.m. (EST). E-mail address: docdelivery@haworthpress.com].

fieldwork performance, and students' perceptions based on their participation.

The information gained during this exploratory study could be useful to other faculty in developing similar web-based resources to promote student success. Additionally, the technology skills gained by the students are hoped to improve their confidence to participate in web-based professional list serves and distance education opportunities in the future. *[Article copies available for a fee from The Haworth Document Delivery Service: 1-800-HAWORTH. E-mail address: <docdelivery@haworthpress.com> Website: <http://www.HaworthPress.com> © 2004 by The Haworth Press, Inc. All rights reserved.]*

KEYWORDS. Distance education, web-based, level II fieldwork

WEB-BASED SUPPORTS DURING LEVEL II FIELDWORK

Occupational therapy (OT) students have long been required to complete level II fieldwork in clinical environments as part of the educational process. This often means a separation from their classmates and for some a geographical relocation. This is often a stressful experience for students (Steward, 1994). These experiences are considered essential to promote the application of the book knowledge they have learned and the development of critical thinking skills. Students are also expected to demonstrate appropriate professional behaviors in this new unfamiliar environment.

The demands placed on the students to perform successfully in real-life environments create new challenges. The thought of working with "real clients," while exciting, can be overwhelming to some students. Nursing students have reported that clinical rotations increase anxiety and fears about confronting the unknown, making errors, unpredictable and stressful situations, and jeopardizing the patient/client relationship (Wong & Wong, 1987). Occupational therapy students have expressed specific fieldwork anxieties to include the change in roles and expectations, dealing with challenging client behavior, and feeling socially isolated when living off-campus (Steward, 1994). Additionally, students may feel vulnerable to the subjective nature of the student/supervisor relationship and suddenly feel less confident in their knowledge and skills (Barr, 1980). Tyrell and Smith (1996) identified that OT students indicated higher levels of psychological stress during fieldwork, which was similar to the stress levels of medical and dental students. The separation from classmates, who may have provided support and structure, is hard for some students. The resources that were at the students' fingertips during the academic program may not be readily available in rural sites. All the realities of the professional responsibilities creep into place. The students strive to attain professional behaviors when they are feeling vulnerable and challenged. This web-based support was implemented as a way to ease the transition and provide peer and faculty supports during level II fieldwork.

METHODS

The University of South Alabama Department of Occupational Therapy decided to offer an optional web-based resource for occupational therapy students who leave campus for two, three-month rotations of level II fieldwork, to provide peer and faculty support. A survey identified that most students had access to a computer with Internet service. The curriculum ensured that all students had successfully completed two required computer courses during their academic program. Students completed questionnaires to identify their perceived needs for success on level II fieldwork. These included:

- Intervention ideas
- Quick access to accurate information
- Reminders for deadlines
- Support and encouragement
- Time Management and professional development for practice

An exploratory resource was created for the fall semester 2000 and voluntarily continued through spring semester 2001. Participation was voluntary and without grades or extra credits. The purpose of this web-based support was to provide peer and faculty support to enhance students' success and confidence on the clinical fieldwork rotations. The web-based resource was designed to provide social and emotional supports to students, to promote critical thinking skills relevant to the profession, and to encourage sharing of resources and information to promote student self-development. Students were encouraged to seek ideas and resources from their classmates using web-based asynchronous formats.

One faculty member acted as the group monitor and established the web group. This faculty member monitored all the discussions and provided the leadership and guidance to the group. Additionally, when specific students needed more supports, this faculty member provided more individual support and notified the academic fieldwork coordinator of any potential problems. Other faculty members listened in and were available to the students.

A group list serve was utilized because it provided the features of "restricted members only" participation, group and individual e-mails, asynchronous communication, files sharing, web link sharing, and a calendar component to provide information about deadlines. Asynchronous communication was permitted between faculty and students and student-to-students. Students were invited to join the group while still attending on-campus courses.

RESULTS

All twenty-three class members were invited to participate in the list serve. The participation varied for each rotation due to accessibility and computer issues as students changed living situations. In the fall semester, eighteen out of twenty-three students (78%) voluntarily participated in the web-based list serve and in the spring semester, seventeen of twenty-three students (74%) voluntarily participated. Twenty-one out of twenty-three students (91%) participated for at least one of the rotations.

The communication messages were saved from both rotations and analyzed by qualitative and quantitative methods. Messages that were duplicates (sent twice) were only counted once and empty messages were not counted. The initial logging in or trial messages were also not counted. All other messages from Sept. 2000-March 2001 were utilized. A total of 334 messages were utilized. The students were encouraged by the list moderator to submit patient cases for discussion, provide ideas for intervention, and to share good quality web site URL addresses they found helpful. The content of e-mail messages allowed students to keep up with each other's lives as they reported their personal changes and challenges, such as pregnancy, engagements, break-ups, and family illness. The contents of the e-mail messages were saved to disk and analyzed for themes using the Nud*ist Program. Eight themes emerged and the percentage of communication based on each theme was noted.

Emerging Themes

The theme that emerged most frequently and accounted for 30% of the communication was *intervention/ treatment*. These communications included case discussions, treatment ideas, discussion of literature that supported specific treatments, and the sharing of treatment resources.

The second largest theme (23%) that emerged was *personal experiences.* This included communication related to narrative storytelling, specifics about personal experiences at a site, funny stories to share, time management strategies for the clinic, documentation strategies and resources, and unusual opportunities they had that week.

The third theme to emerge was *information* and accounted for 20% of the web-based communication. This was mainly information sent to the students from the University of South Alabama reminding them about scheduling for next semester, events they needed to know about, exam information, graduation deadlines, and other relevant information. This was a fast and inexpensive method to disseminate this information.

The fourth theme to emerge was *support of classmates* and this accounted for 13% of the web-based communication. This included personally supportive e-mails to class members, words of encouragement to individuals, and primarily positive and encouraging thoughts to all class members. All this communication was encouraging and supportive of a "can do" attitude. When the moderator identified a student who needed additional supports the information was passed on to the Academic Fieldwork Coordinator for intervention.

The fifth theme to emerge was family/relationships which accounted for 8% of the web-based communication. This information included invitations to classmates to visit each other, sharing phone numbers, making get-together plans, and even planning a baby shower.

The sixth theme to emerge was *research* which accounted for 3% of the web-based communication. Students were working on research projects while on fieldwork rotations and utilized the web to share ideas, discuss problems, share resources, and communicate with others about their experiences.

The seventh theme to emerge was *web site information* sharing which accounted for 2% of the communication. This included sharing of the URL addresses for good informative web sites so classmates could check them out. Many wonderful resources were shared.

The last theme to emerge was *computer and technology problems*, which accounted for 1% of the web-based communication. This was primarily help messages sent out and answers given back. The list serve company switched providers on us during the course and many needed further directions to make the transition to the new provider. Also, some students wanted to expand their computer skills and asked for help with chart making, searching, document sharing, and other computer issues. One student communicated a computer problem and organized to have another classmate call and share information over the phone while the computer was not working so nothing was missed.

Frequency of Web-Based Communication

The range of the number of times each student communicated was from one to twenty-five times during each twelve-week fieldwork rotation. The students who communicated the most for each rotation were in separate and remote locations and were the only OT student at each facility. The student who had the largest change in communication went from six messages one rotation to twenty-three messages (17) the second rotation. This demonstrated the freedom students had to use the web-based communication, as needed, as demands changed from one fieldwork rotation to another.

Effects on Fieldwork Evaluation Scores

The students demonstrated a 100% pass rate on both fieldwork rotations. In previous years, some students had difficulty passing the first clinical rotation. The mean scores as recorded by the Fieldwork Evaluation Form for the Occupational Therapist (AOTA, 1987) for each area evaluated (performance, judgment and attitude) were higher for the Class of 2001 (which received web-based mentoring) than for the Class of 2000 (which did not receive web-based mentoring) by fourteen or more points (see Table 1). T-tests were conducted and determined that these results are statistically significant with performance ($p = .02$), judgment ($p = .017$) and attitude ($p = .015$). These results support the effectiveness of the web-based mentoring on student performance on fieldwork rotations.

Student Perceptions

At completion of both web-based opportunities, students were asked to complete a questionnaire about their experiences. All students who participated in the web-based communication (100%) responded to the questionnaire. Students identified the primary factors that encouraged their participation in this web-based communication were: being eager to hear from classmates, the need for resources, the encouragement from others, the ideas generated and shared, the desire to keep in touch with their classmates, the peer supports provided, and to stay in touch with instructors. Students identified the primary factors that hindered their participation were: limited time, computer malfunctions and problems, other responsibilities, time availability of the Internet access, difficulty accessing the site or specific information on the site, and limited participation of classmates. The new computer skills that students reported they learned from this participation were: how to send e-mail messages

TABLE 1. F.W.E. Mean Scores

	Class of 2000	Class of 2001	Score Change	T-Test
Performance	195.66	210.13	+14.47	.02
Judgment	203.55	219.90	+16.35	.017
Attitude	228.57	244.09	+15.52	.015

to a group, how to establish a user name and password on a list serve, how to access the home page of the list serve, how to open and download files sent electronically or posted on the home page, and how to share files and Internet site addresses. The largest benefits the students perceived from this experience were the sharing of intervention ideas and the ability to stay in touch with their classmates. The students completed a Likert Scale of 1-7 (1 = strongly disagree, 7 = strongly agree) to respond to twenty-one statements. The statements receiving the highest scores were:

> The contacts with classmates made me feel more supported (6.18)
> This group helped me feel less lonely and isolated on FW (6.1)
> It was great to have contact with my classmates (6)
> Keeping in touch with classmates made it easier to come back together as a class now (5.8)
> Getting updated information from the department was helpful (5.7)
> I was able to be supportive to classmates who had family crises (5.6)
> When I got into difficulties on FW, I knew I had a support and resource group to access for help and information (5.5)
> The sharing of client cases helped me process treatment planning (5.5)

Concerns

One issue that arose was the limited and lack of participation by some classmates. This made some students feel like they were contributing and doing more for their classmates than they were getting back in return. Unfortunately, there was some truth to this, since participation was voluntary, and some offered much more to their classmates than others. Others reported missing the classmates who were not participating.

Other reported negatives consisted of time limitations to read all the e-mail messages, technology problems, and individual replies that were broadcast to all group members. Some students reported difficulty accessing the links section of the list serve, so the URL addresses were posted in e-mail messages as well. A questionnaire that was placed in the file section of the course was also sent out as an e-mail attachment. Providing multiple access points helped accommodate the variety of situations and resources available to the students.

DISCUSSION

This data supports that the web-based communication was able to provide students with additional information, support and encouragement for success on fieldwork, calendar reminders of deadlines, and use of the web for expanding educational opportunities. Interestingly, even with little restrictions and no grade associated with this, the students utilized the communication for primarily educational purposes.

The qualitative and quantitative data and the supporting opinions of the students all indicate that the web-based mentoring was successful. Of course, there were the usual technological difficulties experienced by some students. Overall, it seems that students who were isolated and/or in need of supports were able to use the web-based resource to seek what they needed from their classmates and the faculty. The table below (see Table 2) illustrates an analysis of how each perceived need identified by the students through questionnaires was met by the web-based mentoring resource. It appears that the web-based resource was an appropriate strategy for meeting these intended needs. Sharing of strategies for intervention was the most highly communi-

TABLE 2. Needs and Strategies

Identified Need	Did the web-based mentoring meet this need?	How?
Intervention ideas	Yes 30% of content shared on-line	Students posted a variety of treatment ideas, discussed client cases, and shared experiences and successes.
Quick access to accurate information	Yes 2% of content	Faculty and students shared links to relevant resources to minimize the surfing time to access information.
Reminders for deadlines	Yes Part of information theme sent to students on-line	Calendar reminders programmed into course that sent e-mails to remind students of deadlines for academic requirements. Less expensive than mailing or calling.
Support and encouragement	Yes 13%	Students were supported by each other and the faculty. Faculty stepped in to help those in crisis. Everyone was more aware of each others' experiences and needs.
Time management and professional development for practice	Yes–Part of personal experiences (23%) and research	Students shared personal stories that included time management and documentation tips. Research conducted on site was a professional development opportunity. Personal/funny stories shared.

cated content. This seems appropriate since this hands-on skill is the component the occupational therapy students are practicing the most during clinical fieldwork rotations. Students chose to participate in this web-based resource despite the fact that there were no grades or required assignments. Students participated willingly and utilized the web-based resource to promote their self-development. It is hoped that the computer skills gained from this experience will also increase their comfort level for participating in professional list serve activities after graduation.

REFERENCES

American Occupational Therapy Association (1987). *Fieldwork evaluation for the occupational therapist.* Bethesda, MD: Author.

Barr, E.M. (1980). The relationship between student and clinical supervisor. *British Journal of Occupational Therapy, 33* (3), 390-397.

Steward, B. (1994). Researching fieldwork practice in occupational therapy. *Educational Action Research, 2* (2), 259-265.

Tyrell, J. & Smith, H. (1996). Levels of psychological distress among occupational therapy students. *British Journal of Occupational Therapy, 59* (8), 365-371.

Wong, J. & Wong, S. (1987). Towards effective clinical teaching in nursing. *Journal of Advanced Nursing, 12,* 505-512.

Effects of Level II Fieldwork on Clinical Reasoning in Occupational Therapy

Marjorie E. Scaffa, PhD, OTR, FAOTA
Theresa M. Smith, MHS, OTR

SUMMARY. *Objective.* Fieldwork has been described as an educational method that enhances clinical reasoning skills. The purpose of this study was to determine the effects of Level II fieldwork on the development of clinical reasoning skills of undergraduate occupational therapy students.

Method. A quasi-experimental pretest-posttest design was used with a convenience sample of 48 undergraduate seniors. All students participated in two 12-week, full-time rotations of Level II fieldwork. The Self-Assessment of Clinical Reflection and Reasoning (SACRR) developed by Royeen, Mu, Barrett and Luebben (2000) was administered the week before the students left for fieldwork and the first day after they returned from fieldwork.

Results. Paired t-tests revealed statistically significant differences in pretest and posttest scores for 13 of 26 items on the SACRR. In addition, the overall total score increased from 102.55 to 108.41 (p < .01).

Marjorie E. Scaffa is Associate Professor and Chairperson (corresponding author) and Theresa M. Smith is Instructor and Academic Fieldwork Coordinator, Department of Occupational Therapy, University of South Alabama, SHAC Rm. 5108, 1504 Springhill Avenue, Mobile, AL 36604-3273 (E-mail: mscaffa@jaguar1.usouthal.edu).

[Haworth co-indexing entry note]: "Effects of Level II Fieldwork on Clinical Reasoning in Occupational Therapy." Scaffa, Marjorie E., and Theresa M. Smith. Co-published simultaneously in *Occupational Therapy in Health Care* (The Haworth Press, Inc.) Vol. 18, No. 1/2, 2004, pp. 31-38; and: *Best Practices in Occupational Therapy Education* (ed: Patricia A. Crist, and Marjorie E. Scaffa) The Haworth Press, Inc., 2004, pp. 31-38. Single or multiple copies of this article are available for a fee from The Haworth Document Delivery Service [1-800-HAWORTH, 9:00 a.m. - 5:00 p.m. (EST). E-mail address: docdelivery@haworthpress.com].

http://www.haworthpress.com/web/OTHC
Digital Object Identifier:10.1300/J003v18n01_04

31

Conclusion. The results suggest 24 weeks of full-time fieldwork experience, in the senior year of an undergraduate occupational therapy curriculum, can significantly facilitate the development of students' clinical reasoning skills. *[Article copies available for a fee from The Haworth Document Delivery Service: 1-800-HAWORTH. E-mail address: <docdelivery@ haworthpress.com> Website: <http://www.HaworthPress.com> © 2004 by The Haworth Press, Inc. All rights reserved.]*

KEYWORDS. Fieldwork, clinical reasoning, education

INTRODUCTION

The role of occupational therapy educational programs is to prepare students for entry-level practice. All occupational therapy educational programs require students to successfully complete 24 weeks of full-time, supervised Level II fieldwork education (American Occupational Therapy Association [AOTA], 1998). Level II fieldwork is a crucial part of professional preparation that involves the integration of academic knowledge with the direct application of skill and clinical reasoning in a practice setting (AOTA, 1996).

The goal of Level II fieldwork is to develop competent, entry-level, generalist occupational therapists (AOTA, 2000). Effective occupational therapy practice requires not just a solid knowledge base, but the development of a reasoning process to apply knowledge in dynamic practice. Accordingly, Level II fieldwork education is designed to promote clinical reasoning and reflective practice (AOTA, 1998).

The purpose of this study was to determine the effects of Level II fieldwork on the development of clinical reasoning skills of undergraduate occupational therapy students. Neistadt (1996) describes the development of clinical reasoning as following a continuum through the stages of novice, advanced beginner, competent, proficient, and expert. Students are not expected to graduate at competent, proficient, or expert levels of clinical reasoning as these may take years of practice and continuing education to achieve. Neistadt (1996) contends that students can enter practice as novices or advanced beginners if their academic preparation for Level II fieldwork has provided them with an awareness of clinical reasoning concepts.

Several types of clinical reasoning are relevant in occupational therapy. These include narrative reasoning, procedural reasoning, interactive reasoning, and conditional reasoning. Mattingly (1991) suggests narrative reasoning is a primary mode of clinical reasoning in occupational therapy. Therapists use narrative reasoning to guide their therapy with particular clients by imagining where the person is now and where the patient might be in the future after discharge (Mattingly, 1994). Fleming (1994) indicates that therapists use different types of reasoning to address different aspects of evaluation and intervention. Procedural reasoning by therapists concerns addressing the physical diagnosis and treatment techniques. Interactive reasoning involves the collaborative process used by the therapist with the client. Therapists use conditional reasoning to understand the client in the context of their life-world.

Occupational therapy literature suggests several methods of fostering clinical reasoning skills with Level II fieldwork students. Buchanan, Moore, and van Niekerk (1997) propose using a revised case study guide format and reflective writing to improve clinical reasoning of fieldwork students. McKay and Ryan (1995) indicate students can improve narrative reasoning skills on fieldwork by reflecting on treatment sessions before the session, during the session, and after the session. They also suggest students, by sharing personal therapeutic stories with their peers and fieldwork educators, may improve their reasoning processes.

Cohn (1989) presents several strategies to help advance clinical reasoning skills of Level II fieldwork students. She recommends that fieldwork supervisors use probing questions with students to help them develop a range of intervention strategies. Fieldwork supervisors should serve as role models, teaching technical skills and modeling reflection of their practice. She suggests sharing the reasoning process with students by telling intervention stories and using case studies that demonstrate the constant revision of intervention planning over time.

Students should chunk, or cluster, information to increase organization of their reasoning process and review videotapes of treatment sessions to increase understanding of the impact of their behavior on the client (Cohn, 1989). Cohn (1989) also advocates for students to work with a variety of clients with a similar diagnosis to learn routine treatment approaches. She states that students must develop their technical skills before they can begin to reflect on their practice.

Some of these methods have been shown to improve clinical reasoning with Level II fieldwork students. A study by McKay and Ryan (1995) found the use of probing questioning improved narrative reasoning with a student on fieldwork presenting a case study of a client. Initially, the student relied on biomedical information to describe the client and her focus was in the present. She did not seem to have a sense of the client as a person. Through additional questioning and examining the appreciation and interpretation of the client's life story, the student was better able to articulate an image and an understanding of the client.

A research study by Sladyk and Sheckley (2000) presented empirical evidence that significant clinical reasoning skill development occurred during a 12-week fieldwork experience. This result was obtained by using a pretest and posttest Clinical Reasoning Case Analysis Test designed for this study. Their study also examined seven activities believed to improve clinical reasoning (i.e., journal writing, videotaping, reviewing case studies, probing questions, working with a consistent population, role modeling, listening to supervisor stories). ANCOVA used with participation in each of the seven activities revealed two activities improved students' reasoning skills: seeing a steady patient population of not more than three different diagnoses, and videotaping activities (Sladyk & Sheckley, 2000). Their findings suggest that at some point involvement in too many different clinical reasoning activities may interfere with the development of students' clinical reasoning skills.

METHODS

It has long been assumed that Level II fieldwork enhances clinical reasoning skills, at least at the most basic level. The purpose of this study was to test this assumption and determine the effects of Level II fieldwork on the development of clinical reasoning skills of undergraduate occupational therapy students. A quasi-experimental pretest-posttest design was used with a convenience sample of 48 senior undergraduate occupational therapy students. All subjects participated in two 12-week rotations of Level II fieldwork in two different sites. Level II fieldwork consists of two required courses in the curriculum and is sequenced in the last two semesters of the bachelor of science degree program. The Self-Assessment of Clinical Reflection and Reasoning (SACRR), created and tested by Royeen, Mu, Barrett and Luebben (2000), was administered to the students to measure changes in clinical reasoning thought processes and behaviors.

The Self-Assessment of Clinical Reflection and Reasoning (SACRR) was developed as a means of evaluating the clinical reasoning skills of occupational therapy and physical therapy students and practitioners. The assessment items are based on Roth's (1989) hierarchy of 24 behaviors or actions of the reflective process. The SACRR tool demonstrates acceptable psychometric properties, including high internal consistency and moderate test-retest reliability (Royeen et al., 2000). Internal consistency, as measured by Cronbach's alpha, was .87 for the pretest and .92 for the posttest. An examination of test-retest reliability yielded a Spearman rank order correlation of .60, an acceptable level for pilot investigation (Royeen et al., 2000).

The SACRR consists of 26 items that are rated on a five-point Likert scale with a rating of "5" indicating "strongly agree," and a rating of "1" indicating "strongly disagree." Each item addresses a different aspect of clinical reflection and reasoning. According to Royeen et al. (2000), the SACRR can be used to evaluate the effects of different educational methods on clinical reasoning. A limitation of this instrument is that it relies on the subject's self-perception of clinical reasoning skills and behaviors rather than an objective measure of clinical reasoning performance. The SACRR was administered prior to the first day of the first Level II fieldwork rotation as a pretest and after the last day of the second Level II fieldwork rotation as a posttest to determine changes in clinical reasoning.

RESULTS

A total of 48 undergraduate occupational therapy students participated in the study. The participants ranged in age from 20 to 38 years, and the sample included six males and 42 females. Pretest and posttest scores were compared for each of the 26 items on the SACRR using a two-tailed t-test. Of the 26 items, statistically significant improvements were noted on 13 of the items (see Table 1). In addition, the student's total scores (aggregate scores for all 26 items) demonstrated statistically significant improvement upon completion of two 12-week rotations of Level II fieldwork. Overall scores improved 5.86 points from 102.55 on the pretest to 108.41 on the posttest. This improvement was statistically significant at the $p < .01$ level.

CONCLUSION

Clearly, Level II fieldwork had a statistically significant effect on students' self-perception of their clinical reasoning skills and behaviors. Changes were noted in one-half of the items on the SACRR. These 13 items clustered around three general themes: use of theory and frames of reference to understand client problems, questioning the potential efficacy of treatment, and use of specific clinical reasoning strategies. The clinical reasoning strategies that were perceived to have increased in use included developing and testing hypotheses, comparing and contrasting options, and contemplating "what if . . ." scenarios.

In addition, the students' tolerance for uncertainty and ambiguity increased as did their reliance on their own experience to validate their clinical hypotheses and practice decisions. Interestingly, on one item (#24), "I use clinical pro-

TABLE 1. Pretest/Posttest Comparisons

SACRR Items	Pretest Mean	Posttest Mean	P value
1. I question how, what and why I do things in practice.	4.04	4.04	ns*
2. I ask myself and others questions as a way of learning.	4.49	4.65	ns
3. I don't make judgments until I have sufficient data.	4.04	4.20	ns
4. Prior to acting, I seek various solutions.	4.04	4.20	ns
5. Regarding the outcome of proposed interventions, I try to keep an open mind.	**4.31**	**4.61**	**<.01**
6. I think in terms of comparing and contrasting information about a client's problems and proposed solutions to them.	**4.04**	**4.35**	**<.05**
7. I look to theory for understanding a client's problems and proposed solutions to them.	**3.60**	**3.90**	**<.05**
8. I look to frames of reference for planning my intervention strategy.	3.67	3.90	ns
9. I use theory to understand treatment techniques.	3.92	4.00	ns
10. I try to understand clinical problems by using a variety of frames of reference.	**3.70**	**4.06**	**<.01**
11. When there is conflicting information about a clinical problem, I identify assumptions underlying the differing views.	3.96	4.04	ns
12. When planning intervention strategies, I ask "What if" for a variety of options.	4.16	4.31	ns
13. I ask for colleagues' ideas and viewpoints.	4.53	4.71	ns
14. I ask for the viewpoints of clients' family members.	4.22	4.38	ns
15. I cope well with change.	3.88	4.02	ns
16. I can function with uncertainty.	**3.60**	**3.92**	**<.01**
17. I regularly hypothesize about the reasons for my clients' problems.	4.13	4.29	ns
18. I must validate clinical hypotheses through my own experience.	**3.88**	**4.27**	**<.01**

TABLE 1 (continued)

SACRR Items	Pretest Mean	Posttest Mean	P value
19. I clearly identify the clinical problems prior to planning intervention.	4.02	4.39	<.01
20. I anticipate the sequence of events likely to result from planned intervention.	3.94	4.33	<.01
21. Regarding a proposed intervention strategy, I think, "What makes it work?"	3.96	4.29	<.01
22. Regarding a particular intervention, I ask, "In what context would it work?"	3.90	4.31	<.01
23. Regarding a particular intervention with a particular client, I determine whether it worked.	4.16	4.49	<.01
24. I use clinical protocols for most of my treatment.	3.04	2.78	<.05
25. I make decisions about practice based on my experience.	3.88	4.31	<.01
26. I use theory to understand intervention strategies.	3.82	3.94	ns
TOTAL SCORE	102.55	108.41	<.01

*ns means not significant

tocols for most of my treatment," students' scores significantly decreased. A decrease in the use of clinical protocols may indicate an increase in the students' confidence in their clinical judgment with a corresponding decrease in their need to rely on predetermined intervention approaches.

Future studies need to focus on further validation and testing of the SACRR, development of other instruments to measure clinical reasoning, in vivo observation of students' clinical reasoning skills and behavior, and the use of control groups to determine the specific aspects of Level II fieldwork that enhance the clinical reasoning skills of students.

REFERENCES

American Occupational Therapy Association (1996). Statement: Purpose and value of occupational therapy fieldwork education Retrieved 1/11/2003, from the World Wide Web: http://www.aota.org/nonmembers/area13links/LINK07.asp.

American Occupational Therapy Association (1998). Standards for an accredited educational program for the occupational therapist. *The American Journal of Occupational Therapy*, 53, 575-582.

American Occupational Therapy Association (2000). Commission on education guidelines for an occupational therapy level II fieldwork experience. Retrieved 1/11/2003, from the World Wide Web: http://www.aota.org/nonmembers/area13/links/LINK06.asp.

Buchanan, H., Moore, R., & van Niekerk, L. (1997). The fieldwork case study: Writing for clinical reasoning. *The American Journal of Occupational Therapy,* 52 (4), 291-295.

Cohn, E. S. (1989). Fieldwork education: Shaping a foundation for clinical reasoning. *The American Journal of Occupational Therapy,* 43 (4), 240-244.

Fleming, M. H. (1994). The therapist with the three track mind. In C. Mattingly & M. H. Fleming. *Clinical reasoning: Forms of inquiry in a therapeutic practice.* Philadelphia: F. A. Davis.

Mattingly, C. (1991). The narrative nature of clinical reasoning. *The American Journal of Occupational Therapy,* 45 (11), 998-1005.

McKay, E. A. & Ryan, S. (1995). Clinical reasoning through story telling: Examining a student's case story on a fieldwork placement. *British Journal of Occupational Therapy,* 58 (6), 234-238.

Neistadt, M. E. (1996). Teaching strategies for the development of clinical reasoning. *The American Journal of Occupational Therapy,* 50 (8), 676-684.

Roth, R. (1989). Preparing the reflective practitioner: Transforming the apprentice through the dialectic. *Journal of Teacher Education,* 40, 31-35.

Royeen, C. B., Mu, K., Barrett, K., & Luebben, A. J. (2000). Pilot investigation: Evaluation of clinical reflection and reasoning before and after workshop intervention. In P. Crist (Ed.), *Innovations in occupational therapy education* (pp. 107-114). Bethesda, MD: American Occupational Therapy Association.

Sladyk, K. & Sheckley, B. (2000). Clinical reasoning and reflective practice: Implications of fieldwork activities. *Occupational Therapy in Health Care,* 13 (1), 11-22.

Brief or New:
Professional Development
of Fieldwork Students:
Occupational Adaptation,
Clinical Reasoning, and Client-Centeredness

Gina L. Ferraro Coates, MOT, OTR/L
Patricia A. Crist, PhD, OTR/L, FAOTA

SUMMARY. Fieldwork provides occupational therapy students with professional development readiness for entry-level practice. Thus, describing the results of the fieldwork learning process in terms of observed professional behaviors is valuable. This pilot study was initiated as part of program evaluation with the goal to assess fieldwork students'

Gina L. Ferraro Coates and Patricia A. Crist, Chair and Professor, are affiliated with Department of Occupational Therapy, Duquesne University.

Address correspondence to: Patricia A. Crist, Department of Occupational Therapy, Duquesne University, 600 Forbes Avenue, Pittsburgh, PA 15282-0020.

The researchers would like to thank Wendy Starnes, research coordinator and occupational therapist at the Way Station in Frederick, MD, for inviting them to do this program evaluation study and facilitating onsite activities. Thanks also to the fieldwork students who participated, as videotaping oneself is never comfortable, and a special thanks goes to the Way Station members who willingly volunteered to help the researchers learn more about fieldwork student development.

[Haworth co-indexing entry note]: "Brief or New: Professional Development of Fieldwork Students: Occupational Adaptation, Clinical Reasoning, and Client-Centeredness." Ferraro Coates, Gina L., and Patricia A. Crist. Co-published simultaneously in *Occupational Therapy in Health Care* (The Haworth Press, Inc.) Vol. 18, No. 1/2, 2004, pp. 39-47; and: *Best Practices in Occupational Therapy Education* (ed: Patricia A. Crist, and Marjorie E. Scaffa) The Haworth Press, Inc., 2004, pp. 39-47. Single or multiple copies of this article are available for a fee from The Haworth Document Delivery Service [1-800-HAWORTH, 9:00 a.m. - 5:00 p.m. (EST). E-mail address: docdelivery@haworthpress.com].

http://www.haworthpress.com/web/OTHC
Digital Object Identifier:10.1300/J003v18n01_05

performance maturation, clinical reasoning development, and client-centered behaviors as a result of this specific fieldwork experience. Nine occupational therapy students who completed Level II fieldwork at the Way Station, Inc., in Frederick, MD were videotaped administering the *Canadian Occupational Performance Measure* (COPM) to a new client during the 2nd and 10th week of fieldwork to gather descriptions of changes in student professional behavior during the fieldwork experience. Observational analysis demonstrated that primitive and transitional behaviors decreased as mature behaviors increased, clinical reasoning shifted from primarily procedural to interactive and conditional, and client-centered behaviors developed. The findings enhance our understanding of the development of professional behaviors during fieldwork and provide indicants for future studies as well as a methodology for fieldwork supervision. *[Article copies available for a fee from The Haworth Document Delivery Service: 1-800-HAWORTH. E-mail address: <docdelivery@haworthpress.com> Website: <http://www.HaworthPress.com> © 2004 by The Haworth Press, Inc. All rights reserved.]*

KEYWORDS. Fieldwork, professional development, occupational development, clinical reasoning and client-centeredness

INTRODUCTION

The essential goal of fieldwork is the professional development of students leading to entry-level practice readiness (Christie, Joyce, & Moeller, 1985a & b; Crist, 1986; Crepeau & LaGarde, 1991; Garrett & Schkade, 1995; Merrill & Crist, 2000). Thus, describing the results of the fieldwork learning process in terms of observed professional behaviors is valuable as these skills are transferable across sites.

The purpose of this pilot study was to describe the maturation in performance, clinical reasoning and use of client-centered behaviors during a state-of-the-art community mental health placement. One of the primary missions for the Way Station, Inc. in Frederick, MD, is to provide "cutting edge," pre-service education using the community-based, client-centered therapeutic approach to service delivery. This site advocates for the development of client-centeredness in fieldwork students. As part of ongoing program evaluation, the Way Station's administration desired validation that their fieldwork met this important mission.

The Way Station program provides student experiences for a variety of health care disciplines using the clubhouse, community-based approach for individuals with significant mental health problems. Level II fieldwork for occupational therapy is a valued mission of the facility. Between 8-15 students complete Level II during each three-month rotation. The researchers were invited to provide summative program evaluation data regarding the observed outcomes in fieldwork student development as a result of the Way Station's educational experience. Fieldwork sites seldom subject their fieldwork objectives or activities to actual summative measurement beyond the subjective reporting of individual student satisfaction or spontaneous, observational assessment by the fieldwork educator. However, this approach could assist in validating the quality of the experience provided by this site and might suggest methods to promote fieldwork and student development.

Performance Maturation

One objective of this study was to replicate Garrett and Schkade's (1995) study that demonstrated that Occupational Adaptation is an effective way to describe the performance maturation of students in response to adapting to fieldwork challenges. Occupational Adaptation posits that three increasingly adaptive response behaviors are available: primitive (hyperstabilized); transitional (hypermobilized); and mature (the blend of stability and mobility) (Schkade, 1999). Initial responses to new or unfamiliar demands typically result in primitive behaviors such as frozen postures, blanking of previously known information, attempts to escape the situation or anxious behaviors in order to avoid failure. The transitional response phase is observed as random behaviors or activity for the sake of giving any type of response. Attention to relevant stimuli in the environment is ignored and an adequate rationale for responses is not available. Mature responses are goal-directed, efficient in movement, thoughts or interpersonal activities.

Clinical Reasoning Development

The development of clinical reasoning has been a focus of professional development in occupational therapy for almost two decades now. As experience increases, Fleming (1991) believes that the type of clinical reasoning used to direct intervention would also change. Five types of clinical reasoning abilities are most frequently reported in the literature (Fleming, 1991; Mattingly, 1991; and Schell & Cervero, 1993):

- Narrative reasoning: telling the client's story
- Procedural reasoning: selecting the best intervention to address performance problems

- Interactive reasoning: understanding the client's perspective on his or her illness or disability experience
- Conditional reasoning: considering the entire impact of illness or disability on daily performance and how this condition impacts quality of life
- Pragmatic reasoning: utilizing information regarding contextual factors that will influence intervention or performance, or ones that may not be transferable from one environment to another.

One might hypothesize that a novice practitioner would rely more on procedural reasoning while senior practitioners could synthesize pragmatic and interactive reasoning into conditional understanding of their client. Likewise, during fieldwork, procedural reasoning might occur more readily during the early phases of fieldwork and the others would occur near the closure of the fieldwork experience.

Enhanced Use of Client-Centered Behaviors

The *Occupational Therapy Practice Framework* describes the client-centered approach as focusing on the priorities and needs stated by the client as a core element in designing and implementing intervention (American Occupational Therapy Association, 2002). The Way Station's clubhouse model was founded using the client-centered approach as clients and therapists partner to define occupational performance and decipher individually relevant intervention goals. The client takes the lead in this identification process and the therapist helps to empower the client to accomplish these desires (Law et al., 1995). Therapists encourage clients to do independent reasoning and to use resources around them. The client-centered approach posits that enhanced motivation to participate in therapy will promote performance competence and self-efficacy in problem-solving future situations. Thus, clients seen by fieldwork students who practice a client-centered approach might have an increased likelihood for positive, therapeutic outcomes.

As a result of the unique Way Station fieldwork experience, Level II occupational therapy students were hypothesized to demonstrate more mature professional behaviors, more sophisticated clinical reasoning and more frequent client-centered behaviors than was observed initially.

METHODS

A descriptive, program evaluation study of nine fieldwork students during one 12-week rotation at the Way Station, provided an observation of the student's use of the three professional development behaviors: performance maturation using the Occupational Adaptation approach, clinical reasoning, and client-centered behaviors.

Subjects. Nine of 11 occupational therapy students, in either their first or second level II fieldwork, completed the study. One student did not complete the final assessment and one student was an occupational therapy assistant. Neither was included in the final results. No subject had a previous mental health Level II fieldwork experience or one that emphasized using client-centered behaviors. All students were naïve to the specific purposes for this study and came from four different academic programs.

Data Collection. In order to simulate a process to observe the professional development behaviors, a common fieldwork practice, interviewing a client was utilized. In order to ensure that client-centered reasoning was an option to observe the client-centered assessment, the *Canadian Occupational Performance Measure* (COPM) was utilized (Law et al., 1991). At this time, the site did not use the COPM as an assessment tool which meant that the study would reflect changes in student professional behaviors and not be the result of extensive practice in assessment administration.

Since few of the students were familiar with the COPM, the researchers provided a 1.5 hour orientation session using an introductory training method suggested by the instrument's developers. Interviewing, as a skill, per se, was not trained. Individual videotaping occurred during one student-clubhouse member session at the beginning and end of the fieldwork experience (weeks two and 10) and was conducted at a table in a quiet conference room on site.

Each student was videotaped administering the COPM with an unfamiliar member. No clubhouse member participated more than one time in the assessment. No individual assessment results were shared with the Way Station.

Qualitative Analysis of Videotaped Sessions. The two researchers independently reviewed the two and 10 week tapes to observe use of performance behaviors (primitive, transitional and mature types) as derived from Garrett and Schkade (1995); different clinical reasoning uses (narrative, procedural, interactive, conditional and pragmatic) derived from literature; and the development of client-centered skills. An initial list of indicators of each area was developed and expanded later if the researchers agreed to an addition. Client-centered behaviors were defined as student-member interactions that demonstrated:

1. Working together to define:
   - occupational performance deficits
   - the desired focus of treatment
   - the desired outcomes of treatment

2. Encouraging clients to:
   * make their own decisions
   * use their own style of coping
   * build on their own strengths
3. Helping to empower the client to accomplish desires
4. Avoiding judgment of client's values or decisions
5. Encouraging clients' independent thinking skills (Fleming, 1991; Law et al., 1995; Mattingly, 1991; Schell & Cervero, 1993)

Tapes were grouped by the two time frames, and all were studied for one area of professional development within one time frame. The 2nd week tape group was always followed by 10th week tape to observe for behavioral indicators that would support change across the fieldwork for each student. The researchers met regularly to share their observational results.

RESULTS

Performance Maturation

As expected, fieldwork students demonstrated a majority of primitive behaviors in the initial session. Students showed hesitancy and slowness in verbal responses including many pauses. Also, they would interrupt the interview to ask the videotaper for reassurance that they were doing the assessment correctly. Students lead the goal development process with minimal encouragement for client participation or reliance on client validation.

As students sought solutions to their performance problems, transitional behaviors were noted. For instance, one student who was initially confused as to how to start the assessment, followed by transitional behaviors, and talked non-stop about occupational therapy, the assessment purpose and how it would help the client. The majority of students demonstrated some form of anxiety such as leg tremors, foot kicking, clicking their pens repeatedly and rocking back and forth in their chairs. Others wrote nearly every word the client said, asking them to stop so they had sufficient time to write but not to delve further into the problem area. Students ignored important environmental stimuli, as the motivation to finish the assessment was more important than the interview process. Only one student demonstrated a substantial number of mature behaviors during the initial interview, smiling appropriately and trying to build rapport with the client. If a student asked the client to expand a description of their identified problem, they seldom incorporated this additional information into the assessment results.

By week 10, students markedly transformed most behaviors into mature ones. More skilled interviewing was observed. Less extraneous movement was noted as well as improved listening behaviors and body language. Writing down client words verbatim was gone. Conversation flowed easier as students were more articulate and comfortable with problem identification and encouraged idea expansion. Explanation of occupational therapy was succinct and clear. The COPM goal identification process was modified to be more client-centered and supportive.

Clinical Reasoning Development

As performance behaviors changed, so did the qualitative use of clinical reasoning skills. Initial sessions revealed reliance on procedural reasoning to complete the COPM. "Getting the assessment done" was the primary goal. Interactive reasoning was seen in a few students who were able to initiate problem clarification questions with their clients.

By the final tape, students were more at ease and demonstrating less procedural stress. All students exhibited increased use of interactional or conditional styles of reasoning as they provided more open questions than in the earlier session to draw out client insights about their illness experience (interactional reasoning), and encouraged them to be active participants in the decision-making related to goal-setting (conditional reasoning). Students were more adept at reflecting client input to develop a specific plan that would enhance the client's desired quality of life. They listened to client interests and resisted defining them for the clients. Instead, the students provided stimulus questions for the clients to identify and clarify their performance change priorities.

While students did not practice the COPM between the two tapings, interactional reasoning may account for how they acquired these behaviors.

Enhanced Use of Client-Centered Behaviors

In the initial video, attempts to go beyond creating verbatim lists of clients' first reported occupational performance deficits were non-existent. Setting goal priorities for intervention was similar. Few empowering statements were made to clients such as encouraging them to make their own decisions or utilize resources, beyond saying that it was good that they came to Way Station. Only two students demonstrated client encouragement such as building on current strengths, using compliments or being non-judgmental.

By the final session, the six client-centered areas where students demonstrated the most changes were: defining performance deficits; defining the desired outcomes together; empowering the client; encouraging resource utilization; encouraging decision-making; and using the client's style of coping, when appropriate. Client-therapist collaboration was evident. Students asked clients to clarify or describe more thoroughly phrases such as, "Under what circumstances would you . . ." Students used more collaborative interactions when setting goals. All students let the clients rate their own importance, performance and satisfaction with performances they identified instead of the student first suggesting a likely rating. Many of the students chose goals that interested the member. Certainly, more resource utilization was evident including more knowledge about Way Station's community resources. Students encouraged coping and reinforced positive coping strategies identified by the client. Fewer student-suggested ideas for coping and problem-solving were offered and members were encouraged to make their own decisions.

DISCUSSION

Students demonstrated beneficial professional development in performance maturation, clinical reasoning and use of client-centered approaches across this fieldwork experience. Descriptive evidence indicates that the current fieldwork experience results in positive student learning. The descriptions of these professional development behaviors can provide a supervisory guide for other fieldwork.

Videotaping student activities is shown as a viable method to evaluate fieldwork program effectiveness and student performance. Videotape can be used as a self-development tool for supervisory meetings and adapted to facilitate self-development or serve as a common event for reality-based, student-supervisor discussion. Students could use the tape in their portfolio to show others their level of clinical competence or use as a basis for later self-analysis to see how they have developed after a greater amount of practice.

Caution in using this data is noted as this was a program evaluation study. Due to this study's pilot nature, repetition with more students and using a formal research design would be beneficial. Certainly, the independence of the three areas could be tested as multiple observations provided evidence for more than one area at the same time.

One researcher debriefed a group of 14 students during the next three-month cycle after this study. Like the group studied, these students also concluded that they could not be client-centered in other sites. The sole reason was that they would not have sufficient time to talk with clients. This misinterpretation of client-centeredness warrants attention. Understanding how to vary one's client-centered approaches based on context is essential.

Regardless, when Christie, Joyce and Moeller (1985a & b) presented their study at the AOTA conference in 1981, the title was "Fieldwork: The Forgotten Essential." Little has changed over the past 20 years in terms of supportive evidence for differing fieldwork approaches beyond rhetoric. Much is unknown about this learning phase that encompasses 25% or more of a student's required academic time. With fieldwork being left loosely structured, voluntary, and unevaluated or credentialed, much is needed to really understand "best fieldwork practices." Can we afford the risk any longer?

REFERENCES

American Occupational Therapy Association (2002). *Occupational therapy practice framework: Domain & process*. Bethesda, MD: Author.

Christie, B. A., Joyce, P. C., & Moeller, P. L. (1985a). Fieldwork experience, part I: Impact on practice preference. *American Journal of Occupational Therapy, 39*, 671-674.

Christie, B. A., Joyce, P. C., & Moeller, P. L. (1985b). Fieldwork experience, part II: The supervisor's dilemma. *American Journal of Occupational Therapy, 39*, 671-674.

Crepeau, E. B. & LaGarde, T. (1991). *Self-paced instruction for clinical education and supervision*. Rockville, MD: American Occupational Therapy Association.

Crist, P. A. H. (1986). *Contemporary issues in clinical education*. Thorofare, NJ: Slack, Inc.

Fleming, M. H. (1991). The therapist with the three-track mind. *American Journal of Occupational Therapy, 45*, 1007-1014.

Garrett, S. A. & Schkade, J. K. (1995). Occupational adaptation model of professional development as applied to Level II fieldwork. *American Journal of Occupational Therapy, 49*, 103-106.

Law, M., Baptiste, S., & Mills, J. (1995). Client-centered practice: What does it mean and does it make a difference? *The Canadian Journal of Occupational Therapy, 62*, 250-257.

Mattingly, C. (1991). What is clinical reasoning? *American Journal of Occupational Therapy, 5*, 979-986.

Merrill, S. & Crist, P. A. (2000). *Meeting the fieldwork challenge: A self paced clinical course*. Bethesda, MD: American Occupational Therapy Association.

Schell, B. A. & Cervero, R. M. (1993). Clinical reasoning in occupational therapy: An integrative review. *American Journal of Occupational Therapy, 47*, 605-610.

Schkade, J. K. (1999). Student to practitioner: The adaptive transition. *Innovations in Occupational Therapy Education*, 147-156.

INSTRUCTIONAL METHODS

Teaching Undergraduate Neuroscience with Brain Teaser Experiments

Daniel Goldreich, PhD

SUMMARY. Neuroscience knowledge is of fundamental importance to the occupational therapist and other health care professionals, but neuroscience courses are often viewed in schools of health sciences as among the most arduous of the curriculum. To enhance student learning, the author has developed a series of in-class activities, "brainteasers," that are integrated into each subject module of a semester-long undergraduate neuroscience course. In the brain teaser activities, students experience intriguing sensory and motor phenomena, then use inductive reasoning to generate plausible hypotheses concerning the underlying neural mechanisms. Students profit doubly from these activities, learning neuroscience while practicing critical thinking. *[Article copies available for a fee from The*

Daniel Goldreich holds a PhD in Neuroscience, and is Associate Professor, Occupational Therapy Department, Duquesne University.

Address correspondence to: Professor Daniel Goldreich, Occupational Therapy Department, Duquesne University, 600 Forbes Ave., Pittsburgh, PA 15282-0020 (E-mail: goldreich@duq.edu).

[Haworth co-indexing entry note]: "Teaching Undergraduate Neuroscience with Brain Teaser Experiments." Goldreich, Daniel. Co-published simultaneously in *Occupational Therapy in Health Care* (The Haworth Press, Inc.) Vol. 18, No. 1/2, 2004, pp. 49-55; and: *Best Practices in Occupational Therapy Education* (ed: Patricia A. Crist, and Marjorie E. Scaffa) The Haworth Press, Inc., 2004, pp. 49-55. Single or multiple copies of this article are available for a fee from The Haworth Document Delivery Service [1-800-HAWORTH, 9:00 a.m. - 5:00 p.m. (EST). E-mail address: docdelivery@haworthpress.com].

49

Haworth Document Delivery Service: 1-800-HAWORTH. E-mail address: <docdelivery@haworthpress.com> Website: <http://www. HaworthPress.com>

KEYWORDS. Neuroscience teaching, problem-based learning, active learning, inductive reasoning

INTRODUCTION

In an effort to enhance student learning, university teachers in occupational therapy and other disciplines have begun to incorporate problem-based approaches within the classroom. The goal of such approaches is to engage students actively in the subject matter, through the use of cooperative and critical thinking (Myers, 1986; Nolinske & Millis, 1999). Recently, such techniques have been applied to science courses (Liotta-Kleinfeld & McPhee, 2001; Schuh & Busey, 2001; Stokstad, 2001). The subject matter of science courses, as well as the process of scientific discovery, lend themselves to the creation of novel problem-based approaches for the science classroom. One such approach, developed for an undergraduate neuroscience course, is described here.

Neuroscience knowledge is of fundamental importance to the occupational therapist and other health care professionals (Farber, 1989), but neuroscience courses are often viewed in schools of health sciences as among the most arduous of the curriculum. The reason for this is probably not the inherent difficulty of the subject matter, but rather how the subject is normally presented. In a traditional neuroscience course, students passively view a dizzying array of diagrams and charts describing the locations and functions of dozens of brain areas and the tracts connecting them. These are the neural circuits that allow us to see, hear, touch, smell, taste, and, through movement, manipulate our world. Unfortunately, students rarely acquire from lectures alone a full appreciation for the functioning of the fascinating organ that has been called our "three-pound universe" (Hooper & Teresi, 1986).

It is no wonder that passive exposure to scientific knowledge does little to stimulate learning. Science is not a dry collection of facts; it is an exciting method of discovery. Yet students in science courses rarely experience the joy of scientific discovery. In the learning activity described in this article, the brain teaser, students in a neuroscience course experience intriguing sensory and motor phenomena, then, like actual neuroscientists, use inductive reasoning to generate plausible hypotheses concerning the underlying neural mechanisms. It is hoped that this method of active learning will serve as a model, not just for neuroscience courses, but for other science courses within the occupational therapy curriculum.

COURSE DESCRIPTION

Neuroscience is a two-day, five-hour per week comprehensive survey of the human nervous system taken by junior-year students in the occupational therapy and speech-language pathology programs in the Rangos School of Health Sciences at Duquesne University. The course covers the electrical and chemical properties of the neuron, then focuses on the anatomy, physiology, and pathology of sensory, motor, and cognitive neural systems. The course involves two midterm exams and a comprehensive final exam. Class size from 2000 to 2003 has ranged from 34 to 55 students.

Each of the course's 12 subject modules begins and ends with a brain teaser. The module-beginning brain teaser challenges students to discover a specific operation of the human brain prior to receiving any lectures on the topic. Students thus enter the upcoming lectures having already pondered the subject matter. The module-ending brain teaser challenges students to apply the information received in lecture to a novel case. Students thereby actively process, and consolidate, their newly acquired knowledge. Students receive extra credit valuing one-half of one percentage point to be applied to their next exam score for correctly answering a brain teaser.

BRAIN TEASER OBJECTIVES

The specific objectives of the brain teasers are to:

- bring neuroscience alive to students through direct sensory and motor experience.
- provoke in students a sense of wonder regarding the functioning of the human nervous system.
- challenge students to think inductively, as neuroscientists do, in order to generate plausible hypotheses concerning neural mechanisms.
- reward hard-working students with the thrill of scientific discovery.

BRAIN TEASER PROCEDURE

The majority of the brain teasers follow the format of a simple scientific experiment. The instructor describes a sensory or motor procedure that will soon be performed in class. Students confer in small groups for several minutes in an attempt to predict the outcome of this "mystery demonstration." With predictions in hand, the students are naturally curious to experience the demonstration. The demonstration is then performed, often with results that contradict the student's expectations. Working again in small groups, the students attempt to infer the neural mechanism responsible for what they have just experienced. The instructor calls on the groups to report their hypotheses to the class, constructively critiques their reasoning, and finally ends the suspense by identifying the correct explanation. The entire activity typically lasts about 30 minutes. Two representative brain teasers are described below:

- *Starlight* takes place at the beginning of course module 4 (the retina). This brain teaser requires students to generate a plausible hypothesis about retinal function to explain an intriguing visual experience. The classroom lights are extinguished, and all windows covered over, to create a pitch-black environment. Each group receives a sheet of paper to which are attached two dimly glowing luminescent stars. Students are amazed to find that when they look directly at either star, it disappears, leaving visible only the star that is in peripheral vision! (This phenomenon is known to astronomers and amateur stargazers, such as backpackers, who often see dim stars out of the corner of the eye, only to have those stars disappear when they look directly at them!) The explanation for this bizarre result is that the retina contains two types of photoreceptors, rods and cones, of differing sensitivity (rods detect very dim light; cones cannot) and differing placement within the retina (rods are located peripherally; cones centrally).

- *Afterimage* takes place at the end of course module 4 (the retina). Like *Starlight*, this brain teaser requires students to generate a plausible hypothesis about retinal function to explain an intriguing visual experience. To solve this more difficult brain teaser, however, students must draw upon their knowledge of the retina, recently acquired from the preceding lectures. The students are asked to stare for approximately one minute at a projected image of an odd-looking flag. The flag has the structure of a United States flag, but the stars are black against an orange background, and the stripes alternate between black and green. When the instructor suddenly removes the flag from the overhead projector, rather than the bright white screen that is before them, the students perceive a red, white, and blue U.S. flag! The explanation for this surprising result is that the original image created a pattern of color light on the retina that selectively adapted (fatigued) the different cone (color light) receptors. When subsequently bathed in white light (which consists of all visible wavelengths, or colors), each part of the retina therefore responds most robustly to the wavelengths that were not present in the original image. This results in the perception of a vivid color-negative afterimage: the familiar U.S. flag.

FACULTY EVALUATION

In the author's experience, the brain teasers often elicit remarkably sophisticated thinking from the students. A similar conclusion was reached by two faculty observers, as indicated by their comments below:

- [T]he "brain teaser" . . . exercises . . . were introduced on the first day of class, and were used to great effect thereafter. In addition to providing an attention-grabbing introduction to new material, the "teasers" were obviously designed to stimulate critical thinking and did so at a level of sophistication that was frankly surprising to me. The "teasers" were typically introduced by a "mystery demo," in which the instructor, the entire class, or student volunteers would participate in a live experiment. Following the demonstration, students were placed into small groups and were asked to explain the outcome they had just witnessed . . . This strategy was extremely effective. I listened in as groups discussed, debated, and discarded various hypotheses, sounding very much like budding scientific thinkers. (What a joy to hear.) I was so taken by this activity that I immediately incorporated a version of it into the class I taught last summer. (Susan Felsenfeld, PhD, CCC-SLP, 2000)
- The demonstration that began the class was a wonderful example of higher order thinking . . . This demonstration was actually designed like a small experiment. The data . . . gathered from the demonstration was . . . used . . . by the students in small groups to form theories about what they had seen. Each group then presented their theories to the rest of the class and to the instructor. Accurate interpretations were identified and inaccurate interpretations were entertained and disproved by the data. This sort of exercise encourages the highest order of thinking. Students must pull together abstract data, recollect what they know about neuroscience and then assimilate the abstract data and previously mastered material into a novel theory of explanation. (David Somers, PhD, PT, 1999)

STUDENT EVALUATION

Of the 176 neuroscience students who completed written end-of-semester teacher evaluation questionnaires (TEQs) over the last four years (2000 through 2003), 93 (53%) mentioned the brain teasers in answer to the question, "What aspects of this instructor's teaching were *most* effective?" and 126 (72%) commented positively on the brain teasers at some point within their

TEQ. Only two students offered comments that seemed generally negative. A sample of students' written comments are provided below:

- The brain teasers were very helpful in getting us to think on a higher level.
- Brain teasers really helped to bring concepts home.
- Class is wonderful, brain teasers and mystery demos keep us interested and challenge us to think!
- I enjoy our class activities. The brain teasers are really fun and give us a chance to learn in groups and interact.
- I loved the class activities. Not only were they fun, they required inquisitive thinking.
- The brain teasers and mystery demos are wonderful! They really make us think and go beyond what we've learned in lecture.
- The class was unique to any college class I have had before . . . I thought that I learned an enormous amount of material because of the hands on approach of the professor. The mystery demos were very helpful to my learning. . . .
- I really enjoy his use of the brain teasers and mystery demos to help us to discovery on our own.
- Loved the Brain Teasers!! These were fun and effective ways of forcing students to think critically and analytically while earning extra credit.

SUGGESTIONS FOR BRAIN TEASER DEVELOPMENT

For faculty interested in developing their own brain teaser activities, the following suggestions may prove useful:

- In the author's experience, the most effective brain teasers begin with mystery demonstrations that involve the entire class in a shared sensory or motor experience. Demonstrations involving just one or two volunteers called to the front of the classroom usually provoke less interest.
- Students must be given adequate time to interpret the observed phenomena. Usually 15 minutes suffice, but more complex brain teasers may require more time. It is important to recognize that time in which students engage in critical thinking is time well spent.
- It is useful for the instructor to circulate throughout the room to "eavesdrop" on the groups as they engage in deliberations, in order to assess student understanding and to answer questions (whenever this can be done without revealing the solution to the brain teaser).

- Since students are not penalized for incorrect answers in this extra credit activity, the instructor is free to pose particularly challenging brain teasers. Nevertheless, a balance must be struck between brain teaser difficulty and maintenance of student interest. The solution to the brain teasers should be within the grasp of hard-working and attentive students. The author favors brain teasers that are typically answered correctly by at least one-quarter of student groups.
- To encourage the widest variety of student interaction throughout the semester, it is recommended that students be newly (and randomly) assigned to groups for each course module. A group size of five or six students seems to work well, as this number is large enough to generate creative discussion, yet small enough to allow all students in the group to participate.

CONCLUSION

The brain teaser activities appear to substantially enhance student learning. The mystery demonstrations pique student interest, motivating the subsequent period of critical thinking in which students hypothesize about underlying mechanisms. This method of active learning may provide a useful model, not only for neuroscience courses, but also for other science courses within the occupational therapy curriculum.

REFERENCES

Farber, S. (1989) Neuroscience and occupational therapy: Vital connections. 1989 Eleanor Clarke Slagle lecture. *American Journal of Occupational Therapy* 43 (10), 637-646.

Hooper, J. & Teresi, D. (1986) *The three-pound universe*. New York: Macmillan Publishing Co.

Liotta-Kleinfeld, L. & McPhee, S. (2001) Comparison of final exam test scores of neuroscience students who experienced traditional methodologies versus problem-based learning methodologies. *Occupational Therapy in Health Care* 14 (3/4), 35-53.

Myers, C. (1986) *Teaching students to think critically. A guide for faculty of all disciplines*. San Francisco: Jossey-Bass Inc.

Nolinske, T. & Millis, B. (1999) Cooperative learning as an approach to pedagogy. *American Journal of Occupational Therapy* 53 (1), 31-40.

Schuh, K. L. & Busey, T. A. (2001) Implementation of a problem-based approach in an undergraduate cognitive neuroscience course. *College Teaching* 49 (4), 153-159.

Stokstad, E. (2001) Reintroducing the intro course. *Science* 293 (5535), 1608-1610.

Laugh and Learn:
Humor as a Teaching Strategy
in Occupational Therapy Education

Marti Southam, PhD, OTR/L, FAOTA
Kathleen Barker Schwartz, EdD, OTR/L, FAOTA

SUMMARY. Humor use in education has been studied in fields such as psychology and nursing. Research has demonstrated that effective educational humor needs to be integrated into the topic and used in moderation. Used appropriately, humor can gain attention, facilitate creative thinking and memory, motivate students to attend class, and promote learning outcomes. No studies were located in the occupational therapy literature that specifically related to humor as an aspect of teaching. The purpose of this article is to explore the merits of humor as an educational tool and to give examples of ways that occupational therapy faculty and clinical instructors can employ humor. *[Article copies available for a fee from The Haworth Document Delivery Service: 1-800-HAWORTH. E-mail address: <docdelivery@haworthpress.com> Website: <http://www.HaworthPress. com> © 2004 by The Haworth Press, Inc. All rights reserved.]*

Marti Southam is Assistant Professor, and Kathleen Barker Schwartz is Professor, Occupational Therapy Department, San Jose State University, San Jose, CA.

Address correspondence to: Dr. Marti Southam, Occupational Therapy Department, One Washington Square, San Jose State University, San Jose, CA 95192-0059 (E-mail: msoutham@casa.sjsu.edu).

[Haworth co-indexing entry note]: "Laugh and Learn: Humor as a Teaching Strategy in Occupational Therapy Education." Southam, Marti, and Kathleen Barker Schwartz. Co-published simultaneously in *Occupational Therapy in Health Care* (The Haworth Press, Inc.) Vol. 18, No. 1/2, 2004, pp. 57-70; and: *Best Practices in Occupational Therapy Education* (ed: Patricia A. Crist, and Marjorie E. Scaffa) The Haworth Press, Inc., 2004, pp. 57-70. Single or multiple copies of this article are available for a fee from The Haworth Document Delivery Service [1-800-HAWORTH, 9:00 a.m. - 5:00 p.m. (EST). E-mail address: docdelivery@haworthpress.com].

KEYWORDS. Educational humor, teacher immediacy, motivation

INTRODUCTION

Humor has received little recognition in occupational therapy literature, and is especially lacking in writings pertaining to occupational therapy education. Humor and fun, however, are two ingredients that produce a number of beneficial effects in the teacher and the learner. Affect is considered an important domain of learning (Bloom, 1974), and humor is one tool that teachers can use to engage and motivate learners, which relates to learning outcomes. Humor in educational settings can also serve to enculturate novices into the profession of occupational therapy that often has elements of embarrassing intimacy or "reality shocks." Robinson (1991, p. 115) lists four interrelated aspects of education and humor:

1. Enhancing the learning process itself through humor.
2. Facilitating the process of socialization into the health profession through humor.
3. Teaching the concept of humor as a communication and intervention tool.
4. Modeling the use of humor as a vehicle for facilitating the other three.

This article will explore humor and laughter in occupational therapy education by addressing several key points. First, a definition of humor will be offered. Second, it will review literature that addresses humor as an active learning approach related to creative instruction and learning outcomes. Third, it will provide considerations and strategies for employing humor in occupational therapy education,

DEFINITION OF HUMOR

Because humor is different according to the context (persons, places, and times), it can be a difficult concept to define. Southam (in press) defines humor as "any communication that leads to an emotional experience of amusement, pleasure, and/or mirth. It usually involves an element of surprise and results in smiling and laughter." This definition provides an understanding of the affective component, as well as a way to determine whether or not a humorous incident has occurred.

THE ART AND SCIENCE OF TEACHING

Just as occupational therapy has been described as an art and a science, so has teaching. The "science" of teaching refers to the rigorous organization of curriculum and delivery of accurate and timely information. The "art" involves the instructor's passion for the content and his or her ability to convey this passion through teaching. Master teachers are able to bring both the science and the art to the instructional setting in a way that produces relaxation and openness, enhances creativity and problem solving, and encourages interaction between students and the instructor (Allen, 1993; Hillman, 1995).

Enhancing the Learning Process Through Humor

Communicative behaviors that decrease physical and psychological distance between instructor and students are defined as "teacher immediacy" and are positively related to learning outcomes (Gorham & Christophel, 1990; Wanzer & Frymier, 1999). These behaviors often include the use of humor, maintaining eye contact, using vocal variety, smiling, gesturing and moving about in a relaxed manner, using personal stories, and talking with students outside of the instructional situation. Gorham and Christophel (1990) demonstrated a positive relationship between the frequency of humor use and the use of other verbal and nonverbal immediacy behaviors. In addition, the "overall use of verbal and nonverbal immediacy behaviors was highly correlated with learning outcomes" (p. 58).

The humor-learning relationship may be explained by humor's ability to arouse students' interest as well as to gain and hold their attention. Attention and motivation to learn are related to memory, which in turn is necessary for cognitive learning to occur (Frymier, 1994; Gorham, 1988; Loomans & Kolberg, 1993). Because humor appreciation in the educational setting changes according to the age of the learners, the instructor must take care in the selection of humor according to the age of the student (Robinson, 1991; Zillman & Bryant, 1983). The attention of younger children can be gained and maintained through silly, irrelevant humorous materials. However, for the adult learner, humor that is irrelevant to the topic is reported to have detrimental effects on information acquisition and on the relationship between the adult student and the teacher. On the other hand, humor that is relevant and well-integrated into the presentation subject matter makes the experience more enjoyable and adult students may experience superior retention of the material (Zillman & Bryant, 1983). The instructor's appeal is enhanced when humor is used to make pertinent points through wit. Witty, rather than funny, professors are considered interesting, entertaining, and motivating (Wanzer & Frymier,

1999). Interestingly, student demotivation is a result of teachers' lack of humor (Gorham & Christophel, 1990).

Using the theoretical assumption that lowering individuals' anxiety levels through humor would aid learning, Moses and Friedman (1986) conducted a quasi-experimental study of beginning nursing students' performance on a laboratory test (inserting a nasogastric tube). The hypothesis that student anxiety would be lowered and performance improved through the use of deliberate and relevant teacher humor was not supported through statistical analysis. However, the authors did report that posttest interviews with the nursing students revealed that more than half felt the humor was helpful during the task completion. Some confusion was apparent among the participants as they reported being unsure about how to respond to the introduction of humor during a performance test, with some finding it distracting. The authors recommended attempting this research with a larger sample size, using humor that was not only relevant but an integral part of the actual task, and finding more humorous interactions.

To investigate the effects on student learning of humor in teaching, Ziv (1988) conducted an excellent experimental study with replication. A semester course in statistics was planned with humor as the independent variable and learning as the dependent variable. The participants were two groups of students (n = 161) with approximately equal numbers of males and females. Group one was randomly chosen to be the experimental group receiving humorous instruction, and group two became the control group. The same teacher taught both classes. Student learning was measured by a standard departmental final exam. The results showed an average score on the final of 82.5 for the experimental humor group and 72.5 for the control group, a statistically significant difference in mean scores. The author followed up with a replication study using the same methodology but a different student population and a different teacher. The findings were similar with an average on the final exam of 82 for the experimental group and 73.5 for the control group. The author concluded that these results clearly demonstrated the contribution of teachers' uses of humor to student learning.

The Ha-Ha–AHA! Connection

Siegel (1986) reports that the two brain hemispheres seem to communicate unusually well during laughter. Furthermore, in order for something to be perceived as humorous, both hemispheres of the brain operate in concert (Ornstein, 1997). The right hemisphere is especially important in humor because it interprets nonverbal language cues such as facial expressions, gestures, and tone of voice. The linear, focused, and detail-oriented left side hemisphere has the ability to select the right word for speaking or for interpreting. When one is presented with a joke, cartoon, or humorous situation, there is often incongruity to be resolved (Koestler, 1964; McGhee, 1989; Ornstein, 1997). Frequently, there is a sudden shift or surprise that occurs, and a rapid interpretation needs to be made. The hemispheres communicate instantaneously in a complex mental undertaking that makes the humorous intention understandable (Ha-Ha–AHA!).

Cognitive characteristics expected of health care professionals include creative thinking (Robinson, 1991). Richards (1990) states that "affect may be key in motivating and channeling creative cognition" (p. 312). Brain chemistry, such as endorphin release, may facilitate such good feelings in a person, that he or she will continue to seek this "high" through future creative efforts. Also, individuals in an "up" mood tend to be more creative problem-solvers (Jamison, 1993), and an increase in bonding among group members is seen (Kuhlman, 1984; Metcalf & Felible, 1992).

To be a creative thinker requires more than knowledge; it requires an attitude or outlook that encourages manipulation of information for new possibilities. The use of humor and laughter in group brainstorming, which is part of collaborative and problem-based learning, allows participants to try various ideas, see new patterns and connections, and possibly to come up with something unique (von Oech, 1983; Warnock, 1989). Provine (1996) states that laughter occurs 30 times more often when people are in social situations than when they are alone. In a recent study, Provine found that 80 percent of the laughter in his sample took place in naturally occurring conversation, as mutual playfulness, which served to promote an "in-group" positive feeling amongst the participants. "In creative play, there are no wrong answers; there are only possibilities" (Loomans & Kolberg, 1993, p. xi).

Frequency and Types of Humor in Education

Humor is a component of educational presentation that enables the speaker to gain and hold the learner's attention, to impart information in a non-threatening way, to help groups bond, and to increase receptivity to new ideas (Hillman, 1995). Studies on the frequency and type of humor that college teachers use in the classroom demonstrate that it is a common element in lectures and class activities.

Frequency

Bryant, Comisky, Crane and Zillman (1980) found that humor was a normal part of pedagogy resulting in 3.34 humorous episodes per 50-min. class session. The focus of their research was on gender differences in usage of humor. Results indicated that male teachers utilized humor more frequently (over 5 times within a 50-minute class) than females (2.3 times). A later study by Gorham and Christophel (1990) also indicated that male instructors used humor slightly more often, but "the proportional uses of stories, comments, jokes, and tendentious humor were far more similar" (p. 60) between the genders than in the Bryant et al. study. Interestingly, learning outcomes of female students were not as influenced by teacher humor as were male students, although females did indicate a preference for personal stories to illustrate pertinent points (Gorham & Christophel, 1990).

Downs, Javidi, and Nussbaum (1988) conducted two consecutive studies of college teachers' uses of humor. Study 1 tape-recorded 50-minute lectures in courses across a variety of disciplines three times during one semester. Each tape was coded by two trained coders with an interceder reliability of .80. The results showed an average of 13 humorous attempts directed towards course material predominantly playing off course content, but instructors also used humor directed at self, students, others not in class, and "other." Seventy percent of the humor was relevant to course content. A follow-up, comparative study was conducted to describe the use of humor and other verbal behaviors of nine award-winning teachers. They were videotaped for the entire 50-minute period of a class in the second, sixth, and tenth week of the spring semesters of three consecutive years. Two trained people coded the tapes with an inter-coder reliability of .85. Results found an average of seven humorous attempts, aimed at others not in class, self and course material. Sixty-six percent of the humor was relevant to the course content. These teachers showed a downward trend in humor use during the semester, with the highest amount in the second week, less in the sixth week, and least in the tenth week.

Types of Humor Used in Teaching

Bryant, Comisky, and Zillman (1979) categorized humor use by college teachers into six areas: joke, riddle, puns, funny stories, funny comments, and other. Humor was mostly spontaneous and was positively related to subsequent evaluations of teacher competence by students.

Gorham and Christophel (1990) inductively described a typology of 13 types of humor as recorded by college students. Six are "brief tendentious comments" directed at an individual student; the class as a whole; the university, department or state; national or world events, personalities, or popular culture; the topic, subject or class procedures; and the teacher. The remaining types include personal and general anecdotes related to the subject; personal and general anecdotes unrelated to subject; jokes; physical or vocal comedy; and other.

Shade (1996) described four forms of humor that teachers use in the class-room: (1) figural that is displayed through drawings, comic strips, cartoons, TV, magazines; (2) verbal that uses language, often incongruity, through jokes, puns, irony, limericks, tall tales; (3) visual elements that depend on sight for cues to humor (clowning, slapstick, pratfalls, impersonations); and (4) auditory elements that depend on hearing for cues to humor like noises, funny sounds (whistles, beepers, imitation of animals, etc.), and impressions.

HUMOR, LAUGHTER AND HEALTH

Students who consistently attend classes are more likely to learn and retain information better than students with frequent absences. The use of humor by instructors may increase learning enjoyment, but it may also have an actual health benefit for students that could affect their attendance and thus, their learning. Studies have shown that a relationship exists between psychosocial factors, especially stress, and changes in immune status. An experimental study by Cohen (1995) demonstrated a positive relationship between stress level and the development of a cold. Pretests of stress level, health status and practices, and presence of white blood cells were administered to 400 healthy people who were then randomly assigned to an experimental or a control group. Experimental subjects were given upper respiratory viral droplets in each nostril; the control group received saline droplets. After four days of iso-lation, both groups were examined for infection. None of the control group de-veloped a cold. The results showed that there was a positive relationship between stress level and the probability of developing a cold in the experimen-tal group. In other words, when exposed to an illness, the higher one's stress level, the higher the probability of becoming ill.

Educators hold high expectations for students being trained to become oc-cupational therapists. Programs are generally rigorous, and may produce stress. A variety of experts cite humor and laughter's roles as stress reducers and as health enhancers (Black, 1984; Cousins, 1989; Fry, 1992; Lee, 1990; Wooten, 1996). Humor, playfulness, and laughter aid physical health in a number of ways. Hearty laughter increases heart rate and respiratory activity that often leads to coughing, which stimulates and cleans out the lungs. Blood pressure drops after a bout of belly laughter. Muscle physiologists have shown that "anxiety and muscle relaxation cannot occur at the same time and that the relaxation response after a hearty laugh can last up to 45 minutes" (Adams, 1992, p. 17). Muscle tension of the neck, face, and head, which often leads to headaches, may be relieved after laughter. The pituitary gland may also stimu-late release of endorphins and enkephalins, nature's painkillers. According to

Fry (1992), laughter releases hormones, including epinephrine, norepinephrine and dopamine, which alert all the senses.

Researchers (Berk, 1996; Berk, Tan, & Fry, 1993) have conducted numerous studies and have documented the beneficial psychoneuroimmunological effects of mirthful laughter. Their experimental research demonstrated that levels of cortisol, a precursor of stress hormones that produces fight or flight reactions, decreased during and after laughter; and levels of antibodies increased in the experimental subjects when compared to the control group. Gamma interferon, a substance that acts as a modulator of immune function, increased. Natural Killer cells that locate and kill abnormal cells were recorded in larger numbers during and after mirthful laughter. These researchers conclude that laughter may really be the best medicine!

CONCLUSION

Humor is a key teacher immediacy behavior and can be a useful tool in the educator's repertoire to gain attention, facilitate creative thinking and memory, motivate students to attend class and study, possibly promote health, and facilitate learning outcomes. For humor to be effective, however, it must be used in moderation, be appropriate to the adult learner, and be relevant and integrated into the topic. Student gender must also be taken into account. Females (the bulk of occupational therapy students) have less appreciation for jokes than males and prefer anecdotal and personal stories to make points.

CONSIDERATIONS AND STRATEGIES FOR HUMOR USE IN TEACHING

Appropriate and Inappropriate Humor

Humor appreciation is unique to each individual depending upon one's age, culture, intellect, and even physical status at the time (Silberman, 1987). In other words, what might be funny to a person from Africa would not cause a ripple of amusement in someone from Canada (and vice versa). But then again, both people might find the same thing funny, depending upon the circumstances. A person who is tired and sleepy might not find something amusing that he or she would usually think was hysterical, or on the other hand, everything could seem funny and cause riotous laughter. Humor is personal and enigmatic, and must be used appropriately to be effective.

Environment is important to the free expression of humor. Large lecture halls with tiered seating make moving around and forming groups difficult; a room with movable chairs or desks is preferable. Props, overhead projector, flip chart, video and audio equipment, and bulletin boards can enhance the presentation of humorous material (Hillman, 1995). The tone of learning enjoyment needs to be set by a relaxed and approachable instructor who engages students both inside and outside the educational setting.

Activities may include ice breakers, wake-em-up tricks, warm ups, laughing lessons, learning games and play breaks. Many wonderful ideas can be found in numerous books written specifically for teachers who want to implement humor in their instructional planning (Loomans & Kolberg, 1993; Scannell & Newstrom, 1998; Shade, 1996; Sugar, 1998).

Potential problems concerning humor use in teaching may occur if the instructor is not sensitive to inappropriate humor use by him or herself and by students. Inappropriate forms of humor in education include sarcasm, ridicule, racist or ethnic jokes, obscenities, scatological and sexual jokes.

Teacher, Know Thyself

A key consideration for an instructor who wants to use humor in teaching is to know his or her own style of humor. Loomans and Kolberg (1993, pp. 15-19) describe four distinct categories:

1. The Joy Master: includes everyone in uplifting, warmhearted play and laughter that is healing and humanizing.
2. The Fun Meister: entertains through clowning, imitation or slapstick, but may use ridicule that is hurtful and degrading.
3. The Joke Maker: uses wordplay and parodies to show insight, but may use destructive verbal humor that is satirical and insulting.
4. The Life Mocker: uses humor in a dehumanizing, cynical way that excludes others.

The Joy Master, obviously, is the optimal style of humor, but mixing in positive traits of the Fun Meister and the Joke Maker can spice up educational presentations. The Life Mocker is never appropriate in dealing with students. A series of checklists are provided by Loomans and Kolberg (1993) for teachers to determine their individual humor style.

Examples of Possible Humor Uses in Occupational Therapy Education

Visual Media

As the old saying goes, "a picture is worth a thousand words." Cartoons can rapidly get a message across through simplification, exaggeration, and/or distortion (Pease, 1991). Students may be assigned to collect cartoons from newspapers, magazines, and other printed material that illustrate stereotypes (for example, aging, disability, homelessness, etc.) and then share and critique them during a class. Pease (1991) also suggests projecting a cartoon and having students fill in the caption. She states that their stereotypical thinking is often revealed and fosters a lively discussion. After this experience she describes distributing cartoons to students in small groups and asking them to brainstorm as many captions as possible in three minutes. These may be shared with the larger group and awarded prizes for being most creative and funny. Topics range from the stresses of being a student to the really "heavy, various" ideas that are part of a health professional's training.

In a class on "Human Adaptation Across the Life Span" that the author teaches, the topic of loss as it occurs in aging is first experienced by students in an empathy activity. They are told to list the top 10 things that are most important in their lives. Students must then gradually eliminate nine from their list, leaving only their top priority item. Southam leads a discussion of how hard it is to lose people, animals, abilities, and favorite activities, and relates loss to aging as something that people often experience the longer they live. This usually produces a somber, sad and thoughtful atmosphere. To lighten up the learning environment for the next topic, Southam then plays a clip of Billy Crystal from the movie, *City Slickers*. Crystal's character describes what it's like to grow old, putting a funny spin on a serious topic that produces the release of laughter and an openness to move on to the next point in the lecture.

Verbal Humor

In reviewing material for presenting an instructional unit, the instructor may recall a particular incident that can help to make the point through a personal narrative. Stories of the teacher's experiences provide a way for students to learn the material as well as feel closer to the teacher (Hillman, 1995; Parrot, 1994; Watson & Emerson, 1988). This can be an especially useful technique for clinical educators.

Humorous quotations, poems, or songs related to the topic can be introduced into a presentation to gain students' attention, rehearse learning, or add emphasis to a particular concept (Robinson, 1991). Robbins (1994), a creative nursing instructor, turned a laboratory on body mechanics when transferring patients into a fun, songfest. She first taught the proper ways for lifting and moving patients through video and demonstration. Then she played rock music and students followed directions posted on a transparency by singing a song developed by Robbins to teach the steps in a safe bed to chair transfer.

Kinesthetic Humor

Humor that involves movement can alert the senses, facilitate blood flow, release physical tension, encourage interactions, and promote learning. An example from the author's experience comes from a unit on hand skill development. After teaching hand, finger and upper extremity movements required for reach, grasp and release, students are instructed to place their hands palm down on a piece of paper in their manual (an old page left in for this exercise). Next, they must use just that one hand to wad the page into a ball while ripping it out of their manual. Such an unexpected direction yields surprised laughter which is rapidly followed by Southam saying, "Now, let's have a snow ball fight!" Activity and laughter erupt. Once the "snow balls" are retrieved and discarded, debriefing takes place with students describing the hand and upper extremity motions they used during the activity as well as the trunk stability required for distal movements.

Play breaks that include body movements and laughter can energize learners. One example is the "Sixty-Second Mirth Quake" (Loomans & Kolberg, 1993, p. 125). Students are asked to stand and start with a small, silent smile. They then turn to someone and smile. Soon, the instructor requests that students perform laughing motions, but without a sound. The movements build and finally, they are encouraged to add sound and really laugh. Problem-based learning discussion may be facilitated after these few minutes of laughter, which is known to increase blood circulation, promote communication between the brain hemispheres, and increase social bonding.

Role plays and skits have also been used successfully by teachers and students to teach concepts and to demonstrate therapeutic techniques. Exaggeration, costumes, and props can add to the joy (Parrott, 1994). Besides being fun for everyone, these activities encourage group bonding and creative thinking, important aspects of occupational therapy education and practice. For example, as part of the class on the "History of Occupational Therapy," the co-author, Schwartz, requires her students to find a way to present a topic as the founders of the profession might have. They come to class dressed in time-appropriate clothes and speak in the language of the times. One student dressed as Susan Tracy and asked a group of students to be her clients while she taught a craft in Tracy's style (i.e., making use of zero to low-cost items).

In the "Introduction to Occupational Therapy" class that the co-author teaches, Schwartz discusses the concept of the therapeutic use of self. One aspect of the class includes how therapists might use humor in situations with clients to decrease tension and redirect the client's thinking. Small groups of students are given case studies and are asked to develop humor strategies to role play with a variety of clients. The students take turns using humor to intervene, which gives everyone the opportunity to be creative and to see how others might handle the same situation.

CONCLUSION

By using appropriate humor, educators can increase their own enjoyment of teaching as well as promote learning outcomes for students. Humor can nurture the learners' creativity, socialization into the profession and even their physical health. A future challenge for occupational therapy educators is to study empirical evidence regarding the benefits and values of humor as a practice and educational tool.

REFERENCES

Adams, P. (with Mylander, M.) (1992, December). Good health is a laughing matter. *Caring Magazine* (pp. 16-20).

Allen, S. (1993). Foreword. In D. Loomans & K. Kolberg, *The laughing classroom: Everyone's guide to teaching with humor and play*, p. ix. Tiburon, CA: H. J. Kramer.

Berk, L. (1996). The laughter-immune connection: New discoveries. *Humor and Health Journal, 5,* 1-5.

Berk, L., Tan, S., & Fry, W. (1993). Eustress of humor associated laughter modulates specific immune system components. *Annals of Behavioral Medicine, 15,* 111.

Black, D. W. (1984). Laughter. *Journal of the American Medical Association, 252* (21), 2995-2998.

Bloom, B. S. (Ed.) (1974). *Taxonomy of educational objectives: The classification of educational goals.* New York: David McKay Co.

Bryant, J., Comisky, P. W., Crane, J. S., & Zillman, D. (1980). Relationship between college teachers' use of humor in the classroom and students' evaluations of their teachers. *Journal of Educational Psychology, 72* (4), 511-519.

Bryant, J., Comisky, P., & Zillman, D. (1979). Teachers' humor in the college classroom. *Communication Education, 28,* 110-118.

Cohen, S. (1995). Stress and susceptibility to the common cold. In N. Hall, F. Altman, & S. J. Blumenthal (Eds.), *Mind-body interactions and disease: Proceedings of a conference on stress, immunity, and health* sponsored by the National Institutes of Health (pp. 45-51). Tampa, FL: Health Dateline Press.

Cousins, N. (1989). *Head First.* New York: Penguin Books.

Downs, V. C., Javidi, M., & Nussbaum, J. F. (1988). An analysis of teachers' verbal communication within the college classroom: Use of humor, self-disclosure, and narratives. *Communication Education, 37,* 127-141.

Fry, W. F. (1992). The physiologic effects of humor, mirth, and laughter. *Journal of the American Medical Association, 267* (13), 1857-1858.

Frymier, A. B. (1994). A model of immediacy in the classroom. *Communication Quarterly, 41*, 454-464.

Gorham, J. (1988). The relationship between teacher immediacy behavior and student learning. *Communication Education, 37*, 40-53.

Gorham, J. & Christophel, D. M. (1990). The relationship of teachers' use of humor in the classroom to immediacy and student learning. *Communication Education, 39*, 46-62.

Hillman, S. M. (1995). Laugh and learn: Humor in nursing education. *Journal of Nursing Jocularity, 5* (1), 32-34.

Jamison, K. R. (1993). *Touched with fire: Manic-depressive illness and the artistic temperament.* New York: Free Press

Koestler, A. (1964). *The act of creation.* New York: Penguin Books.

Kuhlman, T. L. (1984). *Humor and psychotherapy.* Homewood, IL: Down Jones-Irwin.

Lee, B. 5. (1990). Humor relations for nurse managers. *Nursing Management, 21* (3), 86-92.

Loomans, D. & Kolberg, K. (1993). *The laughing classroom: Everyone's guide to teaching with humor and play.* Tiburon, CA: H. J. Kramer.

McGhee, P. (Ed.) (1989). *Humor and children's development: A guide to practical applications.* New York: The Haworth Press, Inc.

Metcalf, C.W. & Felible, R. (1992). *Lighten up: Survival skills for people under pressure.* Reading, MA: Addison-Wesley Publishing Co.

Moses, N. W. & Friedman, M. M. (1986). Using humor in evaluating student performance. *Journal of Nursing Education, 25* (8), 328-333.

Ornstein, R. (1997). *The right mind: Making sense of the hemispheres.* New York: Harcourt Brace & Company.

Parrott, T. E. (1994). Humor as a teaching strategy. *Nurse Educator, 19* (3), 36-38.

Pease, R. A. (1991). Cartoon humor in nursing education. *Nursing Outlook, 39* (6), 262-267.

Provine, R. R. (1996). Laughter. *American Scientist, 84*, 38-45.

Richards, R. (1990). Everyday creativity, eminent creativity, and health "Afterview" for *Creativity Research Journal* special issue on creativity and health. *Creativity Research Journal, 3*, 300-326.

Robbins, J. (1994). Using humor to enhance learning in the skills laboratory. *Nurse Educator, 19* (3), 39-41.

Robinson, V. M. (1991). *Humor and the health professions: The therapeutic use of humor in health care* (2nd Ed.). Thorofare, NJ: SLACK.

Scannell, E. & Newstrom, J. (1998). *The big book of presentation games: Wake-em-up tricks, ice breakers, and other fun stuff.* New York: McGraw-Hill.

Shade, R. A. (1996). *License to laugh: Humor in the classroom.* Englewood, CO: Teachers Ideas Press.

Siegel, B. (1986). *Love, medicine, and miracles.* New York: Harper and Row.

Silberman, I. (1987). Humor and health: An epidemiological study. *American Behavioral Scientist, 30* (1), 110-112.

Southam, M. (in press). Therapeutic humor: Attitudes and actions by occupational therapists with adult clients in physical disabilities settings. *Occupational Therapy in Health Care, 17* (1).

Sugar, S. (1998). *Games that teach: Experiential activities for reinforcing training.* San Francisco, CA: Jossey-Bass/Pfeiffer.

von Oech, R. (1983). *A whack on the side of the head: How to unlock your mind for innovation.* New York: Warner Books.

Wanzer, M. B. & Frymier, A. B. (1999). The relationship between student perceptions of instructor humor and students' reports of learning. *Communication Education, 48,* 48-62.

Warnock, P. (1989). Humor, a didactic tool in adult education. *Lifelong Learning, 12* (6), 22-24.

Watson, M. J. & Emerson, S. (1988). Facilitate learning with humor. *Journal of Nursing Education, 27* (2), 89-90.

Wooten, P. (1996). Humor: An antidote for stress. *Holistic Nursing Practice, 10 (2),* 49-56.

Zillman, D. & Bryant, J. (1983). Uses and effects of humor in educational ventures. In P. McGhee & J. H. Goldstein (Eds.), *Handbook of Humor Research, Volume II: Applied studies,* pp. 173-193. New York: Springer-Verlag.

Ziv, A. (1988). Teaching and learning with humor: Experiment and replication. *Journal of Experimental Education, 57*(1), 5-15.

FOCUS ON STUDENT PROFESSIONAL DEVELOPMENT

Promoting Professional Reflection Through Problem-Based Learning Evaluation Activities

Martina C. McNulty, PhD, OTR/L
Terry K. Crowe, PhD, OTR/L, FAOTA
Betsy VanLeit, PhD, OTR/L

SUMMARY. To become competent occupational therapy practitioners, students must develop the ability to reflect upon their current and future

Martina C. McNulty is Assistant Professor, and Terry K. Crowe is Professor and Director, Occupational Therapy Graduate Program, Department of Orthopaedics, University of New Mexico. Betsy VanLeit is Assistant Professor, Occupational Therapy Graduate School, Department of Orthopaedics, University of New Mexico.

Address correspondence to: Tina McNulty, Assistant Professor, Health Sciences Center, Occupational Therapy Graduate Program, MSC09 5240, 1 University of New Mexico, Albuquerque, NM 87131-0001.

Readers can write to the first author for a copy of the UNM Student Self-Assessment of PBL Participation.

[Haworth co-indexing entry note]: "Promoting Professional Reflection Through Problem-Based Learning Evaluation Activities." McNulty, Martina C., Terry K. Crowe, and Betsy VanLeit. Co-published simultaneously in *Occupational Therapy in Health Care* (The Haworth Press, Inc.) Vol. 18, No. 1/2, 2004, pp. 71-82; and: *Best Practices in Occupational Therapy Education* (ed: Patricia A. Crist, and Marjorie E. Scaffa) The Haworth Press, Inc., 2004, pp. 71-82. Single or multiple copies of this article are available for a fee from The Haworth Document Delivery Service [1-800-HAWORTH, 9:00 a.m. - 5:00 p.m. (EST). E-mail address: docdelivery@haworthpress.com].

Digital Object Identifier:10.1300/J003v18n01_08

professional development. This paper presents one curriculum's approach (the University of New Mexico) to using evaluation activities in problem-based learning to enhance students' cultivation of professional reflection skills. A description of these evaluation activities and accompanying tools is provided along with a critique of their strengths and limitations. *[Article copies available for a fee from The Haworth Document Delivery Service: 1-800-HAWORTH. E-mail address: <docdelivery@ haworthpress.com> Website: <http://www.HaworthPress.com> © 2004 by The Haworth Press, Inc. All rights reserved.]*

KEYWORDS. Professional development, reflective practitioner, educational assessment

INTRODUCTION

Occupational therapy educators are challenged to implement and evaluate educational strategies that effectively and efficiently teach our profession's evolving and growing core knowledge base. Problem-based learning (PBL) is an innovative educational method that educators can use to facilitate students' efficient learning of critical occupational therapy content and processes. PBL was designed to promote students' professional problem-solving, development of self-directed learning habits, and integration of basic science knowledge into applied scenarios (Barrows, 1986; VanLeit, 1995). PBL affords students the opportunity to develop or remediate noncognitive professional behaviors that have been recognized as important predictors of their future success in fieldwork. These behaviors include successfully problem-solving ambiguities found in practice, responding productively to constructive feedback, and taking responsibility for one's own professional knowledge and growth (Gutman, McCreedy, & Heisler, 1998; Hayes, Huber, Rogers, & Sanders, 1999). One major criticism of PBL has been the difficulty of evaluating its outcomes relative to its perceived labor- and time-intensive requirements (Vroman & MacRae, 1999). In this paper, we will present one curriculum's (University of New Mexico) PBL evaluation process and describe how we believe it supports one of the most important program outcome competencies for PBL: the development of professional reflection skills.

PROFESSIONAL REFLECTION SKILLS

Expert professional practitioners demonstrate an ability to set and solve problems by applying their knowledge and experience to the unique characteristics of a given challenge or problem (Schön, 1983). In a sense, seasoned practitioners are able to instinctively engage in a "conversation" with the problem or challenge at hand. One hallmark of this "conversation" is the ability to reflect while taking action, which often culminates in the discovery of a solution that is relevant and novel (Schön, 1995). This type of flexible and skillful professional reasoning requires intellectual curiosity and an ability to engage in self-directed learning. The reflection process often requires gathering additional professional resources (e.g., books, consultation, etc.) and deliberating critically upon past efforts to resolve the challenge. The nature of providing relevant and meaningful occupational therapy services draws upon this type of professional reflection in action, and is a skill that educators strive to instill in their students.

PBL Evaluation

Educators in occupational therapy and other health science disciplines have described varied efforts to evaluate the outcomes of PBL. Faculty who facilitate PBL grow to appreciate the value of PBL as a unique and worthwhile educational endeavor (Bernstein, Tipping, Bercovitz, & Skinner, 1995). However, designing the definitive evaluation tool for PBL has been notoriously elusive, partly because PBL is designed to promote students' development of complex cognitive and noncognitive professional skills. Occupational therapy researchers have principally utilized qualitative methods to document students' positive perceptions of their experiences with PBL (Hammel et al., 1999; Sadlo, 1997; Stern, 1997). Occupational therapy investigators have also attempted to demonstrate significant differences on tests of critical thinking between students who have participated in a PBL course versus those who have not (Liotta-Kleinfeld & McPhee, 2001; McLeod, 1997, June). Unfortunately, no significant differences in critical thinking were detected with the particular tools used in these studies. Disciplines such as medicine, nursing, and clinical laboratory sciences have found positive outcomes by comparing course evaluations, certification exam performance, and changes in learning styles in students who have and have not been taught with PBL (Teshima, 2001; White, Amos, & Kouzekanani, 1999). However, limitations can be found with each of these chosen outcome measures.

UNM PROFESSIONAL REFLECTION PROCESS

PBL has been an integral part of the University of New Mexico (UNM) Occupational Therapy Program since the program's inception 10 years ago

(VanLeit & Crowe, 2000). PBL was adopted along with other didactic and experiential approaches to support the teaching of the curriculum's three core competencies: professional reasoning, professional communication, and professional reflection and growth. Throughout the history of PBL in the UNM curriculum, the importance of a multidimensional approach to evaluation has been recognized and refined. This continuous process of evaluation and improvement has helped the PBL develop as a rich and integrated component of the entire curriculum. The evaluation process has also grown into an effective model for the type of professional reflection behaviors that we wish to develop in our students. As the faculty demonstrates behaviors consistent with the role of reflective educators, students simultaneously develop their skills as reflective practitioners. Thus, the evaluation or "feedback" process for our PBL curriculum has become conceptualized as the PBL professional reflection process. The PBL reflection and evaluation process is comprised of four different tools to facilitate professional reflection and addresses all the facets of effective PBL: the Student Self-Assessment of PBL Participation, Student PBL Professional Objectives and Growth, Faculty Facilitator Evaluation, and the PBL Focus Group Interview.

Student Self-Assessment of PBL Participation

One tool developed over the years to facilitate students' participation in PBL is the Student Self-Assessment of PBL Participation. This assessment is organized around three core competencies in the curriculum's design: professional reasoning, professional communication, and professional reflection and growth (VanLeit & Crowe, 2000). The tool serves two major purposes. The first is to communicate to students what specific skills related to these three competencies the faculty wants them to develop and demonstrate in PBL. Significant effort was made by the faculty as a whole to codify the 30 specific behavioral skills that students could concretely observe in themselves and others during PBL. Figure 1 is the first page of this evaluation and shows specific skill items developed for the core competency of professional reasoning. For the core competency of professional communication, examples of skill items are: (a) demonstrates professional verbal and nonverbal communication (e.g., makes eye contact with members, projects voice, has confident body language, etc.); and (b) helps group organize agenda and defines the group's goals for the day. Examples for the core competency of professional reflection and growth include: (a) uses group to help identify growth areas and to check out self-perceptions and (b) identifies strengths and areas of concern in the group process with specific examples.

FIGURE 1. Page One of the UNM Occupational Therapy Graduate Program Mid-Semester Student Self-Assessment of PBL Participation

---

Mid-Semester Student Self-Assessment of PBL Participation

Student: _____   Date: _____

Facilitator: _____

Directions: 1. After each section, reflect on your strengths and areas for growth.
2. On the last page, identify your top strengths, areas to develop, and an objective for your professional growth.
3. Please complete this assessment prior to coming to PBL.

PROFESSIONAL PRACTICE

Knowledge and Learning:

- Is prepared for PBL
- Asks questions that clarify concepts and content of case
- Integrates readings and information from other courses (e.g., anatomy, applied kinesiology for occupation, etc.) into case discussions as appropriate
- Discusses information in adequate breadth & depth
- Comments demonstrate understanding of concepts & information presented in the case as well as in the curriculum

Critical Thinking/Professional Reasoning:

- Uses data and information from learning resources to support comments and questions
- Formulates relevant, focused learning issues
- Formulates hypotheses with new and previously acquired information
- Applies occupational therapy models and theoretical frames of references to cases
- Uses a variety of current learning resources
- Critiques & questions resources utilized including own
- Challenges others' concepts and ideas in a constructive way

Overall Rating for Professional Practice Skills: (Check one) ___ Satisfactory ___ Unsatisfactory

Reflect on your strengths and areas for growth:

For each set of skill items under a given core competency, students are directed to write specific examples of when they have performed particular skills well, or when they have demonstrated a need to improve them. The second purpose of the tool is to provide structure for students' careful self-evaluation through identification of their top three strengths and top three areas for growth. Based upon their reflections of their strengths and areas for growth, students then write at least one measurable objective for their future professional growth in PBL. The evaluation's final section includes an area for the student's faculty facilitator to write brief comments on each student's professional growth throughout his or her PBL participation.

Designing relevant and measurable objectives for professional development became a feature of this assessment because faculty recognized students needed more opportunities to expand this skill. The Student Self-Assessment of PBL Participation form requires that students design a measurable objective for their professional growth in PBL at the mid-semester and end of the semester. As students have gained more practice with personal objective writing in PBL, we have also seen their proficiency with writing client objectives in courses and fieldwork improve as well.

Student PBL Professional Objectives and Growth

The end of the semester objectives from the Student Self-Assessment of PBL Participation are recorded on the Student PBL Professional Objectives and Growth tracking sheet (see Figure 2). During each semester, students have the opportunity to review and discuss the progress documented on this form during their designated PBL mid-semester and final reflection group discussions. This document captures each student's progress related to professional objectives across four semesters.

FIGURE 2. Example of One Student's Professional Objectives and Growth Across the UNM Occupational Therapy Program's Curriculum

	UNIVERSITY OF NEW MEXICO Occupational Therapy Graduate Program **Student PBL Professional Objectives and Growth**	
	Objectives	Date Achieved/ Continued
Year 1, Fall	To improve my ability to communicate information succinctly, I will verbally summarize information related to the case at least once during each PBL session.	9/5/01
Year 1, Spring	To improve my ability to communicate information effectively, I will use some type of visual aid/diagram/outline during each PBL session to present my learning issue throughout this semester.	11/1/01
Year 2, Fall	To improve my professional reasoning, I will include class information in my learning issue presentation at least one time each session until the end of the semester.	5/4/02
Year 2, Spring	To increase my group leadership skills, I will summarize the group's progress or assist in providing direction for group one time each PBL session.	12/7/02

Faculty Facilitator Evaluation

Because the role of facilitator is so vital to successful PBL experiences, students complete a faculty PBL Facilitator Evaluation at the end of the semester (see Figure 3). The feedback gleaned from the ratings and students' comments can guide future professional development of facilitators through formal and informal training. The ratings and comments on the PBL Facilitator Evaluation can also be used by faculty to support their promotion efforts.

Time to Reflect, Discuss, and Plan for Future Growth

Meaningful professional reflection can only occur in a learning environment that students perceive as safe and supportive. The tools shown in this paper support, but cannot replace, the skilled facilitation required to engage students in a genuine discussion of their professional strengths and areas for growth. The heart of professional reflection is the time that faculty must create to assist students in verbally reflecting upon what they have written in the previously described documents and to help them to discuss a plan for their future growth in PBL. In our curriculum time is dedicated to these reflective discussions at the end of each PBL session, at the mid-semester, and at the end of the semester.

Specifically, during each two- to-three hour PBL session, 20 to 30 minutes are designated as a reflection time in which all students have the opportunity to discuss their perceptions of how PBL "went for them" during that session. Students review the strengths of their participation and areas for growth as well as those of their peers and faculty facilitator. This discussion can also include comments about how the PBL's group process supported or detracted from their own learning experiences.

Significantly more time is devoted to this reflection and feedback process at the middle and end of the semester, i.e., one to two hours, so that students can take the long view of their PBL participation across the semester and curriculum. Students are supported not only in sharing their own areas for growth, but are encouraged to give constructive feedback to their peers and their facilitator. Once again, the notion of a safe environment must be created by the faculty facilitator if students are to take risks and give each other constructive feedback. The faculty facilitators serve as models for reflecting on group and individual strengths and areas for growth. The faculty must be willing to share their own areas of growth and model the ability to create measurable goals for their professional development. One veteran faculty facilitator tells her students in PBL that it is the highest compliment for her to receive constructive

FIGURE 3. UNM Occupational Therapy Graduate Program PBL Facilitator Evaluation

UNIVERSITY OF NEW MEXICO
Occupational Therapy Graduate Program
PBL Facilitator Evaluation

Facilitator: _____   Date: _____

Semester/Year: _____

Directions: **Use the following scale to rate your PBL facilitator. Please add your comments below.**

RATING KEY :

1	2	3	4	5
Strongly Disagree	Disagree	Neutral	Agree	Strongly Agree

1. Promoted student-directed learning	1	2	3	4	5
2. Promoted critical thinking and evidence-based practice related to case content	1	2	3	4	5
3. Challenged students appropriately	1	2	3	4	5
4. Promoted students' leadership skills	1	2	3	4	5
5. Served as a resource person when appropriate	1	2	3	4	5
6. Sensed problems and assisted in resolution	1	2	3	4	5
7. Facilitated fair and appropriate feedback and reflection	1	2	3	4	5
8. Considered and listened to student feedback and reflection	1	2	3	4	5
9. Demonstrated enthusiasm for educational role	1	2	3	4	5

Additional Comments:

Areas of strength:

Areas for growth:

Other Comments:

feedback from a student in PBL. The student's willingness to do this is an indicator that a safe environment has been created and that students see faculty as reflective educators who welcome the opportunity to learn and grow. Students often articulate a desire to become more proficient in giving constructive feedback in PBL because they recognize it as an important skill they will utilize in their future roles as therapists, team members, and supervisors. Faculty also often need to help students craft clear and relevant objectives for their professional goals. This facilitation and ensuing discussions can powerfully influence how students decide to develop their professional skills in future PBL sessions and in their practice as occupational therapists.

End of Semester Focus Group Interviews

Reflection regarding the strengths and limitations of each case occurs each time a case is completed. In general, cases are revised after each semester. In addition, a focus group interview is held at the end of the semester to provide an opportunity for students to reflect upon their faculty facilitation and how well the timing of the cases integrated with their course lectures and labs. A faculty member who did not facilitate the students leads the students through the standard focus group questions (see Table 1). Students routinely provide constructive recommendations about cases, facilitation, and integration with coursework that are documented and acted upon by faculty in future semesters.

ADVANTAGES AND LIMITATIONS OF THIS PROCESS

The professional reflection process described in this paper assumes a significant commitment on the part of involved faculty and students. Professional reflection takes discipline and time, a precious commodity in educational environments with competing demands for ever-increasing content. We estimate that during an average semester, a faculty facilitator will devote approximately eight to 10 hours to professional reflection activities which includes

TABLE 1. PBL Focus Group Interview Questions

1.	How well was PBL integrated with your coursework this semester?
2.	In general, what did you like/dislike about each of the cases this semester?
3.	How did you feel about the facilitation of your group this semester?
4.	Do you have any recommendations concerning PBL in the curriculum?

three hours outside of the designated PBL time to prepare reflective comments for students and to provide individual written comments on each student's self-assessment form at mid-semester and at the end of the semester. Nonetheless, educational scholars have emphasized the need for faculty to teach students how to apply the knowledge they gain in meaningful contexts to deepen learning and to enhance future meaningful information retrieval (Norman & Schmidt, 1992). Professional reflection in the context of problem-based learning can not only improve students' professional reasoning, but it can serve as a powerful catalyst for students to address noncognitive professional behavior deficiencies that can sabotage their future success in fieldwork. The faculty in the UNM Occupational Therapy Graduate Program have observed specific instances in which students have gained feedback and insight in PBL that initiated important changes in students' professional attitudes and behaviors that likely would not have been addressed until the student was in fieldwork.

One limitation of this model of reflection and evaluation is that it demands program-wide acceptance and commitment. Time must be made to discuss the results of these reflective activities and systematic methods must be used to track needed changes made to the cases, schedules, facilitator training, etc. However, the end result of this level of faculty commitment is that students become inculcated in the value of professional reflection and take active responsibility for making constructive recommendations for PBL in the curriculum. By their second or third semester of PBL, students have made a serious investment in the professional reflection process and they are highly committed to the activities that support their continued growth as well as the development of the curriculum as a whole.

CONCLUSION

The majority of educational assessments most curriculums employ in the classroom evaluate students' cognitive mastery of basic and applied knowledge essential for occupational therapy practice. Unfortunately, these types of paper and pencil evaluations may not provide our students with the kind of learning they vitally need related to their professional behaviors and communication. The thoughtful use of professional reflection and evaluation activities in the context of a Problem-Based Learning curriculum can powerfully and effectively develop both the cognitive and noncognitive behaviors that students must successfully perform in their Fieldwork II practicums. We have proposed an evaluation system that promotes students' taking responsibility for their own professional growth through professional reflection opportunities that are heavily supported by faculty. The outcomes from the evaluation process we have described are students' high investment in professional reflection as well as their documented progress on self-selected objectives in the areas of professional reasoning, professional communication, and professional reflection and growth. We consider the time devoted to facilitating students' reflection upon their professional reasoning, communication, leadership, and growth a critical opportunity to hone skills they will soon need to demonstrate fluently in their future occupational therapy practice.

REFERENCES

Barrows, H. S. (1986). A taxonomy of problem-based learning methods. *Medical Education, 20* (6), 481-486.

Bernstein, P., Tipping, J., Bercovitz, & Skinner, H. A. (1995). Shifting students and faculty to a PBL curriculum: Attitudes changed and lessons learned. *Academic Medicine, 75,* 66-70.

Blake, R. L., Hosokawa, M. C., & Riley, S. L. (2000). Student performances on Step 1 and Step 2 of the United States Medical Licensing Examination following implementation of a problem-based learning curriculum. *Academic Medicine, 75,* 66-70.

Gutman, S. A., McCreedy, P., & Heisler, P. (1998). Student level II fieldwork failure: Strategies for intervention. *American Journal of Occupational Therapy, 52,* 143-149.

Hammel, J., Royeen, C. B., Bagatell, N., Chandler, B., Jensen, G., Loveland, J., & Stone, G. (1999). Student perspectives on problem-based learning in an occupational therapy curriculum: A multiyear qualitative evaluation. *American Journal of Occupational Therapy, 53,* 199-206.

Hayes, K. W., Huber, G., Rogers, J., & Sanders, B. (1999). Behaviors that cause clinical instructors to question the clinical competence of physical therapist students. *Physical Therapy, 79,* 653-671.

Liotta-Kleinfeld, L., & McPhee, S. (2001). Comparison of final exam test scores of neuroscience students who experienced traditional methodologies versus problem-based learning methodologies. *Occupational Therapy in Health Care, 14* (3/4), 35-53.

McLeod, K. (1997, June). *Do problem-based learning courses improve critical thinking? An empirical evaluation of a PBL course in a traditional occupational therapy curriculum.* Paper presented at the Canadian Occupational Therapists Association Conference, Halifax, Canada.

Norman, G. R., & Schmidt, H. G. (1992). The psychological basis of problem-based learning: A review of the evidence. *Academic Medicine, 67,* 557-565.

Sadlo, G. (1997). Problem-based learning enhances the educational experiences of occupational therapy students. *Education for Health, 10* (1), 101-114.

Schön, D. A. (1983). *The reflective practitioner: How professionals think in action.* New York: Basic Books.

Schön, D. A. (1995). The new scholarship requires a new epistemology. *Change, 27* (6), 26-34.

Stern, P. (1997). Student perceptions of a problem-based learning course. *American Journal of Occupational Therapy, 51,* 589-596.

Teshima, D. Y. (2001). Outcome measurement of problem-based learning. *Clinical Laboratory Science, 14* (2), 68-69.

VanLeit, B. (1995). Using the case method to develop clinical reasoning skills in problem-based learning. *American Journal of Occupational Therapy, 49,* 349-353.

VanLeit, B., & Crowe, T. K. (2000). Essentials for successful integration of problem-based learning in occupational therapy curricula. In P. A. Crist (Ed.), *Innovations in occupational therapy education 2000* (pp. 78-94). Bethesda, MD: American Occupational Therapy Association.

Vroman, K. G., & MacRae, N. (1999). The issue is: How should the effectiveness of problem-based learning in occupational therapy education be examined? *American Journal of Occupational Therapy, 53,* 533-536.

White, M. J., Amos, E., & Kouzekanani, K. (1999). Problem-based learning: An outcomes study. *Nurse Educator, 24* (2), 33-36.

Personality Type
in Occupational Therapy Students:
Implications for Teaching
and Learning Strategies

Paula W. Jamison, PhD, OTR
Diane Dirette, PhD, OT

SUMMARY. In this descriptive study, 130 occupational therapy students completed a widely-used personality inventory (the MBTI-M) as part of coursework in their first semester. The majority of students evinced a preference for seven out of the 16 possible personality types; one type was not selected by anyone. These findings closely resembled data from the 1970s on practicing occupational therapists. Common characteristics, such as a high premium on personal connectedness and a dependable working environment, have important implications for faculty. Implications for findings relate to adjusting instructional delivery methods to best match type and learning preferences for this population.

Paula W. Jamison is Assistant Professor of Occupational Therapy, and Diane Dirette is Assistant Professor of Occupational Therapy, Western Michigan University.

Address correspondence to: Paula W. Jamison, Occupational Therapy Department, Western Michigan University, Kalamazoo, MI 49008 (E-mail: *paula.Jamison@ wmich.edu*)

The authors thank Jaclyn West-Frasier, MS, OTR, and Sharon Quintel, MS, OTR, for assistance with data collection.

[Haworth co-indexing entry note]: "Personality Type in Occupational Therapy Students: Implications for Teaching and Learning Strategies." Jamison, Paula W., and Diane Dirette. Co-published simultaneously in *Occupational Therapy in Health Care* (The Haworth Press, Inc.) Vol. 18, No. 1/2, 2004, pp. 83-98; and: *Best Practices in Occupational Therapy Education* (ed: Patricia A. Crist, and Marjorie E. Scaffa) The Haworth Press, Inc., 2004, pp. 83-98. Single or multiple copies of this article are available for a fee from The Haworth Document Delivery Service [1-800-HAWORTH, 9:00 a.m. - 5:00 p.m. (EST). E-mail address: docdelivery@ haworthpress.com].

KEYWORDS. Occupational therapy education, personality types, learning style

Occupational therapy students need tools for understanding both self and others in order to function effectively in academic and clinical settings. According to the literature, self-assessment and monitoring are important keys to becoming a self-directed, "adult" learner (Kasar, 2000; Knowles, 1980). Being able to recognize and honor one's own and others' learning and personal styles is crucial to effective functioning as a team member or group leader (Schwartzberg, 1998; Thompson & Bing-You, 1998). In addition, the transition from an academic environment to practice places demands on new clinicians' abilities to maximize learning strategies and develop a realistic sense of confidence (Lyons, 1997; Tryssenaar, 1997). One means of assisting students in this transition is to help them develop so-called metacognitive strategies for recognizing their progress as they adapt to new roles (Tryssenaar & Perkins, 2001). Understanding personality preferences, and the learning styles that they imply, offers students helpful tools for professional and personal development.

In order to increase awareness of learning styles and heighten respect for differences, students in one occupational therapy program participate in a variety of personal and professional self-assessment activities. Among these is the opportunity to complete the Myers-Briggs Personality Type Indicator (MBTI), selected because it is designed to reflect healthy, adaptive functioning rather than pathology (Myers, McCaulley, Quenk, & Hammer, 1998; Quenk, 2000). The overview of the instrument given to the class and confidential results communicated to each respondent offer students access to research findings pertaining to learning styles as well as approaches to teamwork and other relationships (Ditiberio & Hammer, 1993; Hammer, 1993; Provost, 1990).

The role of personality, aptitude, and attitude in education and professional development has been studied in relationship to a variety of fields (Fisher & Kent, 1998; Hayes & Allinson, 1998; Linares, 1999). However, studies that specifically examine personality and the career of occupational therapy are less common. Lysack, McNevin, and Dunleavy focused on personality traits of practicing occupational and physical therapists using a measure adapted from the MBTI (2001).

More interest has been accorded to the learning styles and preferences of occupational therapy students. However, researchers have favored measures designed specifically to elicit cognitive or learning preferences rather than the broader construct of personality type. The Canfield-Lafferty Learning Styles Inventory (Blagg, 1985; Llorens & Adams, 1978) and a Learning Preference Inventory developed by Rezler (Barris, Kielhofner, & Bauer, 1985) have been used. The MBTI was employed in 1975 to establish correlations with results from Rezler's Learning Preference Inventory (in Rezler & Rezmovic, 1981).

Notwithstanding, personality type has been linked to learning styles by the developers of the MBTI (Myers, 1980; Myers et al., 1998). Subsequent research reports correlations between learning characteristics such as a preference for concreteness versus abstraction (Myers & McCaulley, 1985). Ferguson and Fletcher examined the relationship between personality type as indicated by the MBTI and cognitive constructs such as memory, verbal ability, selective attention, and recall (1987). A review of the literature on brain functioning and type (Power & Lundsten, 1997) confirms that hemispheric function reflects type preferences (Myers et al., 1998).

METHOD

Participants

One hundred thirty occupational therapy students at a state university in the Midwest took part in this study. All of the students had attained at least junior status in the university and were at least 20 years old. Thirteen students were male, 114 were female, and three did not identify gender on the form. Ninety-two participants were undergraduate students, and 38 were graduate students. Because of their standing within the university and their admission to this program of study, it is expected that all of the students had at least an eighth-grade reading level as recommended for administration of the MBTI (Myers et al., 1998).

Instrument

The Myers-Briggs Type Indicator Form M (MBTI-M) was used for this study. The MBTI-M is a 93-item self-report instrument designed to identify personality type as theorized by Carl Jung (Myers et al., 1998). The MBTI is designed to elicit personality preferences and attitudes found in psychologically healthy individuals. The resulting personality type is purported to reflect an innate disposition to favor one polarity on each of four qualitatively distinct categories, called dichotomies (Quenk, 2000). The measure uses a forced choice format designed to elicit a type indicating one pole of each of the four dichotomies. Sixteen combinations of polarities are possible. Each resultant type has its own strengths (Quenk). The results reflect the individual's preferences, not abilities (Ditiberio & Hammer, 1993), and offer a unique but comprehensible way of "describing and explaining certain consistent differences in the ways that normal people use their minds" (Quenk). In addition to eliciting a four-part type, results also indicate the degree of preference, or clarity, exhibited for each pole. Preferences range from slight to very clear (Myers et al., 1998). Table 1 provides a summary of the dichotomies.

Good construct validity has been demonstrated for the four dichotomous preference scales (Johnson, Mauzey, & Annabel, 2001). Since less evidence is available to support the 16 separate types, the four dichotomous preferences were analyzed in addition to the 16 types (Myers et al., 1998). The MBTI-M has been shown to have high degrees of reliability with other samples. Previous studies from 1998 to 2001 have reported coefficients for the four dichotomous scales that range as follows: E/I .74-.95, S/N .78-.97, T/F .48-.97, J/P .63-.97 (Capraro & Capraro, 2002). The instrument is more reliable with samples of people who are over 18 years of age and has higher consistency with higher achieving students (Myers et al., 1998).

Procedures

During their first semester of study, students in the Occupational Therapy Program took the Myers-Briggs Type Indicator Form M (MBTI-M) as part of their coursework to help them identify their learning styles and preferences. The instrument was administered and scored by the instructors according to

TABLE 1. Four Dichotomies

E/I	
Extraversion	Preference for attending to phenomena outside the individual
Introversion	Preference for attending to interior phenomena, e.g., feelings, dreams, thoughts, etc.
S/N	
Sensing	Preference for focusing on physical, sensory phenomena
Intuition	Preference for focusing on what cannot be perceived by the senses, e.g., thoughts, patterns, concepts
T/F	
Thinking	Preference for use of objective, impersonal means to form opinions
Feeling	Preference for reliance on personal values, e.g., group harmony, to form opinions
J/P	
Judging	Preference for coming to conclusions
Perceiving	Preference for ongoing data collection, continuing to weigh pros and cons, options

published instructions (Myers et al., 1998). Individual results were distributed to the students during class. A general discussion of types and learning preferences was included during this session to provide the students the opportunity to review and reflect on the results.

Approval to use the data was obtained from the university's Human Subjects Institutional Review Board. A chart review of all the existing data was done. The data included the student's program of study, gender and type preferences.

RESULTS

Student Characteristics

Data were entered into SPSS 11.0 for analysis. As noted in Figure 1, the most common type among the students was ENFP with 29 students representing 22.3% of the sample. The second most common type was ISFJ with 22 students representing 16% of the sample. The least common type among the students was ISTP with zero students. See Figure 1 for details.

FIGURE 1. Type Preferences of Sample

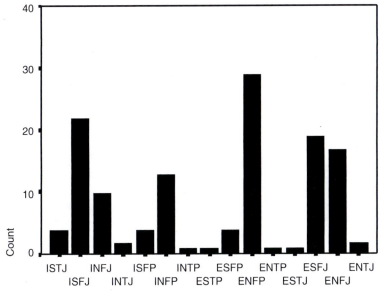

Dichotomy Differences

Although ENFP was the predominant type for these students, analyses of the individual dichotomies reveal other characteristics. As illustrated in Figure 1, the second, third, and fourth type preferences together constitute a higher percentage in the Judging pole of the J/P dichotomy. Chi-square goodness of fit analyses resulted in no significant differences between percentages in the E/I dichotomy ($p = .079$) or the S/N dichotomy ($p = .054$). A significantly higher percentage of students indicated a preference for the Feeling half of the T/F dichotomy ($p = .000$) and for the Judging pole of the J/P dichotomy ($p = .035$). See Table 2 for details.

Figures 2 through 5 indicate the degree of preference that students indicated for each pole of the dichotomies, with the possible options being very clear, clear, moderate, or slight. Scores for the clarity of preference on the E/I, S/N, and J/P dichotomies ranged from clear to slight; similar response patterns were obtained in the level of preference at each pole of these dichotomies, with the fewest number of students exhibiting a very clear preference.

In the T/F dichotomy, the preference for Thinking ranged, in descending order, from slight to clear, while preferences for Feeling were clear, then moderate, and then very clear. Feeling was the only half of a dichotomy for which the fewest students indicated a slight preference. Scores on the T/F dichotomy present an almost inverse relationship to the preferences expressed for the other dichotomies.

Gender Differences

Analyses of the 16 types related to gender are presented in Figure 6. Gender differences were noted for the 16 types in general. The most common types

TABLE 2. Dichotomy Preferences

	Frequency	Percent
Extrovert (E)	75	57.7%
Introvert (I)	55	42.3%
Sensing (S)	54	41.5%
Intuitive (N)	76	58.5%
Thinking (T)	13	10%
Feeling (F)	117	90%
Judging (J)	77	59.2%
Perceiving (P)	53	40.8%

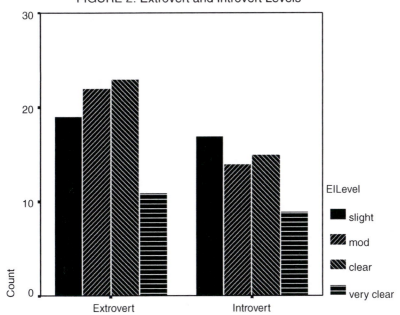

FIGURE 2. Extrovert and Introvert Levels

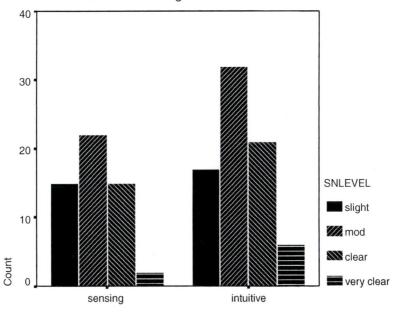

FIGURE 3. Sensing and Intuitive Levels

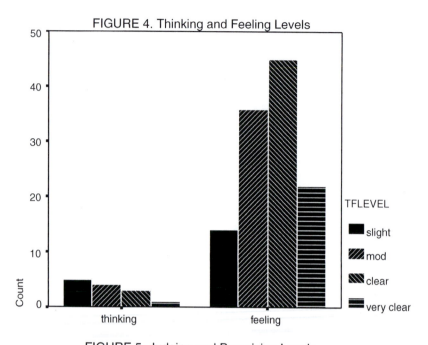

FIGURE 4. Thinking and Feeling Levels

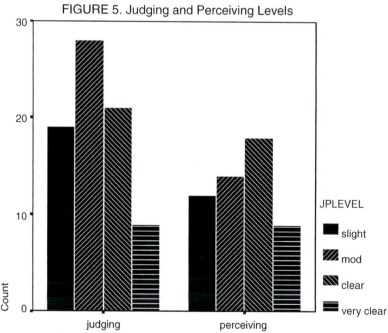

FIGURE 5. Judging and Perceiving Levels

among the male students were ISTJ, ISFJ, and INFJ, with two students in each. Three types had only males, including ESTP, ENTP, and ESTJ, with one male each. Five types were selected by females only.

Although ENFP was the type selected by the most students, the gender difference in this sample is evident. Twenty-five females, three unidentified, and only one male indicated this type. A chi-square analysis was used to examine any differences between the male and female students (see Tables 3-6). Male and female students did not differ significantly on the E/I dichotomy, the S/N dichotomy, or the J/P dichotomy (see Tables 3-5).

The male and female students did, however, differ significantly on the T/F dichotomy (see Table 5). Because one cell had a minimum expected value of

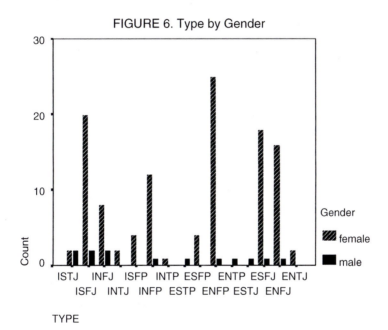

FIGURE 6. Type by Gender

TABLE 3. Gender by Extrovert/Introvert Cross Tabulations

Gender		Extrovert	Introvert
Female	Count	66	48
	(Expected Count)	(64.5)	(49.5)
Male	Count	6	7
	(Expected Count)	(7.4)	(5.6)

TABLE 4. Gender by Sensing/Intuitive Cross Tabulations

Gender		Sensing	Intuitive
Female	Count	48	66
	(Expected Count)	(48.5)	(65.5)
Male	Count	6	7
	(Expected Count)	(5.5)	(7.5)

TABLE 5. *Gender by Thinking/Feeling Cross Tabulations

Gender		Thinking	Feeling
Female	Count	8	106
	(Expected Count)	(11.7)	(102.3)
Male	Count	5	8
	(Expected Count)	(1.3)	(11.7)

* (Fisher's exact test = .004)

TABLE 6. Gender by Judging/Perceiving Cross Tabulations

Gender		Judging	Perceiving
Female	Count	68	46
	(Expected Count)	(69.1)	(44.9)
Male	Count	9	4
	(Expected Count)	(7.9)	(5.1)

less than 5, Fisher's exact test was used as an alternative to the Pearson's chi square (Munro, 2001). The Fisher's exact test was significant at .004. More male students' (38.5%) scores were in the Thinking pole of the dichotomy than female (7%). Likewise, more female student's scores (93%) were in the Feeling half of the dichotomy than male (61.5%).

DISCUSSION

These results offer intriguing similarities to type distribution noted among 245 individuals who had taken the MBTI in the 1970s and early 80s and who had listed occupational therapy as their profession (Myers & McCaulley, 1985). In the present sample of 130 students, two thirds of the students preferred the following types, in descending order: ENFP, ISFJ, ESFJ, and ENFJ.

In the previous sample, over half the respondents exhibited a preference for the following types, in descending order: ENFP, ESFJ, ISFJ, and ISTJ, with ESTJ tying with ENTJ for fifth place (totaling 55.5% of respondents) (Myers & McCaulley, 1985). The first preference in both samples was ENFP, with ESFJ or ISFJ in either second or third place, depending on the sample. The least reported type in both samples was the same: ISTP, with no responses reported in the current sample and 0.41% in 1985 (Myers & McCaulley).

The most prevalent type in both samples, ENFP, is associated with people who are "warmly enthusiastic" and who "make connections between events and information very quickly" and are able to improvise (Myers et al., 1998, p. 64). All of these characteristics fit the profile of a hands-on learner. It should be noted that the dichotomous preference for F/J in the other two most common types is linked to a preference for structured learning with clear goals and personal validation from faculty, in addition to a high reliance on personal values and sense of personal connection with other people (Myers et al., p. 64).

A different type of distribution is found in the survey data of 128 occupational therapists published in 2001 by Lysack et al. Again, ENFP is a commonly reported preference, listed as second in the top five (Lysack et al., 2001). Otherwise, the most commonly reported types in the top 68.2% of Lysack's sample differ. Most notably there is a higher incidence of preferences for Perceiving: ENFP, ESFP, ISFP, and INTP (Lysack et al.). Lysack et al. reported that 7.8% of their sample selected ISTP, while none of their respondents selected ISFJ (2001). These differences may be attributed to the use of a different instrument. Although it was adapted from the MBTI and employs similar terminology and type constructs, the measure used by Lysack et al. presupposes a different theoretical background (Myers et al., 1998).

While there is some diversity among the types most commonly reported by occupational therapy students and practitioners, the similarities are striking. Out of a total of 16 possible types, the majority of occupational therapy students and practitioners selected only nine. All of these types exhibit characteristics that would be useful to a competent therapist, especially a commonsense approach and powers of observation and caring for others (Myers et al., 1998).

The dichotomous preferences offer the most striking similarities and differences among the three groups studied. First of all, approximately two thirds of the two populations assessed with the MBTI exhibited a preference for Judging (Myers & McCaulley, 1985). However, Perceiving was the most common preference in the recent literature (Lysack et al., 2001). The characteristics commonly associated with Perceiving types in the literature–openness to new experience, flexibility, and an "active, experiential learning style" (Myers et al., 1998, p. 94)–represent qualities highly valued among occupational therapists (Lysack et al., 2001). The more commonly expressed preference for Judging (which, incidentally, was characteristic of the physical therapists reported by Lysack et al., 2002) is linked with a desire for a structured and concrete sequential learning style, as well as participant learning and conscientiousness (Myers et al., 1998). It is worth noting that few of the occupational therapy students displayed a very clear preference for either pole of the J/P dichotomy, which indicates at least some degree of comfort with flexibility. This more moderate degree of preference may offer an advantage to such students as they learn to cope with the demands of rapidly accelerating knowledge in the health care fields. Myers et al. note that when it is not tempered by the openness indicating the Perceiving polarity, "Judging may be correlated with closed-mindedness" (1998, p. 183).

One difference between the distributions reported in the different samples is striking. Compared to the other samples in the literature, occupational therapy students in the current study exhibited a surprisingly high preference for Feeling on the T/F dichotomy. Ninety percent of students indicated a preference for Feeling, with a high incidence of a very clear preference. Myers and McCaulley (1985) reported just over 57% of occupational therapists with this preference, and Lysack et al., 54 % (2001). While all three samples are preponderantly female, this distribution surpasses that of the representative population reported in the literature in which 25% of females report a preference for Thinking, and 75% a preference for Feeling (Myers et al., 1998). Individuals who indicate a preference for the combination of Feeling and Judging are said to "derive genuine pleasure from helping others create and maintain harmony in their lives" but may have trouble devoting enough time to themselves (Myers et al., 1998, p. 54). This statement has important implications for students and professionals alike, especially in times of escalating demands for increased productivity in the workplace.

Implications for Teaching Strategies

The call for a "best fit" of teaching and learning styles would optimally facilitate the student's transition into a challenging professional environment (Fisher & Kent, 1998). Characteristics of the learning styles associated with the types selected by occupational therapy students include a need to experience a personal connection to the material, to feel supported and appreciated, and for faculty to be organized (Ditiberio & Hammer, 1993). This majority of students also place a premium on dependability, on being able to plan well in advance, and to work steadily toward goals (Ditiberio & Hammer, 1993). The highly fluid nature of today's health care environment may be especially frustrating to these individuals if they are unable to employ compensatory strategies. According to Jungian theory, healthy adults naturally are drawn to develop such less-preferred choices once they reach midlife (Myers et al., 1998). Faculty need to find ways to respect not just the strengths that students bring to the learning process. The adaptive strategies that faculty may find most personally useful and rewarding in their own lives may not be as effective for younger students.

Educators should also be aware of the most typical responses to stress among the four most-commonly reported types. These include getting upset or angry and not showing it, developing physical symptoms, confiding in someone close, relying on religious beliefs, and exercise (Myers et al., 1998, p. 238). Only one of the four common types (ISFJ) utilizes "trying to think of options" as a coping mechanism for dealing with stress (Myers et al., p. 238). Teaching students effective techniques for stress management and validating their use are vital, particularly to those, such as the FJ's, who may find it difficult to set aside sufficient time for their own needs.

Type preferences of occupational therapy educators have not been examined. While some type of similarity between occupational therapy faculty and students is likely, available evidence about allied health faculty and students indicates that clear variations in styles and even values exist (DePoy & Merrill, 1988; Ditiberio & Hammer, 1993; Freeman & Tijerina, 2000; Joyce-Nagata, 1996; Linares, 1999; Myers & McCaulley, 1985).

Limitations

Even though the profession of occupational therapy is predominantly female, the small number of male subjects (n = 13) in this study makes it difficult to draw conclusions concerning their preferences. Overall, males in this study chose the less-commonly reported types, with only one male out of 13 expressing a preference for ENFP, and two for ISJF. More data on male occupational therapy students would provide greater certainty about their personality types and learning preferences. Additionally, a larger sample of both genders would increase confidence in the generalizability of the current findings about females. The data reported in 1985 corroborate these findings, however (Myers & McCaulley).

Distribution of type by gender has been examined in the MBTI. In a large population sample (n = 3000), preference poles of three of the dichotomies are distributed equally between males and females (Ditiberio & Hammer, 1993). The exception is T/F. Fifty-seven percent of males report a preference for Thinking and 43% for Feeling. Among females, only 25% report a preference for Thinking and 75% for Feeling (Quenk, 2000).

CONCLUSION

Two thirds of the 130 occupational therapy students preferred four of the 16 possible MBTI personality types: ENFP, ISFJ, ESFJ, and ENFJ. Among the dichotomous preferences, the FJ combination is predominant, with a majority of students selecting Feeling over Thinking and Judging over Perceiving. Males, who form a distinct minority in the sample, exhibited a preference for less common types, with only two selecting ISFJ and one, ENFP.

These findings suggest that the majority of occupational therapy students share concerns for the feelings of others and a need for structure and personal validation. Educators and supervising clinicians need to discover ways to respect and honor these needs and build upon these strengths. The gender difference between personality style and learning preferences reported here points to a recurring question for both clinicians and educators: how to meet the needs of individuals with widely divergent learning and interpersonal styles. It is up to educators to discover how to motivate and accommodate the minority of students whose needs and gifts differ. Greater awareness of the differences between occupational therapy faculty personality types and those of their students could also have an impact on instructional delivery. Finally, the personality types and learning styles of graduate students have not been explicitly addressed. This information is highly relevant, as the profession transitions to requiring graduate education for entry-level practice in 2007. Further examination of personality type and learning style has the potential to offer important insight about how to foster the qualities and skills occupational therapists need to adapt effectively to a constantly changing, and often unpredictable, professional environment.

REFERENCES

Barris, R., Kielhofner, G., & Bauer, D. (1985). Learning preferences, values, and student satisfaction. *Journal of Allied Health, 14*, 13-23.

Blagg, J. D. (1985). Cognitive styles and learning styles as predictors of academic success in a graduate allied health education program. *Journal of Allied Health, 14*, 89-98.

Bush, J. V., Powell, N. J., & Herzberg, G. (1993). Career self-efficacy in occupational therapy practice. *American Journal of Occupational Therapy, 47*, 927-933.

Capraro, R. M. & Capraro, M. M. (2002). Myers-Briggs type indicator score reliability across studies: A meta-analytic reliability generalization study. *Educational and Psychological Measurement, 62*, 590-602.

DePoy, E. & Merrill, S. C. (1988). Value acquisition in an occupational therapy curriculum. *Occupational Therapy Journal of Research, 8*, 259-274.

Ditiberio, J. K. & Hammer, A. L. (1993). *Introduction to Type in college.* Palo Alto, CA: Consulting Psychologists Press.

Ferguson, J. & Fletcher, C. (1987). Personality type and cognitive style. *Psychological Reports, 60*, 959-964.

Fisher, D. L & Kent, H. B. (1998). Associations between teacher personality and classroom environment. *Journal of Classroom Interaction, 33,* 5-13.

Freeman, V. S. & Tijerina, S. (2000). Delivery methods, learning styles, and outcomes of physician assistant students. *Physician Assistant, 24,* 43-50.

Hammer, A. L. (1993). *Introduction to type and careers.* Palo Alto, CA: Consulting Psychologists Press.

Hayes, J. & Allinson, C. W. (1998). Cognitive style and the theory and practice of individual and collective learning in organizations. *Human Relations, 51,* 847-871.

Johnson, W. L., Mauzey, E., & Johnson, A. M. (2001). A higher order analysis of the factor structure of the Myers-Briggs type indicator. *Measurement and Evaluation in Counseling and Development, 34,* 96-108.

Joyce-Nagata, B. (1996). Students' academic performance in nursing as a function of student and faculty learning style congruency. *Journal of Nursing Education, 35,* 69-73.

Kasar, J. & Clark, E. N. (2000). *Developing professional behaviors.* Thorofare, NJ: Slack.

Knowles, M. (1980). *The modern practice of adult education: From pedagogy to andragogy.* Chicago: Follett.

Linares, A. Z. (1999). Learning styles of students and faculty in selected health care professions. *Journal of Nursing Education, 38,* 407-414.

Llorens, L. A. & Adams, S. P. (1978). Learning style preferences of occupational therapy students. *American Journal of Occupational Therapy, 32,* 161-164.

Lyons, M. (1997). Understanding professional behavior: Experiences of occupational therapy students in mental health settings. *American Journal of Occupational Therapy, 51,* 686-692.

Lysack, C., McNevin, N., & Dunleavy, K. (2001). Job choice and personality: A profile of Michigan occupational and physical therapists. *Journal of Allied Health, 30,* 75-82.

Munro, B. H. (2001). *Statistical methods for health care research.* Philadelphia: Lippincott.

Myers, I. B., & McCaulley, M. H. (1985). *Manual: A guide to the development and use of the Myers-Briggs Type Indicator.* Palo Alto, CA: Consulting Psychologists Press.

Myers, I. B., McCaulley, M. H., Quenk, N. L., & Hammer, A. L. (1998). *MBTI manual: A guide to the development and use of the Myers-Briggs Type Indicator* (3rd ed.). Palo Alto, CA: Consulting Psychologists Press.

Myers, I. B. & Myers, P. B. (1980). *Gifts differing.* Palo Alto, CA: Consulting Psychologists Press.

Power, S. J. & Lundsten, L. L. (1997). Studies that compare type theory and left-brain/right-brain theory. *Journal of Psychological Type, 43,* 22-28.

Provost, J. A. (1990). *Work, play, and type: Achieving balance in your life.* Palo Alto, CA: Consulting Psychologists Press.

Quenk, N. L. (2000). *Essentials of Myers-Briggs Type Indicator assessment.* New York: John Wiley and Sons.

Rezler, A. G. & French, R. M. (1975). Personality types and learning preferences of students in six allied health professions. *Journal of Allied Health, 4,* 20-26.

Rezler, A. G. & Rezmovic, V. (1981). The Learning Preference Inventory. *Journal of Allied Health, 10,* 28-34.

Schwartzberg, S. L. (1998). Group process. In Neistadt, M. E. & Crepeau, E. B. (Eds.) (1998). *Willard & Spackman's occupational therapy* (9th ed.). New York: Lippincott Williams & Wilkins, 120-131.

Thompson, J. A. & Bing-You, R. G. (1998). Physician's reactions to learning style and personality type inventories. *Medical Teacher, 20,* 10-14.

Tryssenaar, J. (1997). Clinical interpretation of "Understanding professional behavior": Experiences of occupational therapy students in mental health settings. *American Journal of Occupational Therapy, 51,* 693-695.

Tryssenaar, J. & Perkins, J. (2001). From student to therapist: Exploring the first year of practice. *American Journal of Occupational Therapy, 55,* 19-27.

Brief or New:
Student Learning Portfolios:
Balancing Tradition with Innovation

Karen P. Funk, MA, OTR

SUMMARY. For decades, educators have used traditional assessment measures to evaluate student learning and performance. Though these measures may have been successful in the past, the shifting culture of universities requires educators to seek more innovative methods which not only assess student learning but also elicit professional development and higher thinking skills. To keep pace with a rapidly changing health care market, educators not only need to teach better, but also evaluate smarter. Student learning portfolios are one way educators can assess a student's performance based on a learning paradigm which encourages active learning, enhances professional development, and integrates cumulative knowledge. *[Article copies available for a fee from The Haworth Document Delivery Service: 1-800-HAWORTH. E-mail address: <docdelivery@ haworthpress.com> Website: <http://www.HaworthPress.com> © 2004 by The Haworth Press, Inc. All rights reserved.]*

KEYWORDS. Portfolio, education, student-learning

Karen P. Funk is associated with The University of Texas at El Paso.

[Haworth co-indexing entry note]: "Brief or New: Student Learning Portfolios: Balancing Tradition with Innovation." Funk, Karen P. Co-published simultaneously in *Occupational Therapy in Health Care* (The Haworth Press, Inc.) Vol. 18, No. 1/2, 2004, pp. 99-105; and: *Best Practices in Occupational Therapy Education* (ed: Patricia A. Crist, and Marjorie E. Scaffa) The Haworth Press, Inc., 2004, pp. 99-105. Single or multiple copies of this article are available for a fee from The Haworth Document Delivery Service [1-800-HAWORTH, 9:00 a.m. - 5:00 p.m. (EST). E-mail address: docdelivery@haworthpress.com].

http://www.haworthpress.com/web/OTHC
© 2004 by The Haworth Press, Inc. All rights reserved.
Digital Object Identifier:10.1300/J003v18n01_10

If you always do, what you've always done;
You'll always get, what you've always got.

Few would argue that the ethos of the university has changed over the past 25 years. Students are older, more culturally diverse, with higher expectations of what their education should provide. However, students are also entering colleges less academically prepared, less autonomous, and less aware of the professional skills needed for today's job market (Spence, 2001). Educators have developed innovative teaching strategies for this generation of students; however, studies show that assessment of student learning continues to follow traditional methods in which students advance at the same rate regardless of interests, abilities, or prior experience (Jeffries, Rew, & Cramer, 2002). Criticism warns that these traditional methods do not fully prepare students to enter the work force, nor do they influence professionalism, higher level thinking, or motivation to become life-long learners (Lumsden, 2002). The question becomes: How do educators design innovative student assessments which capture the mastery of course content, yet promote and support professional development skills required for higher level thinking and life-long learning?

The purpose of this article is to describe a unique advancement in pre-service education regarding student learning and assessment. This advancement, known as student learning portfolios, is gaining national attention from the educational community and, when used correctly, could be a catalyst for improving occupational therapy education.

WHAT ARE STUDENT LEARNING PORTFOLIOS?

Student learning portfolios are organized anthologies of a student's work used to optimize learning and provide a realistic assessment of a student's progress, accomplishments, and competencies either in a particular class, fieldwork experience, or throughout an entire curriculum. Portfolios are product- and process-oriented (Darling, 2001; Guillaume & Yopp, 1995). As a product, they serve as an extended resume, highlighting a student's accomplishments and achievements. As a process, they expose natural strengths and weaknesses of a student, encourage self-responsibility, stimulate reflective thought, integrate cumulative knowledge, and develop complex, multidimensional problem-solving and reasoning skills (Smith & Tillema, 2001). When combined, the product and process unite to create a productive and powerful method of professional development and student assessment.

Benefits of Portfolios

One of the primary reasons student portfolios are so useful is that they employ principles of active learning. Depending upon learning objectives, past experiences, abilities, personal needs, and professional desires, students collaborate with their instructor to determine their optimal learning experience. Since students actively learn when they are engaged in what they study, the process makes learning meaningful and more transferable to practice than test scores or scheduled reading assignments (Lumsden, 2002).

Secondly, student portfolios facilitate ongoing assessment that is critical to professional development and life-long learning. By eliminating assessments based primarily on instructor-created assignments and tests, students are better able to participate in opportunities that examine the learning process and encourage interactive communication, critical analysis, creative problem-solving, autonomy, self-responsibility, and reflective thinking. Students compare samples of their work in various developmental stages to reflect upon improvement, changes in perceptions/attitudes, perceived strengths and weaknesses, and personal growth experiences (Smith & Tillema, 2001).

Thirdly, portfolios help students integrate individual coursework and synthesize it into a whole. Often, theories and concepts are lost when students are left on their own to assimilate information and apply it to realistic situations. According to Spence (2001), students traditionally do not transfer classroom learning to realistic situations outside of the classroom and, more surprisingly, often do not transfer learning from one class to the next. He asks the question: Is it learning if students cannot use or remember it? Student learning portfolios can be a method to achieve a more student-centered learning paradigm of education. By using portfolios that provide opportunities to reflect on development and performance over a longer period, students better understand how classes work together to provide a continuum of learning which is successive and cumulative.

Limitations of Portfolios

There is no question that student learning portfolios have certain disadvantages. Portfolios can be cumbersome and determining a student's full learning experience can be challenging. Students must be organized, interactive, and willing to reflect honestly about their work. Some students may require more time to articulate learning objectives while other students may require more time to honestly explore personal feelings, beliefs, and attitudes about what they are learning. Students also may not immediately see the value of learning portfolios, which can result in feelings ranging from uncertainty to resentment (Weiss, Cosbey, Habel, Hanson, & Larsen, 2002). Lastly, student portfolios require the instructor to shift roles from teacher to mentor, which is sometimes difficult and requires additional faculty time per student for offering feedback and measuring performance.

CREATING A PORTFOLIO

Student learning portfolios can vary greatly in arrangement and composition. They are highly adaptable and should assume the shape and structure of the course(s) they are designed to assess or the purpose they intend to appraise (Brown, 2002). They can be used for clinical fieldwork experiences, individual classes, or as a program evaluation measure. A comprehensive assessment portfolio includes an arrangement of information that captures a student's learning goals, insights, feelings, beliefs, knowledge, skills, and commitments towards learning, while illustrating efforts, progress, achievements, accomplishments, and professional competencies (Guillaume & Yopp, 1995). In this respect, a portfolio becomes a narrative that slowly unfolds, illuminating the developmental learning and personal growth of a student (Darling, 2001).

Creating a portfolio involves five steps: (1) identification, (2) collection, (3) feedback, (4) reflection, and (5) presentation. Portfolios begin with students identifying and establishing their learning objectives and goals. From the learning objectives, students collaborate with the instructor to decide which methods best meet their objectives. Table 1 outlines examples of contents typically found in student learning portfolios.

The student selects what is included in their portfolio, thus taking ownership and becoming more motivated to learn and master the course material. As the semester progresses, students continue to collect items to add to their portfolio.

Although portfolios are self-directed, students need feedback for optimal growth. Feedback from instructor, peers, and self is useful to expand learning opportunities and gain skills for evaluating self and other's work. Feedback can take the form of analytical peer review, self-evaluation, or instructor comments on work produced. The significance of feedback is for each student to

TABLE 1. Contents of a Student Learning Portfolio

Learning goals and objectives	Work samples
Essays/professional papers	Personal position papers
Instructor/student communications	Personal reflections
Individual and group projects	Self-evaluation
Presentations	Peer comments
Pictures/videotapes	Articles influencing learning

judiciously reflect upon how his or her work is progressing, create opportunities for change, and develop confidence in his/her abilities.

Student reflection is an essential part of the portfolio process. Students should consistently reflect upon professional growth, which extends beyond what they are achieving to what they are actually learning. This process promotes students to develop critical thinking, identify strengths and weaknesses, connect meaning to their learning, and apply learning to situations outside the classroom. Additionally, it gives insight into the student's intrinsic motivation for learning and guides the instructor in communicative feedback.

Presentation of the portfolio is the final step. Students should be free to organize their portfolio according to their unique personalities and creative spirits. Typically, they are contained within a three-ring binder with dividers separating the various content sections. Themes, colors, titles, graphics, etc., are at the discretion of the student and often play a vital role towards the synthesis of the materials. Upon completion of the course(s), students have a comprehensive product of their efforts, accomplishments, achievements, and professional competencies as well as a documented record of their learning process.

GRADING STUDENT LEARNING PORTFOLIOS

There are no universal rules or standard procedures in grading student learning portfolios; however, they need not be any more difficult than grading papers or tests. Since student portfolios involve active learning, they are best assessed by determining the extent of learning that has occurred. This can be accomplished in a variety of ways; however, experts agree that it should largely rest upon the stated learning objectives written collaboratively by the student and instructor (Arter & TcTighe, 2001). Although the purpose of the portfolio is to capture growth and change in student thinking and learning, instructors have the responsibility of grading the portfolio. Some common ways they have been graded are: (1) score on a pass/fail system; (2) assess individually weighted assignments which are then averaged to achieve a final portfolio grade; and (3) evaluate the portfolio as a single unit based on how well the student met their learning objectives. Pass/fail portfolios appear to be the easiest of methods since the grading criteria is less complicated; however, with the possible exception of fieldwork, occupational therapy courses are not constructed on the pass/fail system. Grading individual assignments often falls prey to traditional evaluation methods whereby students are more involved with the outcome than the process of what they are learning. Assessing the portfolio as a single entity based on learning objectives may be the best option, but is more challenging to establish fair guidelines. In this case, using a scoring rubric can assist. Rubrics are grading grids for evaluating student work and beneficial in evaluating projects that have no "correct" answer (Gross-Davis, 1993). Point systems such as 1-4 or word descriptors such as excellent-strong-adequate-unacceptable are then used for scoring. The overall portfolio score is the extent to which the student has met their learning goals. Table 2 provides useful Internet links to scoring rubrics, many of which provide examples and samples of scoring rubrics used in education.

CONCLUSION AND FUTURE IMPLICATIONS

Higher education today requires richer and more complex learning environments to keep pace with a changing health care market. Greater expectations, challenging work environments, and multiple job responsibilities will require occupational therapists to have more advanced cognitive and professional development skills by which to compete and practice. Portfolios offer an innovative and contemporary framework for assessment, which aligns with the profession and the pedagogical paradigm shift from passive learning to active participation. Used to replace traditional assessment or to balance existing outcome measures, student learning portfolios can be instrumental in impacting occupational therapy education by developing professional competencies, enhancing professional development, integrating occupational therapy theory and practice, and developing enthusiasm for life-long learning.

Making learning useful, purposeful, meaningful, and self-directed parallels the tenets of occupational therapy and client-centered practice. If the profession agrees that active involvement in choices and decisions is best for clients, why can that not be extended into the classroom by giving students input into

TABLE 2. Websites for Developing Scoring Rubrics

http://edresearch.org/pare/getvn.asp?v=7&n=3
http://eric-ba024.umd.edu/pare/getvn.asp?v=7&n=25
http://edweb.sdsu.edu/triton/tidepoolunit/Rubrics/reportrubric.html
http://www.ericfacility.net/databases/ERIC_Digests/ed446111.html
http://www.interactiveclassroom.com/articles_006.htm
http://www.calpress.com/rubric.html
http://curriculumfutures.org/assessment/a06-01.html
http://www.bethel.edu/~tanswe/ens102/Rubric.html#Quizzes

what they learn, how they learn it, and how they apply it to practice? This does not assume occupational therapy educators are not striving to meet the challenges placed upon them; it only suggests that assessing student learning requires further research. Documenting the value of learning portfolios in specific contexts is the next logical step in improving best practice methods in occupational therapy education. Whether used for fieldwork education, course-specific learning, or throughout an entire curriculum, student learning portfolios are worth investigating.

REFERENCES

Arter, J. A. & TcTighe, J. (2001). *Scoring rubrics in the classroom: Using performance criteria for assessing and improving student performance.* Thousand Oaks, CA: Corwin Press.

Brown, J. O. (2002). Know thyself: The impact of portfolio development on adult learning. *Adult Education Quarterly, 52* (3), 228-245.

Darling, L. F. (2001). Portfolio as practice: The narratives of emerging teachers. *Teaching and Teacher Education, 17,* 107-121.

Gross-Davis, B. (1993). Grading practices. *Tools for teaching.* Retrieved January 13, 2003, from *http://teaching.berkeley.edu/bgd/grading.html*

Guillaume, A. M. & Yopp, H. K. (1995). Professional portfolios for student teachers. *Teacher Education Quarterly, 22,* 93-101.

Jeffries, P. R., Rew, S., & Cramer, J. M. (2002). Student centered versus traditional methods of teaching basic nursing skills in a learning laboratory. *Nursing Education Perspectives, 23* (1), 14-19.

Lumsden, L. (2002). Motivating today's students: The same old stuff just doesn't work. *ERIC Clearinghouse on Educational Management.* Retrieved November 25, 2002, from *http://eric.uoregon.edu/publications/text/portraits1.2.html*

Smith, K. & Tillema, H. (2001). Long-term influences of portfolios on professional development. *Scandinavian Journal of Educational Research, 45,* 183-203.

Spence, L. D. (2001). The case against teaching. *Change, 12,* 11-19.

Weiss, G. L., Cosbey, J. R., Habel, S. K., Hanson, C. M, & Larsen, C. (2002). Improving the assessment of student learning. *Teaching Sociology, 30,* 63-79.

Student Development in an Online Post-Professional Master's Program

Pamela Richardson, PhD, OTR/L, FAOTA

SUMMARY. Students' perceptions of personal and professional development in an online post-professional Master's degree program in occupational therapy were investigated. In-class postings, reflection papers, and e-mail surveys completed by 14 occupational therapists throughout the course of an online Master's program were coded and analyzed. Three themes were identified: the developmental process of post-professional education, the value of the online learning community, and the influence of positive and negative characteristics of online pedagogy in creating lifelong learners. Results indicated that the students perceived personal and professional growth that enhanced their clinical practice,

Pamela Richardson is Assistant Professor, Department of Occupational Therapy, San Jose State University, One Washington Square, San Jose, CA 95192-0059.

The author wishes to acknowledge Dr. Kay Schwartz and Dr. Anne MacRae for their assistance with this study, and for their vision and energy in creating the online Master's program. Her deep gratitude also goes to the students who participated in this study and who shared this learning experience.

[Haworth co-indexing entry note]: "Student Development in an Online Post-Professional Master's Program." Richardson, Pamela. Co-published simultaneously in *Occupational Therapy in Health Care* (The Haworth Press, Inc.) Vol. 18, No. 1/2, 2004, pp. 107-116; and: *Best Practices in Occupational Therapy Education* (ed: Patricia A. Crist, and Marjorie E. Scaffa) The Haworth Press, Inc., 2004, pp. 107-116. Single or multiple copies of this article are available for a fee from The Haworth Document Delivery Service [1-800-HAWORTH, 9:00 a.m. - 5:00 p.m. (EST). E-mail address: docdelivery@haworthpress.com].

and that the online learning community supported and enhanced this growth. Online pedagogy was effective in creating a cooperative learning environment that facilitated personal and professional development at the post-graduate level. *[Article copies available for a fee from The Haworth Document Delivery Service: 1-800-HAWORTH. E-mail address: <docdelivery@haworthpress.com> Website: <http://www.HaworthPress.com> © 2004 by The Haworth Press, Inc. All rights reserved.]*

KEYWORDS. Occupational therapy, online learning, post-professional education

Access to the Internet has resulted in a proliferation of post-graduate programs offered online. Flexibility of access is one of the most important reasons that students choose online programs, as well as a characteristic students most value about online coursework (Barab, Thomas, & Merrill, 2001; Kearsley, Lynch, & Wizer, 1995; McAlpine, Lockerbie, Ramsay, & Beaman, 2002; Udod & Care, 2002). High levels of critical thinking, reasoning, and analysis have been observed in students in online courses (Hansen & Gladfelter, 1996; Kearsley et al., 1995; Lally & Barrett, 1999; McAlpine et al., 2002).

The asynchronous nature of the online discussion allows time for greater reflection (Lally & Barrett, 1999). Disadvantages of online discussions include lack of spontaneity, lack of visual cues, and slow discussion speed (Lally & Barrett; Simons, Baron, Knicely, & Richardson, 2001). However, the quality of responses and the level of class participation often outweigh these disadvantages (Kearsley et al., 1995; Tiene, 2000). The discussions facilitate a strong sense of community and a high level of social interactivity (Barab et al., 2001; Fahy, Crawford, & Ally, 2001; Lally & Barrett, 1999; McAlpine et al., 2002; Rovai, 2001). Establishment of the online cooperative learning community combined with immediate application of coursework can result in a co-evolution of educational and personal development that creates deep and meaningful learning (Barab et al., 2001). A cooperative learning framework is advocated as the most effective structure for online learning (Lally & Barrett, 1999).

Dickerson and Wittman (1999) found that occupational therapists interested in graduate education wanted coursework that would improve their clinical skills and knowledge. Only one study in the occupational therapy literature has addressed online pedagogy (Simons et al., 2000), and no studies have investigated whether online education can meet the post-professional learning needs of occupational therapists. The purpose of this study was to explore students' perceptions of their learning experience in a Master's program where all content was delivered online, as well as how the online teaching environment contributed to this learning. The following research questions were addressed:

1. What personal and professional changes did students report as a result of participating in the program?
2. What characteristics of the online program did students feel contributed to or detracted from their professional and personal development?

METHODOLOGY

Participants

Participants were 14 female registered occupational therapists who composed the first cohort of the online post-professional Master's program. Number of years in practice ranged from three to 30, with a variety of practice areas represented. Seven states were represented.

Program Description

The San Jose State University online post-professional Master's program is a part-time (two courses per semester) program for working professionals that is completed in five semesters. All coursework is delivered online through a web-based platform. The first year courses focus on examination of clinical practice, exploring clinical problems, and grounding practice in historical and theoretical contexts. The second year coursework focuses on examining influences on practice and extending analytical skills to critique the professional literature, while developing a focus for inquiry. The final semester centers on completion of the Master's thesis project.

The teaching philosophy is constructivist (Farquharson, 1995), and is based in social learning theory. It is expected that assimilation of material occurs through the process of group discussion, where students and instructors participate on a more or less equal basis. Course material is presented in a modular format (McKeachie, 1986). Student learning is evaluated through written assignments and discussion participation.

In addition to in-class discussion groups, there is a "Town Square" for students and faculty where information of general interest is posted. There are also "cafés" accessible only to students, which are intended as a site for social interaction (Lauzon, 1992; Udod & Dean, 2002). Students also attend two onsite sessions of 2-3 days. A final optional onsite session occurs at the end of the fifth semester, where students present their research, and graduate.

Data Collection

Data were collected at four points: at the end of the first year, at the end of the second year, during the final semester, and eight months after graduation. At the end of the first year students summarized in writing the growth they experienced during the previous year. A focus group was held during the second onsite session to further explore students' responses. At the end of the second year, students participated in a discussion in the Education course on their perceptions of online learning. During the final semester research seminar students reflected on their learning and growth through the program. Discussion content from these two courses was included. An open-ended e-mail survey addressing perceptions of growth and current professional activity was conducted eight months after graduation. Eleven students responded to the survey.

Data Analysis

The written first year feedback data and focus group data were transcribed. The discussion responses and results of the post-graduation e-mail survey were collated and printed. Constant comparative analysis (Glaser & Strauss, 1967) was used for the initial data analysis to identify categories of responses. Pattern codes were developed that reflected both the process and the outcomes of the educational experience (Miles & Huberman, 1994). Two faculty members reviewed the data and coding scheme and suggested refinements of categories and pattern codes. Two of the participants reviewed an initial draft of the paper for representativeness of the data.

RESULTS

Through pattern analysis of the data three themes were identified. These included the developmental process of post-professional education, the value of the online learning community, and the influence of positive and negative characteristics of online pedagogy in creating lifelong learners. The interaction of these themes in creating student outcomes is represented in Figure 1. The themes are discussed below in relation to how they affected students' personal and professional development, as well as how the online learning process contributed to this development.

Students who pursue online education are typically motivated, self-directed, and organized (Frisby & Jones, 2000; Lally & Barrett, 1999). These students were ready to engage in activities to promote their personal and professional development. Through the first year coursework they acquired a

FIGURE 1. The Process of Transformational Learning in an Online Program

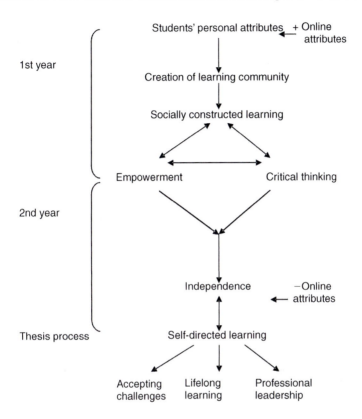

deeper understanding of the foundations of occupational therapy, and developed an awareness of the effect this could have on them as a professional. Their statements from the end of the first year indicate recognition of the transformational learning process that was beginning: "This year I have been reminded of what OT is really about and that has increased my ability to communicate what we do"; "I have discovered an increased energy and enthusiasm for the field, as well as for advanced education"; "I am more energized to move to an occupation-based practice."

A key component in the developmental process was the formation of the learning community. The online technology proved to be an effective vehicle for the students to develop collegial relationships with classmates and instructors. Instructors took on the roles of facilitators, providing a structure within which the students could construct their own learning. The asynchronous discussion format facilitated this process. Quieter students could respond without feeling dominated by more vocal students. Those who preferred to reflect on a question before answering had time to do so. At the end of the first year students reflected on the value of constructivist learning: "Reading the various viewpoints of others on a multitude of topics gave me valuable insight and an appreciation of the different perspectives"; "A distance program fosters support and encouragement and ensures that there is no competition between students, as you are likely to find in a traditional academic setting. This was a very pleasant surprise!"

Just as important as the academic learning were the personal relationships that were forged in class discussions and in the student café. These relationships were central to students' satisfaction, success, and confidence in their ability to complete the program.

> Despite the fact that most of our contacts have been online, the support and encouragement that all members of this cohort have offered each other has been wonderful. We have had babies, been through divorce and illness, turned to each other for advice, helped each other hang on–it is pretty amazing.

The first year experience helped students to develop their critical thinking and problem-solving skills. The confidence they developed created a feeling of empowerment as they began to see their growth as learners and professionals. They learned how to make adjustments in their personal lives to support their academic efforts. They developed proficiency in technology. They were immediately able to apply the concepts they were learning to their work, and in so doing perceived themselves to be more skilled, reflective therapists. These skills, attitudes, and practices prepared them for the second year emphasis on critical analysis and creating change.

During the second year, the learning community provided support as students initiated the independent learning process of developing a research proposal. By the end of this year they showed high levels of self-knowledge regarding their working and learning styles, and were able to reflect on the pros and cons of online learning.

> There is real value in face-to-face learning. There are times when I miss not being able to connect in person with the instructor or with the others in the class. However, the advantage of flexibility, independence, and the diversity of being able to interact with motivated, experienced, self-directed peers from a variety of geographical and practice specialty areas far outweighs any disadvantages.

I think another benefit of distance learning is that everyone gets to speak. Although it is time consuming to read everyone's responses, it was important for my learning and I felt like I really got to know a little bit about everyone through their responses and comments.

As the students progressed through the thesis process during the final semester, student-facilitated discussions provided a forum to reflect on their learning. At this point the negative attributes of online education were discussed in detail. Interestingly, these negative attributes (primarily the lack of physical access to instructor and classmates) were perceived as having a positive benefit: increased self-confidence in themselves as independent, lifelong learners. The thesis project itself was perceived as being essential to the independent learning process.

I agree that one of the greatest learning experiences and eventual accomplishments of completing a distance research project is the degree of confidence you obtain by expanding your skill with learning how to independently seek out answers . . . this program demanded that we take the initiative to seek out the answers when we needed more information. I have gained a much greater appreciation for the resources and networks I know are out there for the future.

Now that I know how to go about it, I will continue to spend time online searching for and reviewing available literature that is relevant to my work and can help me expand my own knowledge base and guide my clinical reasoning.

The responses in the post-graduation survey demonstrated that students felt that they had integrated their academic experiences into a personal and professional identity that was more reflective, analytical, and confident than when they had entered the program. The graduates felt more self-assured about presenting and defending their opinions. They reported increased pride and confidence in their professional role and valuation of their contributions in their workplace. They attributed this to improved critical thinking skills obtained through coursework and research. Graduates reported a strong interest in exploring scholarly literature, and many had taken local and regional leadership roles in a variety of professional activities. Comments included: "I have an increased confidence to take on projects that I would have turned away prior to the program. I have broadened my interests in occupational therapy and no longer feel 'assigned' to my practice area only"; "I feel honored to be a part of a group of professionals who had the same passion for occupational therapy that I have"; "The online Master's program was one of the best things I ever did personally and professionally!!!!!!!"

DISCUSSION

The results of this study illustrate both the developmental process experienced by students engaged in post-professional education, and the unique characteristics of the online environment in facilitating this process. Transformational learning occurs when students experience a change in the way they view themselves as persons and as professionals (Farquharson, 1995). The data indicate that students perceived that transformational learning had occurred. Their developmental trajectory also helps to understand the learning path for the adult student returning to school. The process of successfully fitting school into a busy life gave students confidence in their coping skills. Support from classmates and instructors empowered students to tackle higher-order cognitive and professional challenges as the program progressed.

The contribution of online pedagogy to the learning experience revolved around the ability of the technology to act as a medium for the construction of shared knowledge (Barab et al., 2001). The dichotomy of online pedagogy was also apparent in the many statements relating to feelings of isolation and the wish to have more face-to-face contact. This finding is in line with prior research, as is the students' perceptions that the flexibility of this teaching approach outweighed the negative attributes (Kearsley et al., 1995; Tiene, 2000). Somewhat unexpected was the finding that online instruction promoted more independent learning, which in turn facilitated the pursuit of ongoing lifelong learning. In the follow-up survey, graduates cited specific instances where they used information gathering and critical thinking skills to contribute new knowledge at work. The skills developed in online research and the confidence in analyzing and presenting information converged to enhance their clinical practice.

The experience of these students has reinforced to us the value of post-professional education. By reflecting on and analyzing their practice, students were able to enhance their critical thinking skills and develop a stronger foundation in occupational therapy theory. Only eight months after graduation a number of these graduates had advanced their professional activities. This counters the opinion of many in Dickerson and Wittman's (1999) study who felt that post-graduate education would not advance their careers. These students felt strongly enough about their educational experience to respond in a letter to the editor (Johnson et al., 2000).

Limitations

This small sample of students represents a minority of bachelor's-trained therapists (Dickerson & Wittman, 1999). The experiences of these students do not represent all therapists engaged in post-professional education. However, the developmental trajectories of the subsequent three cohorts in this program show strong similarities to this group, suggesting that these findings are consistent with the experiences of others enrolled in our online program.

Implications/Further Research

This study suggests that online instruction can be a viable teaching methodology for post-professional coursework, and that it can enhance, rather than detract from the post-professional learning experience. Further research on curriculum and teaching methods would help determine which configurations of online and onsite coursework promote optimal learning in post-professional education.

CONCLUSION

Online courses taught using a constructivist approach provide a structure where participation can be maximized and socially constructed learning can occur. The flexibility offered by the online program has encouraged therapists to pursue postgraduate education who otherwise would not be able to do so. These students have shown us that an online post-professional program can provide a transformational learning experience that expands personal and professional horizons, and offers the opportunity for therapists to contribute to the growth of professionalism in occupational therapy.

REFERENCES

Barab, S. A., Thomas, M. K., & Merrill, H. (2001). Online learning: From information dissemination to fostering collaboration. *Journal of Interactive Learning Research, 12* (1), 105-143.

Dickerson, A. E., & Wittman, P. P. (1999). Perceptions of occupational therapists regarding postprofessional education. *American Journal of Occupational Therapy, 53*, 454-458.

Fahy, P. J., Crawford, G., & Ally, M. (2001). Patterns of interaction in a computer conference transcript. *International Review of Research in Open and Distance Learning, 2* (1). Retrieved July 16, 2002, from *http://www.irrodl.org/content/v2.1/fahy.html*

Farquharson, A. (1995). *Teaching in practice: How professionals can work effectively with clients, patients, and colleagues.* San Francisco: Jossey-Bass.

Frisby, A. J., & Jones, S. S. (2000). The initiation of distance learning at Thomas Jefferson University: The library as integral partner. *Medical Reference Services Quarterly, 19* (3), 19-37.

Glaser, B., & Strauss, A. L. (1967). *The discovery of grounded theory: Strategies for qualitative research.* Chicago: Aldine.

Hansen, N. E., & Gladfelter, J. (1996). Teaching graduate psychology seminars using electronic mail: Creative distance education. *Teaching of Psychology, 23* (4), 252-256.

Johnson, M., Spitz, P., Nelson, L., Bowman, M. T., Devine, C., Kanazawa, L., & Rang, G. (2000). Perceptions of occupational therapists regarding postprofessional education [Letter to the editor]. *American Journal of Occupational Therapy, 54,* 444-445.

Kearsley, G., Lynch, W., & Wizer, D. (1995). The effectiveness and impact of online learning in graduate education. *Educational Technology, 35* (6), 37-42.

Lally, V., & Barrett, E. (1999). Building a learning community on-line: Towards socio-academic interaction. *Research Papers in Education, 14* (2), 147-163.

Lauzon, A. C. (1992). Integrating computer-based instruction with computer conferencing: An evaluation of a model for designing online education. *The American Journal of Distance Education, 6* (3), 32-46.

McAlpine, H., Lockerbie, L., Ramsay, D., & Beaman, S. (2002). Evaluating a web-based graduate level nursing ethics course: Thumbs up or thumbs down? *The Journal of Continuing Education in Nursing, 33* (1), 12-18.

McKeachie, W. J. (1986). *Teaching tips: A guidebook for the beginning college teacher* (8th ed.). Toronto: D. C. Heath & Company.

Miles, M. B., & Huberman, A. M. (1984). *Qualitative data analysis: A sourcebook of new methods.* Newbury Park, CA: Sage Publications.

Rovai, A. P. (2001). Building classroom community at a distance: A case study. *Educational Technology Research and Development, 49* (4), 33-48.

Simons, D. F., Baron, J. A., Knicely, K. S., & Richardson, J. S. (2001). Online learning: Perspectives of students and faculty in two disciplines–occupational therapy and teacher education. *Occupational Therapy in Health Care, 14* (2), 21-53.

Tiene, D. (2000). Online discussions: A survey of advantages and disadvantages compared to face-to-face discussions. *Journal of Educational Multimedia and Hypermedia, 9* (4), 371-384.

Udod, S. A., & Care, W. D. (2002). Lessons learned in developing and delivering web-based graduate courses: A faculty perspective. *The Journal of Continuing Education in Nursing, 33* (1), 19-23.

Brief or New:
The Benefits of On-Line Learning
in Occupational Therapy

Heather A. Gallew, MS, CEES, OTR/L

SUMMARY. This paper discusses the benefits of incorporating an on-line program, such as Blackboard, into occupational therapy education to enhance the learning experience. An occupational therapy department at a midwestern university piloted the use of Blackboard in two classes in the spring semester of the junior year. Students (n = 16) ranging in age from 20-28 years participated in the pilot study, which lasted a period of 12 weeks. The students were given various assignments on Blackboard involving discussions, answering questions related to the lecture topic, and sharing evidence-based practice. Overall, the student perceptions of incorporating Blackboard into a traditional classroom were positive. Eighty-one percent of the students felt that Blackboard was easy to access, 75% felt that they could share thoughts and stories that they would not necessarily have shared in a classroom setting, and 81% felt that Blackboard expanded on lecture topics and relevant practice information. Data suggest that on-line learning can en-

Heather A. Gallew is Assistant Professor of Occupational Therapy, Xavier University, 3800 Victory Parkway, Cincinnati, OH 45207-7341 (E-mail: gallew@xavier.edu). She is completing her doctoral work at Creighton University.

The author would like to thank the students who participated in this pilot project for their hard work and dedication, and Stephen J. Page, PhD, Research Assistant Professor of Physical Medicine and Rehabilitation at University of Cincinnati.

[Haworth co-indexing entry note]: "Brief or New: The Benefits of On-line Learning in Occupational Therapy." Gallew, Heather A. Co-published simultaneously in *Occupational Therapy in Health Care* (The Haworth Press, Inc.) Vol. 18, No. 1/2, 2004, pp. 117-125; and: *Best Practices in Occupational Therapy Education* (eds: Patricia A. Crist, and Marjorie E. Scaffa) The Haworth Press, Inc., 2004, pp. 117-125. Single or multiple copies of this article are available for a fee from The Haworth Document Delivery Service [1-800-HAWORTH, 9:00 a.m. - 5:00 p.m. (EST). E-mail address: docdelivery@haworthpress.com].

hance the educational experience by building upon student fieldwork experiences, evidence-based practice, discussion of key concepts in the profession, and clinical reasoning. *[Article copies available for a fee from The Haworth Document Delivery Service: 1-800-HAWORTH. E-mail address: <docdelivery@haworthpress.com> Website: <http://www.HaworthPress.com> © 2004 by The Haworth Press, Inc. All rights reserved.]*

KEYWORDS. On-line learning, Blackboard, education

INTRODUCTION

Technology is part of everyday life. More individuals are using computers, personal digital assistants, and the Internet to increase efficiency, organize daily activities, enhance communication, and build knowledge. Recognizing the importance of technology and virtuality in people's lives, the new Practice Framework (2002) identifies the use of technology and the "virtual" world as one of its context areas. The virtual context is described as an "environment in which communication occurs by means of airways or computers and an absence of physical contact" (Occupational Therapy Practice Framework, 2002, p. 623). Not surprisingly, technology is becoming an essential part of occupational therapy curriculum as evidenced by the Standards for an Accredited Educational Program for the Occupational Therapist (American Occupational Therapy Association, 1998), which requires students to be competent in basic computer use for communication, intervention, research, and management. Reflecting the advances in technology, the National Certification Examination has also become computerized.

The profession of occupational therapy recognizes that computer use and technology are a vital part of people's lives bringing meaning and a sense of self. Technology not only allows practitioners to interact with and rehabilitate clients in new and exciting ways; it also serves as a tool to enhance occupational therapy education. This paper will discuss the use of Blackboard, a software program that takes teaching on-line, opening vast opportunities to enhance learning.

ON-LINE LEARNING

When incorporating on-line learning it is important that the instructor has a clear understanding of its benefits and challenges in order to facilitate the student's experiences. When developing on-line course components, it is important to remember that you are *producing* learning (Barr & Tagg, 1995). The on-line learning experience should be dynamic and collaborative allowing the students to engage in exploration, reflection, and the application of their knowledge. In creating this, the instructor must be aware of the influences of personal characteristics of the students such as learning styles, personalities, home environments, and internal drive (Simons et al., 2001). These factors along with others will influence the level of participation and depth that students reach in on-line learning activities.

The mission of occupational therapy education is to produce learning in all students by designing exciting and varied experiences that allow students to explore, discover, and reflect on new knowledge (Barr & Tagg, 1995). Currently, over 2,600 organizations, many of which are educational institutions, use Blackboard to enrich the educational experience (Blackboard Inc., 2003). In master and doctoral level education, students have a responsibility for their own independent learning. On-line learning programs hold students accountable for the quality and depth of their participation. The discussion elements of the on-line programs establish a collaborative learning environment. On-line learning programs can also enhance classroom coursework by creating a virtual atmosphere that accommodates the busy life of our students as well as an environment where students may express themselves and engage in self-reflection.

METHOD

The occupational therapy department at a midwestern university piloted the use of Blackboard in two classes offered in the spring semester of the junior year. Seventeen students ranging in age from 20-28 years participated in the pilot study, which lasted for a period of 12 weeks. The majority of the students were traditional college students. One student was married and three held degrees in other areas. Upon completion of the pilot study, students voluntarily completed a survey gathering information on their perceptions of using Blackboard (n = 16).

Instrument

Students completed a voluntary survey which was distributed on the last day of classes. The instrument contained eight statements with a 5-point Likert scale anchored by 1 = strongly disagree and 5 = strongly agree (see Table 1 for list of items). The questions sought to gain insight on the student's perception of Blackboard as a learning tool through statements such as "Blackboard allowed me to expand on lecture topics and other related topics that are important to the profession." There were also five open-ended questions asking the students for their recommendations regarding what they liked best, what they liked least, and how much time they spent per week on Blackboard assignments for each class.

TABLE 1. Summary of Student Responses (n = 16)

Questions	Strongly Agree	Agree	Undecided	Disagree	Strongly Disagree
1. Blackboard was a helpful learning tool	1	10	4	1	0
2. Blackboard was user-friendly	5	7	2	2	0
3. I had difficulty accessing Blackboard most of the time	0	2	0	8	6
4. Able to share thoughts and stories I would not have shared in class.	4	8	1	3	0
5. Expanded on lecture topics and other practice related issues	3	10	3	0	0
6. Useful tool to retrieve class information	8	5	2	1	0
7. Would have liked more discussion on Blackboard with my classmates and instructor	0	3	6	7	0
8. Blackboard is a good tool to use in regards to technology and education	7	6	5	1	0

Procedures: Incorporating Blackboard

Blackboard was incorporated into two classes, one addressing neurological conditions, and the other neurological theories. Blackboard participation in the conditions class was worth 5% of the students' final grade. In the theory class, it was worth 15% of the students' final grade. All course materials were posted on Blackboard. The students were given a handout provided by the Information Services Department explaining the steps of accessing Blackboard for each class. Assignments were posted in the Course Document area of the Blackboard website.

The instructor used Blackboard to enhance the classes in numerous ways. Throughout the semester, the instructor posted relevant material on Blackboard for quick communication and efficient course updates. For some lectures, the instructor posted questions on required readings. The students completed this prior to class, thus making class time more effective as they were prepared to engage in discussions and explore the topic in greater depth. Often, students could choose to answer two questions from a list. They were then responsible to engage in discussion with at least two classmates applying fieldwork experiences. The instructor varied the weekly discussion by focusing on topics such as specific neurological conditions, client-centered intervention, ethical practice, context, and spirituality. As students shared their experiences and discussed various topics, the instructor would prompt students with questions to facilitate self-reflection and critical thinking.

EBP was incorporated into Blackboard specifically through the theory course. The instructor posted an EBP lecture on Blackboard, which the students were responsible to read. Using Holm's (2000) Eleanor Clarke Slagle lecture as a guideline, the students were required to research articles on topics relating to class discussions such as constraint-induced therapy, motor re-learning, occupation-based practice, and feeding techniques. Using Holm's suggested format, students posted their findings in the discussion area. During the remainder of the week, the students would respond to one or two of their classmate's postings. The instructor encouraged students to critically analyze the articles and apply them to their clinical experiences to guide practice.

RESULTS

Table 1 shows the student responses to the survey questions. Eighty-one percent of the students felt that Blackboard was easy to access. Seventy-five percent of students felt that they could share thoughts and stories in Blackboard that they would not necessarily have shared in class. Eighty-one percent of the class felt that Blackboard expanded on lecture topics and other relevant information important to the profession of occupational therapy. The majority of the students did not want more discussions on Blackboard. Lastly, 81% felt that Blackboard was a good tool to incorporate technology into the curriculum.

In the open-ended responses students recommended decreasing some of the assignments as their Blackboard work was in addition to other course assignments. Half of the class recommended more questions that allowed them to share their fieldwork experiences and engage in discussions rather than answering "book-related" questions. Two students reported that what they liked best about Blackboard was the ability to retrieve class notes and information whenever they needed it. One student claimed, "being able to go and get research topics of your choice and share them with others" was the best part of Blackboard. Blackboard enhanced classroom learning; it "made me keep up with the material." Other students commented that Blackboard helped them to communicate more professionally with their classmates as they shared their experiences, posed questions, and presented articles on evidence-based practice.

One student commented, "It was great to read other students' experiences and hear their perspectives on different areas of practice." Another stated, "Hearing comments back from students and the professor about my thoughts, experiences, and opinions. It is nice to see a variety of answers and two sides of the coin on matters I previously would have looked at one way." The ambiguity of cyberspace created an atmosphere that allowed the students to share more freely than in the atmosphere of a classroom.

Figure 1 summarizes the students' estimated time spent on Blackboard per week. In the conditions class, 79% reported spending one hour or less reading the assignments, posting their answers, and responding to classmates for the conditions class. In the theory class, 57% reported spending 30 minutes to one hour reading, posting, and responding to their classmates and 29%, one to two hours. The remaining students spent one to three hours. Regarding total time spent on Blackboard per week, half of the students estimated that they spent a total of one hour or less, whereas the other half ranged from one to four hours per week.

Qualitative Data: Building Concepts of Occupational Therapy

Blackboard is a tool that can be used to allow students to explore and discuss important concepts in the practice of occupational therapy. In one session, the students were asked to share their experiences of spirituality on their fieldwork. One student responded, "I think that spirituality has to do with your sense of wholeness and sense of self. I think that part of a person's spirituality is related to their religious beliefs, but also part comes from within yourself . . ." Another student shared her view of the value of occupation. "To me, occupa-

FIGURE 1. Estimated Time Spent on Blackboard per Week (n = 14)

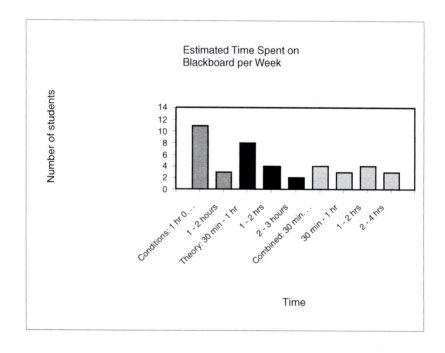

tions are the activities that people engage in that give their life meaning. Occupation is specific to each person and their context. Occupations are what allow us to fulfill our roles everyday . . ." This student has synthesized and applied her knowledge of occupation to use a holistic and client-centered approach. This is a foundation that she will continue to build on through her coursework and clinical practice.

Blackboard, as well as other on-line learning programs, is also used to facilitate clinical reasoning and critical thinking. Clinical reasoning involves a process of thinking that one uses to guide practice and intervention (Neistadt, 1998). Similarly, on-line learning encourages the use of critical thinking as students question, explore, and engage in discussions by analyzing the topic and attempting to apply or explore its possibilities. These are essential skills for the occupational therapy practitioner (Neistadt, 1998).

The Blackboard assignments for this pilot test required a combination of clinical and critical reasoning as the students researched the literature to determine best practice. It also allowed students to engage in self-reflection, and explore the value of research and life-long learning. One student passionately commented on the value of research:

> Research is invaluable to the field of occupational therapy. Research and evidence-based practice validates the need and importance of OT in different settings and with different clients. EBP backs up our profession! The benefits of OT services can be shown to 3rd party payers, families, physicians, and other health professionals; the research currently available and research yet to be conducted is priceless to the growing OT profession.

Another student commented, "I don't think that there is a way to be a successful OT without being a lifetime learner. I see myself learning from my own experiences . . . but also from my patients. I have already learned a lot from clients on fieldwork." Another student stated, "I see myself as a life-long learner, not only in the field of OT, but within every aspect of my life. There is always more to learn and room for growth, so although I learn more each day, I don't feel that I will ever stop learning either."

DISCUSSION

Blackboard did enhance the student learning experience. Blackboard facilitated communication, the delivery of course information and materials, student synthesis of readings and fieldwork experiences, clinical reasoning, and it required students to keep up with their coursework. It provided an atmosphere in which all students could equally participate and share, which is sometimes limited in the classroom. This was an interesting finding as one might think that the virtual environment would create an impersonal, isolated atmosphere.

When designing on-line components it is important to consider the student time involved in its preparation and participation in conjunction with other course assignments. In regards to questions, some students liked ones that forced them to do their readings and review course material, while others preferred questions that facilitated thought and application of fieldwork. To most effectively reach the students given their varying needs and learning styles, and to meet the objectives of the course, it may be most beneficial for the on-line program to incorporate a variety of learning strategies.

Given the increased use of technology in our society and the diverse lives of our students, the positive results in this pilot study show the need for further research on the effectiveness of incorporating on-line learning into occupational therapy curricula. Educators should also be mindful that the National Certification Examination is now computerized, thus on-line course components can provide opportunities for students to practice taking on-line quizzes and tests. Not only would it help prepare students for the National Certification Examination, it would also save class time and require students to stay abreast of their readings.

CONCLUSION

Educators have a mission to facilitate their students' ability to discover knowledge and engage in critical thinking (Esdaile & Roth, 2000), thus leading them towards becoming an occupational therapy practitioner. The students participating in on-line learning showed growth, insight, and passion as they discussed and shared their experiences. The traditional classroom accompanied by on-line learning creates a dynamic learning environment for students.

The results suggested that Blackboard enhanced the learning in the classroom by serving as an additional tool in which students engaged in discussions with each other on topics and concepts such as client-centered practice, EBP, occupation-based practice, habits and routines, spirituality, and culture. As occupational therapy education enters master and doctorate levels, educators must strive to create challenging and dynamic learning experiences for the students. On-line learning is an essential tool to fulfill our mission of instilling knowledge, self-reflection, and growth in our students so that they may become competent practitioners of occupational therapy.

REFERENCES

American Occupational Therapy Association (1998). *Standards for an accredited educational program for the occupational therapist, 53* (6), 575-582.

Barr, R., and Tagg, J. (1995). From teaching to learning–A new paradigm for undergraduate education. *Change, 27* (6), 13-26.

Blackboard, Inc. (2003). Blackboard Learning System. Retrieved June 20, 2003 from www.blackboard.com/docs/wp/LSR6WP.pdf.

Esdaile, S., and Roth, L. (2000). Education not training: The challenge of developing professional autonomy. *Occupational Therapy International, 7* (3), 147-152.

Holm, M. (2000). Our mandate for the new millennium: Evidence-based practice. Eleanor Clarke Slagle Lecture. *American Journal of Occupational Therapy, 54* (6), 575-585.

Neistadt, M. (1998). Teaching clinical reasoning as a thinking frame. *American Journal of Occupational Therapy, 52* (3), 221-229.

Occupational therapy practice framework: Domain and process (2002). *American Journal of Occupational Therapy, 56* (6), 609-639.

Simons, D. F., Baron, J. A., Knicely, K., and Richardson, J. (2001). On-line learning: Perspectives of students and faculty in two disciplines–Occupational therapy and teacher education. *Occupational Therapy in Health Care, 14* (2), 21-53.

Brief or New:
WebQuests:
An Instructional Strategy
for the Occupational Therapy Classroom

Donna Wooster, MS, OTR/L, BCP
Kathy Lemcool, MA, OTR/L

SUMMARY. WebQuests are an innovative teaching activity that promotes students to actively engage in their learning and work cooperatively in small groups. WebQuests have been widely used in K-12 environments in a variety of subjects and are gaining respect in universities. This paper will briefly describe the basic concept of a WebQuest and provide two examples of WebQuests developed for use in an occupational therapy curriculum. *[Article copies available for a fee from The Haworth Document Delivery Service: 1-800-HAWORTH. E-mail address: <docdelivery@haworthpress.com> Website: <http://www.HaworthPress.com> © 2004 by The Haworth Press, Inc. All rights reserved.]*

Donna Wooster is Assistant Professor, University of South Alabama, Department of Occupational Therapy, 1504 Springhill Ave., Room 5108, Mobile, AL 36604-3273 (E-mail: *dwooster@jaguar1.usouthal.edu*). Kathy Lemcool is Assistant Professor, University of South Alabama, Department of Occupational Therapy, Mobile, AL (E-mail: *kgifford@jaguar1.usouthal.edu*).

[Haworth co-indexing entry note]: "Brief or New: WebQuests: An Instructional Strategy for the Occupational Therapy Classroom." Wooster, Donna, and Kathy Lemcool. Co-published simultaneously in *Occupational Therapy in Health Care* (The Haworth Press, Inc.) Vol. 18, No. 1/2, 2004, pp. 127-135; and: *Best Practices in Occupational Therapy Education* (ed: Patricia A. Crist, and Marjorie E. Scaffa) The Haworth Press, Inc., 2004, pp. 127-135. Single or multiple copies of this article are available for a fee from The Haworth Document Delivery Service [1-800-HAWORTH, 9:00 a.m. - 5:00 p.m. (EST). E-mail address: docdelivery@haworthpress.com].

KEYWORDS. WebQuest, occupational therapy curriculum, active learning, cooperative learning, instructional strategies

INTRODUCTION

Most allied health educators are not familiar with WebQuests as an educational activity, but it could be utilized in allied health programs to promote active student learning. WebQuests have been utilized as educational strategies in many educational environments. The availability of quality information and databases on the World Wide Web (WWW) has helped make this activity accepted and utilized. The instructor provides web site addresses to the students, therefore little time is wasted surfing for non-significant information. Instead, students are given tasks to perform and the resources to consult to assist them in the task. This educational strategy should be explored further as an appropriate method for engaging allied health students in active small group cooperative learning processes.

OVERVIEW

WebQuests contain six elements: introduction, task, information sources, description of the process, guidance, and a conclusion. A WebQuest is "an inquiry-oriented activity in which some or all of the information that learners interact with comes from resources on the Internet" (Dodge, on line, 2000, *http://www.edweb.sdsu/courses/edtec596/about_webquests.html*). WebQuests can be of either short duration or longer duration. Short duration WebQuests usually involve knowledge acquisition and integration. The learners will have examined a significant amount of new information and made sense of or summarized it. This usually takes from two to four class periods. The focus of this paper will be limited to describing and giving examples of short-term WebQuests.

Students will be given a topic, a specific task or product to produce, and the information sources they will utilize. Most often some type of guided questions or specific tasks are provided to assist students in the group process and to organize the product (Marzano, 1988). Often students are given a role to play during the exploratory process. They may be asked to examine the information from the perspective of a patient, a doctor, a scientist, a reporter, etc. . . . This tends to increase the students' motivation to participate since it can be authentic in nature in relationship to their future lives or jobs.

One consideration in using WebQuest is that the teacher must determine the web sites and resources students will explore ahead of time and provide the students with the web addresses or links to these sites. This eliminates the wasted time of surfing the net so often done by students who end up frustrated and with poor quality information. These sites become the information sources that students will explore and examine.

WebQuests incorporate strategies that increase student motivation by offering authentic, relevant tasks, cooperative learning, scaffolding, critical thinking, and authentic assessments (March, on line, *http://www.ozline.com/webquests/intro.html*). Students must take charge of their learning and actively participate in this group process. WebQuests are inquiry-oriented activities that require students to access, integrate, and extend their knowledge (Ritchie & Hoffman, 1996). Students must read and scrutinize the information and rearrange or summarize it according to the guiding questions provided and the expected outcome or product.

These learning strategies can be designed from within a single discipline or they can be interdisciplinary in design. This can make it easily customized for use within a particular field in allied health or be interdisciplinary, asking students to view the issues from multiple perspectives.

WebQuests require students to work in cooperative learning groups. Research about cooperative learning indicates it is successful for promoting problem-solving skills when teaching mathematics (Kilpatrick, 1985; Mayer, 1985; Noddings, 1985; Palinscar & Brown, 1989; Schoenfield, 1985). Students think aloud and share information, clarify their understanding of concepts and issues, and can learn from their classmates thinking-aloud skills (Mayer, 1985; Noddings, 1985). The above-cited studies were not focused on web-based learning but rather on cooperative learning. The next step in the utilization of WebQuests would be to study the effectiveness of this web-based technique.

GRADING

A grading rubric for this assignment should be developed in advance and shared with the students as part of their orientation to the assignment. The rubric will vary based on the nature of the product you ask the students to produce. There are three steps to creating a rubric (Dodge, 2000, available online *http://webquest.sdsu.edu/rubrics/rubrics.html*):

1. Generate a number of potential dimensions to use
2. Select a reasonable number of the most important dimensions
3. Identify benchmarks for each level of each dimension

For example, if the product of the WebQuest is an oral presentation one might consider use of voice and visuals as important dimensions. However, if the product is a resource guide, the relevant dimensions might include resources selected and organization of the guide.

ADVANTAGES AND DISADVANTAGES
OF WEBQUESTS AS A LEARNING TOOL

One positive aspect of WebQuest is that it tends to promote active student learning. Students are engaged in the task in classrooms with web connections so that students start the research immediately. This speed facilitates the process and avoids the wasted surf time that so often frustrates students. Another positive aspect of WebQuest is that it allows students to access a vast amount of information available on the World Wide Web. This knowledge is ever increasing.

The main disadvantage of using this assignment is the time involved for the instructor to keep web addresses current. Instructors must check each uniform resource locator (URL) address for currency of information prior to giving the assignment to make sure the site is still a functioning legitimate site. Once the addresses are established it is actually quite simple to check on the link and see if it is still active.

EXAMPLE OF A WEBQUEST

The following example is provided as a model to assist educators in the development of WebQuests for use in occupational therapy (see Appendix A for another example). This example is an assignment for occupational therapy students enrolled in an applied neuroanatomy class. The assignment requires students to work in small groups, while the cerebral palsy WebQuest example also requires the students to take on an assigned role. Students are required to share their information with each other at the completion of each assignment to learn from each other's research efforts and summaries.

Evaluation

Points will be earned based on each group's efforts and final products. The final products will include both the written products and final presentations. Points in the grading rubric will be as follows:

1. Accuracy and depth of informational resources utilized
2. Ability to synthesize information into professional written documents
3. Quality of finished written product–informative, accurate, succinct, appearance, spelling, grammar, neatness
4. Organization of presentation format that flows well and reinforces key points of information to audience

5. Process of presentation to include quality of visual aides, ability to be heard and understood, audience involvement, and accuracy of information presented
6. Individual contribution to the group as evaluated by other team members

EXAMPLE–WEBQUEST ON THE IMPACT OF NEUROLOGICAL DISORDERS ON OCCUPATIONAL FUNCTIONING

Issue
How is daily functioning impacted when people have neurological disorders?

Objectives
1. Explore web resources students can use independently to supplement classroom learning.
2. Enhance students' knowledge and appreciation of neurological conditions through the use of multimedia.
3. Build on students' ability to seek out and find sources of information they will need as future clinicians.
4. Familiarize students with web-based patient educational and supportive information they can share with their patients.
5. Facilitate life-long learning by providing students experience with the WWW as a learning tool for professional growth.

Process
a. Entire class generates a list of common neurological disorders in children, adolescents and adults.
b. Divide the disorders up into group tasks. Students are placed in groups of ten in a group. We will have three groups, one for each age category listed.
c. Students in groups generate aspects of daily living they think are impacted by the disabling condition.

Products
1. Students will compile a resource guide for clinicians and students by printing out all printable online materials for self and patient/family education.
2. Students will complete a webliography for future references. Each semester they will add information to the reference that they gained from other course work.

Web Resources

General Information

1. This is a great overview page of the structures and functions of the CNS:
   http://www.neurogate.com/neuro/redirect.php3?search=Speech&select=and&table=neuro&n=30&url=http://www.caregiver.org/factsheets/als.html&id=991
2. The target audience for this site is children; however, the over simplification is nice to aid understanding. It has lots of good information about all the neural systems:
   http://thalamus.wustl.edu/course/
   Other site for general information on neuroanatomy
   http://www.brain.com

Developmental Disorders

3. Site depicting developmental defects in the CNS. Includes athetoid CP, focal cortical dysplasia, developmental language disorder:
   http://www.crump.ucla.edu/lpp/clinpetneuro/deverrors.html#DevErrors
4. This site talks about neural tube defects and how to prevent them by increased dietary intake of folic acid:
   http://www.neurogate.com/neuro/redirect.php3?search=Neural+Tube+Defects&select=and&table=neuro&n=0&url=http://www.babybag.com/articles/wh-folic.htm&id=904

Disorders of Adolescents/Young Adults

5. This site addresses the neurological deficits associated with AIDS:
   http://www.caregiver.org/factsheets/Hiv.html

Disorders in Adults

6. This site has a fact sheet on diagnosis and treatment of Parkinson's disease:
   http://www.caregiver.org/factsheets/parkinsons.html

Evaluation

Points will be earned based on each group's efforts and the final products. The final products will include both the resource guide and the webliography products. Points in the grading rubric will be for the following:

1. Value of web information selected for the resource guide and the webliography
2. Synthesis of information for the webliography and the WebQuest activities
3. Quality of resource guide–depth, spelling, grammar, neatness

4. Organization of resource guide–useful information, easy to use
5. Organization of the webliography
6. Peer evaluation–students will evaluate the quality and quantity overall of each other's work on this project

CONCLUSION

Educators want students to think and solve problems independently. WebQuests provide such an opportunity and are easily carried out as in class assignments. Additionally, WebQuests give students an opportunity to learn about the resources available on the web. Some of the sources can help them answer their questions about an issue while others may serve as a reference they can share with clients and their families.

REFERENCES

Dodge, B. (2000). WebQuests (On line). Available *http://www.edweb.sdsu/courses/edtec596/about_webquests.html*

March, T. (2000). Why WebQuests? An introduction (On line). Available *http://www/ozline.com/webquests/intro.html*

Marzano, R. J., Brandt, R. S., Hughes, C. S., Jones, B. F., Presseisen, B. Z., Rankin, S. C., & Suhor, C. (1988*). Dimensions of thinking: A framework or curriculum and instruction.* Alexandria, VA: Association for Supervision and Curriculum Development.

Mayer, R. E. (1985). *Implication of cognitive psychology for instruction in mathematical problem solving.* In E. A. Silver (Ed.) *Teaching and learning mathematical problem solving: Multiple research perspectives.* Hillsdale, NJ: Erlbaum.

Noddings, N. (1985). *Small groups as a setting for research on mathematical problem solving.* In E. A. Silver (Eds.), *Teaching and learning mathematical problem solving: Multiple research perspectives.* Hillsdale, NJ: Erlbaum.

Palinscar, A. S. & Brown, A. L. (1989). Classroom dialogues to promote self-regulated comprehension. In J. Brophy (Ed.), *Advances in research and teaching.* Greenwich, CT: JAI Press.

Ritchie, D. & Hoffman, B. (1996). Incorporating instructional design principles with the World Wide Web. In Khan, B. (Ed.) *Web-based instruction.* Englewood Cliffs, NJ: Educational Technology Publications, Inc.

SUGGESTED WEB RESOURCES FOR FACULTY

Bernie Dodge is the creator of the WebQuest. He teaches at San Diego State University and has created a website with a WebQuest that teaches you the design steps for constructing WebQuests. This site also has links to guidelines for grading rubrics. *http://www.edweb.sdsu/courses/edtec596/about_webquests.html*

Tom March's website explains WebQuests, dispels myths, and gives rationales for using WebQuests. *http://www/ozline.com/webquests/intro.html*

APPENDIX A
Example–WebQuest on Cerebral Palsy

Issue
You have just been assigned to work at the local children's hospital for your next clinical rotation. You will be working in occupational therapy with families of children with cerebral palsy (CP). You will provide both inpatient and outpatient services. You must research and prepare for this clinical rotation. The class will divide into four small groups, each completing one of the tasks below. You will report your findings back to your classmates in two weeks and provide handouts for all.

Task
Each group will play the role of an OT with a slightly different focus.

Group One–Medical Information/Diagnostic Summary
Your task is to obtain information about medical procedures, diagnosis, prognosis and other relevant information. Focus your efforts on medical interventions for CP and associated problems and therapeutic interventions. You must prepare an in-depth diagnostic summary that includes diagnosis criteria, prognostic indicators, incidence, prevalence, signs, symptoms, associated problems, medical interventions and therapeutic interventions.

Group Two–You have been assigned to the parent support group. This meets weekly at the hospital. You must find out about resources for families with children with CP in your geographical area. You will prepare this month's newsletter that identified resources that includes the contact person's name, phone number, any eligibility criteria, and services offered to families and children with CP.

Group Three–You will be working closely with a physician in the spasticity reduction clinic. You must research the more common methods of reducing spasticity, indications for their use, and the role of OT in intervention. Provide a chart for your classmates that compares and contrasts the various spasticity reduction techniques including medications, injections, and surgical procedures and the indications, contraindications, outcomes, and therapy interventions.

Group Four–Your focus is on locating literature that supports promoting independence in activities of daily living. Locate literature that supports specific techniques used by occupational therapists to promote independence in these skills. This should include feeding, dressing and toileting skills specifically. Prepare a two-page handout that includes a synopsis of the researched literature in a table format. This may include information about commonly recommended assistive devices.

Cerebral Palsy Resources

Facts/ Medical Information
http://gait.aidi.udel.edu/res695/homepage/pd_ortho/clinics/c_palsy/cpweb.htm
Parent Support Groups
Parents helping parents
http://php.com
Specific types Info
Hemiplegic CP–website by parents and for parents
http://www.hemikids.org
Websites written by families/ patients
Susie's website
http://www.susiecphome.com/home.html
Local/ State Agencies
Alabama State Agencies
http://www.nichcy.org/stateshe/al.htm
United Cerebral Palsy Association with links to states
Spasticity Management
Hyperbaric Oxygen Therapy

http://www.hbot.com/
The Information Exchange by Dr. Fredrickson
http://www.askdrmark.com
Cerebral Institute of Discovery-Non-surgical Interventions for CP
http://www.cerebral.org/cptreat.html

Process
Each member of the team is responsible for collecting data on the subtopics. Besides the web sites listed above, students are expected to review peer reviewed journal articles and relevant textbooks. If in your search, you discover another wonderful web site, please share the address with the course instructor. Also, if any of the links above are no longer working, let the course instructor know that as well. Think about all the resources available to you within department, on campus, and in the library.
You will need to meet as a group to discuss your findings and summarize the information in an organized format. Your final products as a group should be a synthesis of information based on your findings.

Products
You are to gather information and create the following:
1. The required paper documents expected for each group as outlined above. These should be presented professionally, i.e., typed, checked for spelling and grammar errors and complete with references.
2. A professional presentation for about 20 minutes that includes visual aids and each member contributing to the presentation process. Be sure to highlight the important discoveries and synthesis of information you found. This should be professional, well rehearsed, and contain accurate information. Be prepared to answer questions about your topic.

Evaluation
Points will be earned based on each group's efforts and final products. The final products will include both the written products and final presentations. Points in the grading rubric will be as follows:

7. Accuracy and depth of informational resources utilized
8. Ability to synthesize information into professional written documents
9. Quality of finished written product–informative, accurate, succinct, appearance, spelling, grammar, neatness
10. Organization of presentation format that flows well and reinforces key points of information to audience
11. Process of presentation to include quality of visual aides, ability to be heard and understood, audience involvement, and accuracy of information presented
12. Individual contribution to the group as evaluated by other team members

Conclusion
You were able to use the small group process to locate relevant information and learn about CP and occupational therapy. In real world situations, the occupational therapists are expected to have all this knowledge and assume all these roles. Knowing these resources are available should help you stay current in your knowledge and abilities.

PREPARATION
FOR COMMUNITY-BASED PRACTICE

Constructing a Program Development Proposal for Community-Based Practice: A Valuable Learning Experience for Occupational Therapy Students

Barbara Kopp Miller, PhD
David Nelson, PhD, OTR, FAOTA

SUMMARY. Skills required to develop and fund programs can advance an occupational therapist professionally, and innovative occupation-based programs are necessary for the future of occupational therapy. This paper describes a community-based learning experience embedded within the occupational therapy curriculum of the Medical

Barbara Kopp Miller is Associate Professor, Departments of Occupational Therapy, Medicine and Physician Assistant Studies, Medical College of Ohio, Toledo, OH 43614. David Nelson is Professor, also at Department of Occupational Therapy, Medical College of Ohio, Toledo, OH.

[Haworth co-indexing entry note]: "Constructing a Program Development Proposal for Community-Based Practice: A Valuable Learning Experience for Occupational Therapy Students." Kopp Miller, Barbara, and David Nelson. Co-published simultaneously in *Occupational Therapy in Health Care* (The Haworth Press, Inc.) Vol. 18, No. 1/2, 2004, pp. 137-150; and: *Best Practices in Occupational Therapy Education* (ed: Patricia A. Crist, and Marjorie E. Scaffa) The Haworth Press, Inc., 2004, pp. 137-150. Single or multiple copies of this article are available for a fee from The Haworth Document Delivery Service [1-800-HAWORTH, 9:00 a.m. - 5:00 p.m. (EST). E-mail address: docdelivery@haworthpress.com].

http://www.haworthpress.com/web/OTHC
Digital Object Identifier:10.1300/J003v18n01_14

College of Ohio. While developing the Program Development Proposal, each student practices needs assessment; marketing; goals- and objectives-setting; occupation-based programming; budgeting; staffing; program evaluation; and grantsmanship. Outcome surveys of graduates indicate that the experience was positive and provided graduates with a solid foundation for program development. The experience also enhanced partnerships with community-based sites. *[Article copies available for a fee from The Haworth Document Delivery Service: 1-800-HAWORTH. E-mail address: <docdelivery@haworthpress.com> Website: <http://www. HaworthPress.com> © 2004 by The Haworth Press, Inc. All rights reserved.]*

KEYWORDS. Community-based practice, grant-writing, program development

Today's health care and academic systems place high value on program development skills in health care professionals. Possession of the skills required to develop and fund programs has the potential to advance an occupational therapist professionally, and innovative new occupation-based programs are necessary for the future of the profession of occupational therapy. Every profession needs areas of growth. Occupation has broad applicability, and staying within the medical model deprives society of the full benefits of an occupational approach. Naturalistic occupation is most effective, and community-based occupation is more naturalistic than medical model sites. To this end, it is highly desirable for occupational therapy students to learn the skills required to construct program development proposals, especially those oriented to community-based practice. The present paper describes a learning experience embedded within the curriculum of the Master of Occupational Therapy (MOT) Program at the Medical College of Ohio and reports on documented learning outcomes.

SKILLS FOR THE CONTEMPORARY
OCCUPATIONAL THERAPY STUDENT

Two skills will be reviewed in this section: program development proposal skills and community-based practice skills. The 1998 Standards for an Accredited Educational Program for the Occupational Therapist require that occupational therapy programs provide students with a "basic understanding of the process of securing grants" (OT Standard B.8.9; Accreditation Council for Occupational Therapy Education [ACOTE], 1998). This standard requires the curriculum to help the student understand the role of grants, gain information about grants, and appreciate funding mechanisms for grants. The assignment described here meets this standard and includes many additional skills (e.g., in the areas of needs assessment and program evaluation) that the student will be able to use in a variety of settings. We believe it is desirable for curricula to exceed the ACOTE standard in the area of grants and program development so that students are prepared for future changes in the health care environment. Merryman (2002) states that internal forces (e.g., professional standards) and external forces (e.g., federal legislation, hospital cost-containment policies) have created new opportunities for occupational therapy services. The changing field of occupational therapy and the financial realities of health care make it necessary for students to be prepared to develop, implement, and evaluate new programs.

The first recommendation of the Pew Health Professions Commission's Fourth Report (O'Neil & the Pew Health Professions Commission, 1998) proposes that all health professional groups adjust their training to meet the demands of the new health care system. According to this report, "Most of the nation's educational programs remain oriented to prepare individuals for yesterday's health care system" (p. iii). The Commission continued by stressing that educational programs should prepare students to work in emerging practice environments. Healthy People 2010, the national public health initiative document, devotes an entire focus area (#7) to educational and community-based programs (U.S. Department of Health and Human Services, 2000). The goal for this focus area is to "increase the quality, availability, and effectiveness of educational and community-based programs designed to prevent disease and improve health and quality of life" (U.S. Department of Health and Human Services, 2000, pp. 7-3).

Fazio (2001) maintains that there is a natural blend between occupational therapy and community-based programs: "Few professions have an agreed-upon belief system strong enough to organize their interventions without losing their sense of purpose in what can be a complex and demanding care environment–that of the community" (p. 19). Scaffa (2001) reminds us that community practice in occupational therapy is not new. In her book, *Occupational Therapy in Community-Based Practice Settings*, she outlines the historical timeline of community practice, which began in 1914 by two founders of the profession, George Barton and Eleanor Clarke Slagle. Indeed, according to Diffendal (2003), fieldwork supervisors have been utilizing community-based settings for fieldwork placements for many years.

Baum and Law (1998) have eloquently supported the need to prepare occupational therapists for emerging practice arenas, particularly those that are community-based. These authors have advocated for additional skills beyond basic management skills to include an understanding of the mechanisms for service delivery in community-based settings. A crucial skill, according to Baum and Law (1998), is the ability to work in communities as a member of a team that may include traditional disciplines (e.g., physical therapist, nurse) but also new members such as architects, public health officials, and case managers. Paul and Peterson (2001) suggest implementing community-based programs as a strategy for training students for interdisciplinary collaboration.

Based on ACOTE Standards, federal initiatives, and the recommendation of occupational therapy leaders, the Program Development Proposal assignment was designed to: (1) generate basic program development skills in graduate-level occupational therapy students, and (2) bring students, instructors and community-based professionals together to collaboratively design programs to serve clients in the community.

PROGRAM DEVELOPMENT PROPOSAL ASSIGNMENT

The Program Development Proposal Assignment is required in the last year of the program, in the semester prior to six-months level II fieldwork. The class in which the assignment is housed focuses on emerging and community-based models of practice within occupational therapy. The rationale for course sequence reflects the faculty's belief that community-based practice and program development are enhanced by knowledge and skills gained through prior studies in relatively traditional models of practice. For example, a sound understanding of the potentials of assistive technology can help the student start to find a valued role in the community with many populations who have or who are at risk for disabilities. Community-based sites typically involve special challenges to the student's interpersonal skills. Maturity, self-confidence, cultural competence, and the ability to initiate are more likely in the advanced student as opposed to the new student.

The version of the Program Development Assignment described here is the result of an annual process of refining that has taken place over the past five years. These annual changes have been made based on student and faculty evaluations, supplemented by the recommendations of community partners who have helped the students at the sites.

Core texts for the course include *Occupational Therapy in Community-Based Practice Settings* (Scaffa, 2001) and *Developing Occupation-Centered Programs for the Community: A Workbook for Students and Professionals* (Fazio, 2001). Core texts are supplemented with additional readings on such topics as community-based practice (e.g., Baum & Law, 1998) and evaluation (e.g., Valluzzi, 2002). In addition to emerging practice sites, the course also has objectives dealing with group process and cultural competence.

The fieldwork component of the course requires the student to identify a community-based setting in which they would like to develop an occupational therapy program. The two instructors assist students in this process as necessary. The types of settings have varied greatly over the past five years. Examples include agencies responsible for housing of seniors or persons with disabilities; a foundation-based gardening program interested in outreach to children; a homeless shelter; several senior centers; a hospice setting; vocational rehabilitation programs; a supportive home for persons with AIDS; a YMCA; a convent serving older nuns; and a farm-based residence for adolescents and adults with autism and pervasive developmental disorders. A minimum of 24 hours are to be spent on the Level I fieldwork component, with at least half of the time devoted to interactions with the potential recipients of the proposed program. Because the student is not under the supervision of a licensed therapist, it is essential that the student explain his or her role as a student and to explain that he or she is not qualified to provide occupational therapy services. However, the student is qualified and expected to interact with those who might need occupational therapy services. A fieldwork log that documents the student's experiences and time is required.

Once a setting is identified, the student must communicate with the professionals at the setting to become familiar with the agency's mission, programs, and personnel. Usually occupational therapy is not well-understood at the site, and the student must learn how to discuss the potential role of occupational therapy. We believe each student and graduate must be able to educate others about occupational therapy and advocate appropriately for the unique contributions of occupational therapy.

Initial and subsequent meetings with agency professionals contribute to the early stages of a needs assessment. Unstructured and semi-structured interviews with agency personnel are supplemented by beginning interactions with and observations of potential recipients of planned services. At this phase, the student identifies, reads, and analyzes relevant literature concerning the demographics of the population and potential needs for services. Classroom lecture-discussions at this phase focus on relevant resources and models of what past students in the program have done. Once the student completes and hands in an initial needs assessment, the student is matched to a faculty mentor who will work on the Program Development Proposal throughout the remainder of the semester. Both faculty mentors are established grant writers. Their expertise ranges from federally-funded research and training grants to private foundation funding for research and evaluation grants. It is the opinion of the authors that faculty mentoring is a necessary component to aid the student to-wards successful completion of the Program Development Proposal.

The second phase of needs assessment is guided by a formal workshop pro-vided to the students by an evaluation consultant. In this workshop, various forms of needs assessment methodology are presented, both in theory and by example. At this stage the student must identify the relevant stakeholders for a potential program, and must write coherently about the methods that would be used for a comprehensive needs assessment. The student must develop and hand in one structured needs assessment tool, along with a justification for the methods used (e.g., interview, questionnaire, focus group, etc.). The student is required only to plan the second phase of the needs assessment, not to carry it out.

Another early assignment requires the identification of potential funding sources. Using resources such as lecture, a well-stocked, easily accessible li-brary oriented to health care funding, and faculty resources, the student identi-fies three potential funding sources (private and public) for a proposed program. The assignment also requires a rationale as to why each potential funding source is appropriate and a summarized description of the application process.

The next assignment deals with core issues: goal-writing, objectives, and programming. As with the other assignments, lectures are supplemented by past student examples and by examples from funded programs. For most pro-jects, a single focused goal with multiple objectives is desirable. Working with feedback from the faculty mentor, the student typically refines and revises the goal several times. The student learns that writing a goal, defining objectives, and imagining programming is an iterative process, whereby a new program-ming idea can lead to the modification of an objective and sometimes even the re-statement of the goal. A conceptual model of practice or a set of comple-mentary models of practice is selected as the basis for programming. Empha-sis is placed on time-oriented, measurable objectives reflecting changes in occupational performance in potential service recipients. Programming is to be described in sufficient depth that an experienced occupational therapist could carry out the proposed program as planned. Each student's project also specifies the required occupational nature of the planned intervention. The Medical College of Ohio curriculum emphasizes a particular conceptual framework for occupation and this assignment is an example of putting the framework into operation.

The final, written Program Development Proposal that includes or summa-rizes all of the above components as well as some new components is handed in at the end of the semester. The most important new component is the plan for program evaluation, but this task is made relatively easy by having clear measurable objectives to be evaluated. Other new components to the final written proposal include applied managerial topics such as budgeting, timelines, a job description for the occupational therapist, marketing, an organizational chart, and supplemental documentation such as letters of support. The final paper is structured and graded according to detailed, preestablished criteria. Please see Figure 1 for an excerpt from the four-page evaluation form. Our experience is that the MOT student can accomplish marvelous things if provided clear, specific, measurable expectations; if mentored reliably; and if assured that prior students have survived and prospered from the experience.

The final assignment is a poster session, where each student presents the Program Development Proposal to current students, school faculty, college administrators, and personnel from the community sites where their projects were designed. The poster should have interesting visual qualities in addition to communicating the essence of the program. The poster session allows the student to discuss the program with other students and faculty in addition to showcasing the program to personnel from the community site. This not only allows the student to learn from the other students but also serves as a venue for bringing the personnel from the site to campus so that faculty mentors may formally thank them and solicit feedback on the project.

In summary, the overall project involves four mid-semester assignments, a final program development proposal, and a poster. Mid-term assignments keep students on track as they learn more about the community sites and the potential service recipients, as they develop new knowledge and skills in class, and as they make ongoing revisions based on the mentor's comments. The project takes the student approximately 12 weeks to complete.

EVALUATING THE PROGRAM DEVELOPMENT PROPOSAL AS AN ASSIGNMENT

Participants. Graduates from the classes of 1998, 1999 and 2000 were eligible for participation in the evaluation study. These classes represent the first three years the assignment was conducted and allows for a sufficient amount of time to have passed for the graduates to reflect on the value of the assignment as well as to potentially utilize the skills developed through the assignment. There were 56 total graduates, 50 of whom had voluntarily provided telephone numbers to the department and/or alumni affairs. Graduates were randomly selected from the list and contacted for participation in accordance with an exempt ruling from the Institutional Review Board. Data collection occurred during a five-week period. Participation included nine graduates from 1998, six graduates from 1999 and 11 graduates from 2000 (N = 26).

FIGURE 1. Excerpt from Grading Criteria for the MCO MOT Program Development Proposal. This Is Page 2 of 4. Altogether, 100 Points Are Assessed in the Following Areas: Executive Summary; Introduction and Need; Recruiting and Marketing; Objectives; Programming; Budgeting and Staffing; Program Evaluation; Timeline; References; Appendices (Including Agency Mission Statements, Instruments, Job Descriptions, Advertisements, Letters of Support); and Writing Style.

	Weight	Yes	No	Inc
Objectives				
22. Are the objectives logically related to the goal (note: re-state the goal)?	1			
23. Are objectives occupation-based and reasonable, given the literature review?	1			
24. Does each objective pertain to a specific gain to be achieved by participants?	1			
25. Are all objectives oriented to time?	1			
26. Are objectives stated in terms of level of performance (clear standard) to be observed after participation in the program?	1			
27. Are all objectives observable and measurable?	1			
Marketing and Recruitment of Participants				
28. Is the rationale clear as to which stakeholders should be approached in the marketing campaign?	.5			
29. Are marketing materials clear, succinct, cost-effective, and attractive?	.5			
30. Are the marketing strategies appropriate for the target population(s)?	.5			
31. Is there an appropriate promotional mix, given budget constraints?	.5			
32. Is the pool of potential participants/beneficiaries described?	.5			
33. Are inclusion criteria specified and appropriate, and is expected N for the new program clearly specified?	1			
34. In addition to inclusion criteria, will the participants be described in other ways?	.5			
35. Are the methods (who, what, when?) of participant recruitment clearly specified?	.5			
Programming				
36. Is programming logically related to objectives?	1			
37. Does programming reflect cited literature?	.5			
38. Does programming match up to identified model(s) of practice?	1			
39. Are adequate assessments identified (individual, group, and/or environmental)?	1			
40. Are intervention occupational forms described adequately (in principle, and by example)?	1			
41. Is it clear what direct and/or indirect services are provided?	1			
42. Is the documentation system described (including protections for confidentiality)?	.5			
43. Is the sequence of programming described adequately?	.5			

To supplement graduate perceptions, nine community-based site supervisors were identified for possible interviews. Four of the nine were available to participate in telephone interviews.

Methods and Procedure. Upon contacting the graduate, the interviewer described the purpose of the study and informed the participant of his/her rights and the confidential and anonymous nature of the study. The interviewer took notes of the date and the information gathered in the interview but did not record the participant's name or other identifying information. It is important to note that the interviewer was one of the course instructors who is also a psychologist with training in interviewing. All interviews were conducted by the same interviewer. Six questions were asked of the participants. They were first asked to describe their program proposal assignment. A description of tasks required in the assignment was then provided, and the participants were asked if they had employed the skills since graduation. Information regarding whether the assignment was helpful to the participant and recommendations concerning the assignment were solicited. Finally, the participants were asked whether the assignment should be continued and whether an assignment such as this would be useful at other schools of occupational therapy. In accordance with the nature of a semi-structured interview, the interviewer used paraphrasing and re-sequencing of questions and follow-up questions in order to gather the most accurate information possible.

Supervisors of past students were asked to describe the program proposal written at their facility and to discuss the usefulness of the assignment. Supervisors were also asked to evaluate the assignment as an educational experience. In addition, supervisors were asked whether the assignment helped them to understand the possible roles that occupational therapists might take on in their facility or elsewhere. Finally, they were asked if the time they spent working with the student was worthwhile, whether they would participate in future assignments, and whether the assignment should be continued. Again, in accordance with the nature of a semi-structured interview, the interviewer used paraphrasing and re-sequencing of questions and follow-up questions in order to gather the most accurate information possible (Patton, 1990, Chap. 7).

Both interviews took 10 to 20 minutes. Notes were taken during the interview and then transcribed.

RESULTS

Student Learning Outcomes

Employment of Skills Learned. Eighty-five percent of the graduates interviewed stated that they had employed the skills learned through the assignment. In fact, 42% of the graduates reported that they had written/assisted in writing grants or developed new programs since they had graduated. Several graduates stated that the experience gave them the opportunity and confidence to pursue grants. For example, one graduate stated, "I applied for a grant at work. Because of the grant experience at school, [I] felt confident to apply for the grant." Another graduate replied, "I felt comfortable and confident writing the grant. [I] have been asked to be the grant committee chair [at my place of employment]." This graduate also has provided grant writing inservices to other employees.

Five of the 26 graduates indicated that they had started new programs at their places of employment and that the assignment had helped them do so. One graduate commented that she had " . . . recently started a urinary incontinence program. [I] had to budget for personnel and equipment. [I] used the needs assessment skills to determine the need for the program."

Helpfulness of the Assignment. All graduates indicated that the assignment was helpful to them. Some indicated that they felt that it gave them a competitive edge in the job market. For example, one graduate said that the assignment "gave me a competitive edge for jobs because of having the experience." Another commented, "[I] used the . . . experience in interviewing and feel it gave me a leg up." Other graduates reported that the experience was useful because it broadened their knowledge on program development and the diversity of occupational therapy. One graduate said that the Program Development Proposal "helps to realize what needs to be done prior to program implementation. . . .[It is] valuable to see the business side of programs." Still another said that the assignment was "helpful because it taught me not to focus on traditional settings. . . . All the projects showed diverse areas where occupational therapy could be implemented."

Recommendations for the Assignment. The majority of the graduates (65%) did not have recommendations for improving the assignment. Three students suggested working in pairs while one person suggested working with an individual who was currently writing a grant. Other recommendations opposed change in the assignment. Two graduates commented, "Continue to encourage students to stay in a focused direction," and "Continue to make the sky the limit. Encourage students that they can develop programs in whatever area they are inspired."

Continuation of the Assignment. Ninety-two percent of the graduates indicated that the assignment should be continued. One graduate reported that the assignment puts you in the role of "a professional and clinician and is a good resource for future opportunities." One graduate stated that the assignment was a lot of work for a student at that level of education while another one commented that the assignment should be continued depending upon the focus of the class. The value of the assignment might not be apparent until one is employed: "Overall I thought it was an excellent assignment. It was stressful as you were doing it, but it was an assignment that you looked back at almost immediately–what a great assignment!"

Usefulness of Assignment at Other Schools of Occupational Therapy. Fully 92% of the graduates indicated that the assignment would be useful at other schools of occupational therapy. As one graduate stated, "The field of occupational therapy is changing everyday and if [graduates] are not prepared to develop a program independently, they are not prepared for the field that they are getting ready to enter." Another graduate answered, "Everybody should! Reality is that reimbursements are becoming more stringent. By creating a program and getting it funded you perpetuate the industry." Others stated that it would be helpful to have a common knowledge in occupational therapy regarding program development and funding. For example, ". . . to have coworkers have a similar base of knowledge would make it easier to develop programs together."

Community Site Outcomes

Usefulness of the Assignment at the Facility. The value of the assignment to the community sites was apparent through the interviews. One site supervisor said, "[It was] a learning experience for the organization. [We] had the opportunity to learn how to increase the quality of life of patients through occupational therapy." It was also clear that the students had lasting impressions on the site. For example, one supervisor stated, "We were thinking of a children's garden and we have gone forward with it. The student's project gave us more reason to pursue it." Another supervisor reported that because of the experience she now routinely brings in an occupational therapist to speak at their caregiver education group about home environments for individuals with dementia.

Increased Understanding of the Role of Occupational Therapy. When asked if the assignment helped the supervisors to understand the role that occupational therapists might take on in their facilities or elsewhere, all answered affirmatively. One supervisor enthusiastically stated, "Most definitely. Helped me to think outside the box because you are familiar with [occupational therapy in] the traditional setting. I can now see the practicality [of occupational therapy] within a community-based setting."

All supervisors indicated that it was worthwhile helping the student, that they would participate in future assignments, and that the assignment should be continued. One supervisor stated that the Program Development Proposal "opens the possibility of occupational therapy in different settings. My exposure of occupational therapy was limited. Now I see it as a broader discipline that can increase the quality of life."

DISCUSSION

Summary of Results

The results from the evaluation process indicate that the Program Development Proposal assignment had wide-ranging impact, especially in the area of student learning outcomes. Graduates were able to understand the value of the assignment, employ skills learned through the assignment and provide arguments for incorporating such an assignment in other schools of occupational therapy.

The assignment also contributed to tangible outcomes in terms of program development and grant-writing by the graduates. Forty-two percent of the graduates had written or assisted in writing a grant or developed a new program since they had graduated. It is clear that the skills learned through the assignment are worthwhile and transferable to opportunities in the workplace.

The assignment allows students to advocate for occupational therapy while providing the profession opportunities to grow in underserved areas. These are priorities advocated by Baum and Law (1998) and Merryman (2001). Not only do the students learn how to successfully promote occupational therapy but the personnel at the sites learn about occupational therapy and its many facets. It was apparent through the site supervisors' interviews that students have the potential to foster changes that promote occupational therapy and its services.

Lessons Learned and Recommendations for Replication

We believe that the typical student needs one-on-one mentoring by an experienced faculty member in order to develop a high-quality program proposal. Mentorship is a time-consuming, albeit worthwhile, responsibility for an instructor; a time commitment on the faculty member's part is beneficial from the outset. We believe that mentorship by faculty members with experience in program development and grant-writing is necessary for the experience to be valuable for all involved. Perrin and Wittman (2001), who promote a similar occupational therapy assignment, also recommend that faculty have expertise in quantitative and qualitative research methodologies.

There are potential problems that can occur with the fieldwork component of the project. Not all community-based organizations are willing to host students for assignments such as this one. Clear communication with the potential site regarding occupational therapy, the goals of the assignment, and potential benefits to the site are needed from the outset of the assignment. Sometimes the faculty mentor will need to intervene at an early stage. Perrin and Wittman (2001) have stressed the importance of preparing community agencies with regards to expectations and knowledge of occupational therapy services. Another issue is the importance of negotiation with the community site concerning the final disposition of the Program Developmental Proposal. Some agencies have been interested in pursuing funding for the program that the student developed, and the responsibilities and roles of the student, the institution, and the community site need to be determined prior to funding submission.

The most common recommendation provided by the students was to work on the assignment in pairs or groups. This is not without its own set of problems. Perrin and Wittman (2001) conducted their assignment within peer groups and reported that, although many students enjoyed the opportunity, there was also feedback indicating difficulty in working with groups. It is the opinion of the current authors that the students gain more skills and knowledge when they complete the assignment individually under a faculty mentor's guidance. Although more community sites need to be available when working individually, it has potential benefits for the sites. First, it may be easier for site supervisors to work with one student as opposed to two or more. Second, the number of community-based sites exposed to the assignment and value of occupational therapy is increased when each student has his or her own site.

Limitations

Limitations related to the evaluation process must be acknowledged. First, the survey of students and site supervisors employed a retrospective design. This did not permit a comparison of graduates' pre- and post- assignment perceptions. In addition, because the study utilized a semi-structured telephone interview, the duration of the interview was limited, and visual aids could not be used, as in in-person interviewing (Frey & Oishi, 1995). Although random selection of graduates of the program was a strength of the evaluation of the assignment, random selection of agency supervisors was not possible because of job mobility among so many site supervisors. Finally, the interviewer for the study was also one of the course instructors. Although she is a psychologist with experience in interviewing, it is possible that the student responses were affected by this previous relationship. Great care was made to adhere to the interview protocol to decrease the effect of this limitation.

CONCLUSION

Outcome data from graduates indicate that the Program Proposal Development Assignment was a positive learning experience that provided graduates with a solid foundation for program development. Community-based site supervisors agreed that the Program Development Proposal enhanced student understanding of community-based practice and procedures needed in the development of innovative programs in occupational therapy.

REFERENCES

Accreditation Council for Occupational Therapy Education (1998). *Standards for an accredited educational program for the occupational therapist.* Bethesda, MD: American Occupational Therapy Association.

Baum, C., & Law, M. (1998). Community health: A responsibility, an opportunity, and a fit for occupational therapy. *American Journal of Occupational Therapy, 52*, 7-10.

Diffendal, J. (2003). Shelter in South Bend: A homeless center builds its success on OT students. *ADVANCE for Occupational Therapy Practitioners, 19*, 37-38, 46.

Fazio, L. S. (2001). *Developing occupation-centered programs for the community: A workbook for students and professionals.* Upper Saddle River, NJ: Prentice Hall.

Frey, J. H., & Oishi, S. M. (1995). *How to conduct interviews by telephone and in person.* Thousand Oaks, CA: Sage Publications.

Merryman, M. B. (2002, May 13). Networking as an entrée to paid community practice. *OT Practice, 7*, 10-13.

O'Neil, E. H., & the Pew Health Professions Commission (1998). *Recreating health professional practice for a new century.* San Francisco: CA: Pew Health Professions Commission.

Patton, M. Q. (1990). Qualitative evaluation and research methods (2nd ed.). Newbury Park, CA: Sage.

Perrin, K., & Wittman, P. P. (2001). Educating for community-based occupational therapy practice: A demonstration project. *Occupational Therapy in Health Care, 13*, 11-21.

Scaffa, M. (2001). *Occupational therapy in community-based practice settings.* Philadelphia, PA: F. A. Davis.

U.S. Department of Health and Human Services (2000). *Healthy People 2010 (Conference Edition, Two Volumes).* Washington, DC: Author.

Valluzzi, J. L. (2002, February 11). Evaluating and monitoring community-based programs. *OT Practice, 7*, 10-13.

Educating for Community-Based Practice: A Collaborative Strategy

Jaime Phillip Muñoz, PhD, OTR, FAOTA
Ingrid M. Provident, EdD, OTR/L
Anne Marie Witchger Hansen, MS, OTR/L

SUMMARY. This paper describes creative instruction strategies that prepare students for community-based practice. These educational innovations are designed to prepare graduates to understand occupation-based service delivery in community settings, to develop community-built programs that are responsive to community needs, and to understand how to both secure funding for and market occupational therapy services in the community. The process and products of collaboration between instructors in an administration and a community-based practice course are described. Outcome data from students and community partners are presented. Strategies for successful community partnerships and recommendations for continued development of these educational approaches are presented based on these data. *[Article copies available for a fee from*

Jaime Phillip Muñoz is Assistant Professor, Department of Occupational Therapy, Duquesne University, 219 Health Sciences Building, Pittsburgh, PA 15282 (E-mail: munoz@ duq.edu). Ingrid M. Provident is Instructor and Fieldwork Coordinator, Department of Occupational Therapy, Duquesne University, 220 Health Sciences Building, Pittsburgh, PA (E-mail: provident@duq.edu). Anne Marie Witchger Hansen is Instructor and Director of the Practice Scholar Program, Department of Occupational Therapy, Duquesne University, 225 Health Sciences Building, Pittsburgh, PA (E-mail: hansen@duq.edu).

[Haworth co-indexing entry note]: "Educating for Community-Based Practice: A Collaborative Strategy." Muñoz, Jaime Phillip, Ingrid M. Provident, and Anne Marie Witchger Hansen. Co-published simultaneously in *Occupational Therapy in Health Care* (The Haworth Press, Inc.) Vol. 18, No. 1/2, 2004, pp. 151-169; and: *Best Practices in Occupational Therapy Education* (ed: Patricia A. Crist, and Marjorie E. Scaffa) The Haworth Press, Inc., 2004, pp. 151-169. Single or multiple copies of this article are available for a fee from The Haworth Document Delivery Service [1-800-HAWORTH, 9:00 a.m. - 5:00 p.m. (EST). E-mail address: docdelivery@haworthpress.com].

http://www.haworthpress.com/web/OTHC
Digital Object Identifier:10.1300/J003v18n01_15

The Haworth Document Delivery Service: 1-800-HAWORTH. E-mail address:
<docdelivery@haworthpress.com> Website: <http://www.HaworthPress.com>
© 2004 by The Haworth Press, Inc. All rights reserved.]

KEYWORDS. Community-based education, instructional approaches, community-university partnerships

INTRODUCTION

Loukas (2000) has said, "the future lies in the community" (p. 9). However, given changes in health care systems, health care funding, and our own professional educational accreditation standards, community-based practice is more common and is one of the most promising directions for the profession. The future is clearly here now. In 1998, the Accreditation Council for Occupational Therapy Education (ACOTE) adopted new standards that focused on the competencies necessary for community and population-based services (ACOTE, 1998). Some of the current ACOTE requirements include an expectation that educational programs include content that builds a student's knowledge of sociocultural factors influencing occupational choices, the role of occupation in health promotion and disease prevention, the skills needed for community-based interventions at both an individual and a population level, and the advanced knowledge of contextual factors influencing population-focused and community-based service delivery.

Many leaders within the profession have given voice to the need for occupational therapists to return to our roots in community-based practice (Baum & Law, 1997; Fidler, 2000, 2001; Scaffa, 2001). Scaffa (2001) has argued, "to produce competent practitioners for the future, professional education must develop some new curricula and fieldwork models" (p. 374). Faculty at the Duquesne University Occupational Therapy Department in Pittsburgh, Pennsylvania have taken this challenge and infused principles of community practice throughout their curriculum in service learning, community-based experiential teaching/learning activities, and in a course specifically designed to focus on community health. During the Fall 1999 semester, the authors collaborated to introduce an educational strategy designed to integrate the content in an Occupational Therapy Administration course and Community and World Health course, and to develop specific knowledge, skills, and attitudes that support community-based practice. This paper describes the focus and major learning assignments of these two courses, outlines the process of collaboration leading to the educational innovations, provides outcomes and plans for further refinement of this project, and provides recommendations for educational programs seeking to incorporate community-based education in their curricula.

TRAINING FOR COMMUNITY-BASED PRACTICE

McColl (1998) has argued that a knowledge base in medical and biological sciences is insufficient for supporting community-based practice and that occupational therapy curriculums need to expand their knowledge base relative to community-based practice by drawing on social sciences such as sociology, organizational psychology, epidemiology, public health, politics, and systems theory. Training students to work in the community is not a new idea. Using the community as a context for training students appeared in the literature in the mid 1970s (Cermak, 1976; Cromwell & Kielhofner, 1976; Grossman, 1974; Menks, Sittler, Weaver, & Yanow, 1977). In the profession's current discourse on training for community-based practice, the most frequent educational method discussed has been to change the context for training Fieldwork students from traditional to more innovative community-based settings (Donohue, 2001; Dunbar, Simhoni, & Anderson, 2002; Heubner & Tryssenaar, 1996; Mason, 1998; Rydeen, Kautzmann, Cowan, & Benzing, 1995; Scott, 1999; Shordike & Howell, 2001; Totten & Pratt, 2001; Walens, Helfrich, Aviles, & Horita, 2001).

Another approach used by occupational therapy programs has been to secure grant funding to support the integration of community-based training projects into their curricula. For example, Friedland and her colleagues used a grant from the Ontario Ministry of Health to place students in community agencies with the aim of providing community placements for the students, educating the community sites about occupational therapy, and building partnerships for future community-based fieldwork sites (Friedland, Polatajko, & Gage, 2001). Faculty at Columbia University teamed up with a New York City government agency on aging to support a health promotion project for seniors (Miller, Hedden, Argento, Vaccaro, Murad, & Dionne, 2001), and the University of Southern California secured internal university funding to support an occupational therapy after-school enrichment program for 5th and 6th graders in a low income neighborhood in South Central Los Angeles (Frank, Fishman, Crowley, Blair, Murphy, Montoya, Hickey, Brancaccio, & Bensimon, 2001).

In the past few years, descriptions of educational strategies directed at building skills for community-based practice have begun to appear in the occupational therapy literature. Perrin and Wittman (2001) at the University of Mary in North Dakota discuss their Community Partners in Service Project, which is designed to introduce students to community practice over several semesters. This project culminates in the design and implementation of a research project completed at the community agency. At the University of Minnesota, Schaber (2001) has students in her management class create their own job description at local community agencies. At East Carolina University (ECU), faculty have collaborated with a community group, the Concerned Citizens of Tillery, to provide educational, intervention, and research opportunities to their students (Wittman, Conner-Kerr, Templeton, & Velde, 1999). The educational strategy at ECU is designed to build students' competencies for community-based practice over several semesters. In one of the first textbooks on contemporary community practice, Scaffa (2001) describes a program at Washington University in St. Louis, and a service learning approach that emphasizes training for community-based practice at the University of South Alabama.

The literature describing strategies that occupational therapy educational programs are employing to train students to practice effectively in community settings is small but growing. At Duquesne University, the faculty has made training for community-based practice a primary element of their curriculum. Duquesne faculty integrate community-based training into their curriculum through the use of a variety of educational strategies including expectations for volunteerism, community-based experiential learning assignments in a majority of the courses, service learning, the development of a community-focused practice scholar program, and the inclusion of a separate course in community health. What follows are descriptions of one of the educational strategies used at Duquesne that provides an opportunity for students to integrate and apply knowledge, and explore professional roles and service delivery models in community-based settings.

THE COMPONENTS

There are three primary components to this educational strategy. These include an Occupational Therapy Administration course, a Community and World Health course, and a Practice Scholar Program. The courses are the only ones delivered in the fall semester of the student's fifth year in our basic Master's program. Both courses are formatted to be delivered in a condensed five-week period and meet three times a week for 2½ hours. The condensed Fall semester is followed immediately by two Level II fieldwork internships. The students return to Duquesne six months later for a five-week wrap-up that includes post-fieldwork reflection, capstone graduate seminars, and graduation.

Occupational Therapy Administration

At Duquesne University, students' administrative and managerial skills are developed in an Occupational Therapy Administration course. This course provides an introduction to the basic principles of designing and administrating occupational therapy programs and covers topics such as budgeting, quality management, staffing, and program development. Students completing this course are expected to differentiate between managers and leaders, identify various forms of organizational structure, describe the human resource process with respect to recruitment, interviewing and candidate selection, and create and critique performance evaluations. The major learning assignments include: (1) Development of a Proposed Occupational Therapy Program, (2) Creation of a Professional Resumé, and (3) Identification and Discussion of Contemporary Administrative Issues.

The program development assignment was designed as a group project where the students created a hypothetical program containing the following major sections: general purpose, mission statement, Strength- Weaknesses- Opportunities- Threats (SWOT) analysis, program description, needs assessment, budget, organizational structure, implementation plan, position description, performance standards, marketing plan, and program evaluation. This program development assignment assisted students in developing competencies relative to administration, but did not offer the students the opportunity to gain the experience and feedback needed to test the viability of their program ideas in a real-world context.

Community and World Health

The Community and World Health course at Duquesne University focuses on building competencies for community-based practice and covers topics such as community assessment, models of community practice, grant-writing and funding for community practice, community-based programming, indirect service delivery models such as consultation, case management, and education, and cross-cultural and international perspectives on health care delivery.

Class sessions cover content relative to community health care, and incorporate active learning exercises in the classroom, the computer lab, and the community. One class session each week is spent in the community. During this time, students meet with the executive director or staff at their assigned community agency, and complete structured experiential exercises in community assessment, data collection, program development, and grant-writing. In the preceding semester, community agencies are identified and the instructors negotiate student placements. The initial meeting between the students and the directors of their assigned agency is also pre-scheduled by the instructors for the first week of class.

The major learning assignments in Community and World Health include: (1) Analysis of the Literature on occupational therapy community-based practice, (2) a Community Agency Profile including a needs assessment of the agency and surrounding community, and (3) a basic Grant Application focused on funding the program the students have designed in their Occupational Therapy Administration course.

Practice Scholar Program

The seeds for developing the Practice Scholar program were planted more than a decade ago when the Duquesne Occupational Therapy Department was founded. The curriculum is designed to integrate service learning projects and experiential class assignments that place students into community agencies serving various populations such as at-risk youth, physically and mentally challenged men, women and children, homeless and/or incarcerated populations, and the frail elderly.

The Practice Scholar program was created in 1999 as an extension of our community-focused curriculum. The Practice Scholar program is designed to provide opportunities for our students to connect curriculum content, service learning, and fieldwork opportunities with "best practice" models in emerging community-based practice areas. The goals of the practice scholar program are to integrate theory and scholarship in everyday practice, to demonstrate active engagement in responsible fieldwork education, and to live a commitment to the mission of Duquesne University–"Serving God, by serving our students"–who serve the community, and those populations who are most marginalized and underserved.

The primary role of the director of the Practice Scholar Program is to build community-university partnerships that address the comprehensive health and wellness needs of the community with a holistic, innovative, occupation-based approach that improves the quality of life for the community across the life span. The director seeks to develop collaborative, community-built programs that address specific, community-identified needs and then works with community partners to submit funding proposals that support community-based Duquesne University occupational therapy practice scholars. As of this writing, the director has secured over $750,000 in grants funding and has created seven community-based occupational therapy positions.

THE PROCESS OF COLLABORATION

The motivation to integrate these two courses with the practice scholar program arose from several sources. First and foremost was a genuine desire to develop professionals who were prepared to forge their own paths in a community health care context that is dynamic and challenging. As educators, we have a sincere commitment to prepare Duquesne graduates not only to be competitive in these community job markets, but to be the best trained and clearly superior candidates for these positions. The faculty at Duquesne University had only recently established a Practice Scholar Program with the goal of building community-based practice in our region and developing community partnerships that supported the service, educational, and research mission of our department. The integration of these two courses with the Practice Scholar Program allowed us to revision our major learning assignments in these courses to allow for real world application in a community context. Retooling the courses also created an effective synergy with the efforts of the director of the Practice Scholar Program. The students acted as ambassadors from the occupational therapy department and laid the foundation for future community-university partnerships.

Finally, we were motivated to create learning opportunities that could serve as transitional events between the classroom environment and the practice context. Past experience had alerted us to the fact that most students experienced considerable anxiety during this condensed five-week schedule. In addition to coursework, the students were preparing for a significant role transition from student to fieldwork intern. Many students gave voice to their wavering sense of self-efficacy by verbalizing that they "weren't ready" or that they "wouldn't remember anything" once they were in their intern role. The integration of these two courses represented an educational strategy that could address the role transition from a volunteer in a service-learning project to a professional capable of creating his or her own opportunities for community employment. We wanted the students to experience a professional role that required the integration and application of their classroom learning and preparation.

The course assignments provided a means to support student learning by concretely connecting the learning objectives in the two courses. Thus, we collaborated to create learning events that were designed in such a way that discovery in one class supported synthesis and application in the other. The ongoing development of this strategy has been a dynamic process (see Figure 1). The development of and critical reflection on our educational strategies is informed by feedback and outcome data from the students and the community agencies we have partnered with.

FIGURE 1. The Dynamic Process of Refining the Educational Strategy

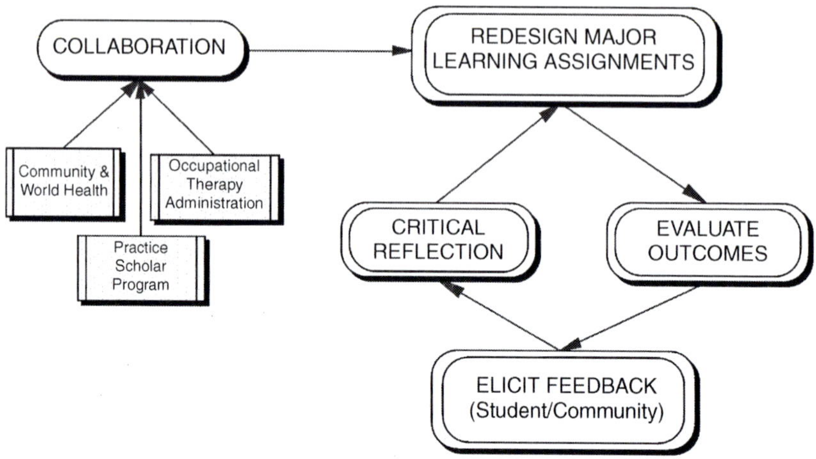

Year One

In the fall of 1999 we integrated the major learning assignments in these two courses. The Practice Scholar Program Director identified two communities (Hill District and East Liberty) that were geographically close to the University, but which had very different economic and social structures, and where she had already begun to develop community connections. The integration of the learning across courses was supported by assigning the students to the same working teams in each of the courses.

In Community and World Health the major learning assignment was a life-span focused, holistic, community assessment. Students were trained and charged with developing an in-depth understanding of the two separate communities by gathering data on key components of the communities including economic development, education, safety, communication, transportation, housing, politics/government, recreation, and health, social and faith-based services. In the Occupational Therapy Administration course, the primary assignment was the development of a Program Development Project. The project the students created included general purpose and mission statements, a SWOT analysis and needs assessment, and a program description that specified the budget, organizational structure, implementation plan, position descriptions, performance standards, marketing plan, and program evaluation methods.

The courses were designed so that the Community Assessment and population-based analyses of health problems completed in one course generated program recommendations that became the basis for Program Development Project proposals in the other course. In this first year, student groups focused their community assessment of health, social, and faith-based services on one of six segments of the community's population (e.g., Infancy and Early Childhood, Middle and Late Childhood, Adolescence, Early Adulthood, Middle Adulthood, and Late Adulthood). Students then proposed an occupational therapy program designed to address the needs of this segment of the population in their assigned community.

The outcomes from both courses included comprehensive assessments of both the Hill District and East Liberty communities in Pittsburgh and 12 occupational therapy program proposals. Since each student team had been assigned a different age group, the communities were presented with proposals that addressed a health need in every segment of the population from birth to old age. The results of the community assessment were delivered to a panel of community representatives in a culminating session held in each community during the students' fifth week of class. Community representatives were presented with a hard copy report of the entire community assessment.

Overall, the evaluative feedback we received from both the students and the community representatives was mixed. The feedback we received from the community representatives was overwhelmingly positive. These representatives appreciated the comprehensiveness and the overall quality of the community assessments. The librarian at the Hill District Library requested a copy of the final community assessment report for their library, stating that people often come into the library asking for this type of information about the community and nothing like the students' assessment existed. The director of the Uptown Community Action Group, a community that borders the Hill District, asked that their community be included in the next set of community assessments. Finally, one Reverend who leads a community group called Clergy and Churches United was pleased that the students' report clearly described what services were currently available and what needs exist. He also shared that he felt the students' assessment had hit upon the heart of one of the community's biggest problems–communication between agencies. On the other hand, some community representatives and agency directors noted that the students demonstrated a certain cultural naiveté and that the tone of some parts of their reports lacked sensitivity to the cultural realities of the community context.

The feedback from students was also mixed. Key findings from an anonymous feedback evaluation found that students were primarily concerned over time constraints, gaining access in the community, and the challenge of completing such a comprehensive population-based assessment. On the other hand, students overwhelmingly reported that the organization, structure, and instructor directives for the Program Development Project significantly supported their learning, and the vast majority (80%) reported that the learning event would give them an edge in future employment. Analysis of students' responses to open-ended questions suggested that students perceived the learning as "real-world," appreciated time built into class for working on assignments and receiving feedback, and felt that they learned lessons that prepared them for their transition from student to intern. However, the results also suggested that many students found building programs in a community context was a very challenging task and a third of the students questioned the relevancy of the assignments, reporting that the community-based project did not provide them the opportunity to develop the administrative skills needed in more traditional settings. Finally, two thirds of the students felt that there was little likelihood that the community agency would actually implement their ideas.

The instructors in the two courses met with the Practice Scholar to critically reflect on the course outcomes and feedback. We recognized that the students' responses might have reflected some lack of self-efficacy as well as some limitations in our educational pedagogy. Since this was a new and unique challenge, students may have been less self-assured about their program ideas and we may have been less effective in building the competencies we were asking the students to apply including how to access community resources, develop culturally responsive programming, and apply administrative principles to the funding realities of community-based programming.

Year Two

Our reflections on course outcomes in year one helped us recognize that a comprehensive community assessment was perhaps too broad, that program proposals that generally addressed the needs of a segment of the population were not focused enough, and that we needed to develop critical competencies for funding community-based programming in our students. In the fall of 2000, we modified the major learning assignments. Instead of a full community assessment, student groups each focused on a particular community agency and created a Community Agency Profile that portrayed the agency's organizational structure, community and cultural context, major programs, and program needs. Similarly, the Program Development Project was restructured to create a proposal that addressed one of these defined needs. Finally, we added an expectation for the students to support their program development ideas by searching for ways to fund these ideas, and incorporated the expectation for the students to complete a basic grant application. For this component we based the assignment around the Pennsylvania Common Grant Application, which is an application used by a consortium of private granting agencies in Southwestern Pennsylvania (http://www.cmu.edu/develop/infoserv/prop/cgaf.html).

We assigned student groups to 12 agencies in a variety of communities in the Greater Pittsburgh area. The Practice Scholar Program Director identified agencies that had expressed an interest in partnering with the university. In order to address the concern that the community agencies were often unaware of the efforts of other agencies with similar missions, we hosted a networking meeting for the executive directors of all 12 agencies at Duquesne University. Community partners from the previous year were also invited to attend as were new contacts identified by the Practice Scholar Program Director. During this meeting, students delivered poster presentations and presented the director of their assigned community agency with a report including the agency profile, program proposal, and grant application materials. The grant applications the students generated were not polished documents ready for submission. They provided the student the opportunity for hands-on development of a grant proposal and the community agency with a grant application framework and potential funding agency from which to solicit funds for the occupational therapy program proposed in the grant.

We solicited written feedback from all the agency directors, which was overwhelmingly positive. Every agency felt the program proposal met a defined need in their agency and all reported that they would consider a partnership with Duquesne University. Ten of the 12 agencies reported that they would hire an occupational therapist if funding could be secured. Some agency directors pointed out that a relative weakness in the grant proposals was the accuracy of the budget projections. Student feedback collected in anonymous post-course evaluations was mostly positive. Students reported that the projects had helped them develop a deeper understanding of the context of community practice, had increased their capacity to create their own community-based position, and had improved their understanding of grant-writing processes. On the other hand, while students reported an increased investment in their projects because it had a "real life" application, nearly two-thirds continued to question if the agency would consider moving forward on their proposal. Concerns about time and access to the community continued to be voiced. Negotiating cross-cultural issues remained a background theme in some of the feedback, particularly students addressing their own cultural awareness and managing the cultural differences between "community time" and "university time."

Critical reflections on our educational strategies resulted in modifications the following year. Specifically, we addressed the students' concerns about time by adding on-line components to the Administration course that were completed asynchronously. We also gave students the option of selecting community agencies in their own communities, added content to better prepare students for the culture shock many were experiencing as they assumed professional roles in community-based settings, and expanded efforts to build grant-writing competencies.

Year Three

One of the most significant adjustments in year three was converting one-third of the Occupational Therapy Administration course for delivery in an on-line environment to support the classroom experience and give the students more flexibility for when they visited community agencies. Student discussions of selected content were shifted to the on-line environment and monitored by the instructor. Sample programs from the past years' projects were uploaded to offer students samples to refer to at any time. Finally, quizzes were given and graded on-line eliminating the need to use class time to test content knowledge. Several students' groups opted to select a community agency in their local community. We contacted and negotiated with these agencies prior to the beginning of the semester.

As in the past year, we hosted a networking meeting for the executive directors of all the agencies at Duquesne University. Past community partners were again invited and we also invited grant reviewers from local private foundations and city government departments as well as the university president, provost, and other key administrative staff. The feedback we received from community agencies was again overwhelmingly positive. Overall, agencies were pleased that the proposals were custom-designed for clients in their agency. Every agency responded that they wanted to maintain and build upon the relationship they were developing with the Duquesne University Occupational Therapy Department. Student feedback was mostly positive. Students continued to report feeling time pressures, but also reported that they liked the flexibility afforded them in the on-line environment and felt that it offered them more time to work around community agency schedules. Overall, students were very positive about the integration of the assignments across the courses and reported that addressing real needs motivated them. One student group was asked and accepted an invitation to present their proposal for a project addressing the needs of parents with disabilities to the executive board of the agency. Another agency reported that the students' proposal for individualized respite services for families of children with disabilities was being used as the basis of a proposal being presented to the Vicariate overseeing services throughout the diocese in North Central West Virginia.

In our own reflections we felt the addition of the on-line environment had been a success in that students seemed to be engaging in richer and deeper discussions of issues relative to administration and community practice. These on-line discussions seemed to support classroom discussion as students were noted to reference materials that they had read or discussed on-line into round table discussions held in the classroom. We also noticed that the student groups that presented the most polished products emphasized the process of collaboration with their community agency contacts as much as the products they were assigned to deliver. We decided to stress the importance of the collaborative process by providing strategies for and examples of effective collaborative relationships. Finally, we realized that providing the students the opportunity to select their own community sites resulted in an extremely diverse group of community settings, which offered variety but challenged the students and the instructors to understand the needs of widely differing populations. Further, some agencies that the director of the Practice Scholar program had negotiated with were not assigned student interns when students selected an agency in their own community, and these agencies expressed disappointment at not being selected.

Year Four

In 2002 we narrowed our focus to community agencies serving one of three specific populations: homeless men and women, people who were incarcerated and/or ex-inmates, and at-risk children and youth. These populations were selected because the Practice Scholar Program Director had been most successful in creating community partnerships with agencies providing services to these populations.

The assignments were fine tuned, but the essential structure of each remained the same. The grant application was modified to encourage students not only to consider securing funds that covered services, but also propose research projects studying the efficacy of community-based interventions. Students were also expected to identify both private foundation and governmental funding sources. Experiential and computer lab exercises were enhanced to support the development of competencies related to grantsmanship, community-university collaboration, and the integration of health promotion and Healthy People 2010 objectives into program proposals.

Our capstone event was again a networking meeting and poster presentation and the feedback we received from community agencies was again overwhelmingly positive. Agencies evaluated the proposals as highly relevant and professionally done and two agencies reported that the students' work was being integrated into background information for grant proposals they planned to submit. Agency partners and students alike responded positively to the focus on a limited number of populations. The staff from community agencies reported that they enjoyed hearing about the programs designed for their agency as well as for other agencies that served the same or similar populations.

Students reported that the more constricted focus allowed them to share resources and information with students from other groups working with the same population. The issue of time resurfaced again, though many students reported satisfaction that their concentrated focus for the five-week period resulted in a product that the community agency valued. The vast majority of the students (92%) reported that being in the community agency helped them understand the challenges and rewards inherent in creating their own job in community practice, that they felt more prepared to create their own employment opportunities in the community, and that the skills they had developed for exploring community health agencies would support them even if they didn't take a position in community-based practice. Just over half (57%) of the students reported that the issue of building a collaborative working relationship with staff in these community agencies proved to be a significant cross-cultural challenge. The major learning activities, key outcomes, feedback, and adjustments based on the author's critical reflection on educational pedagogy over the past four years are highlighted in Table 1.

FUTURE PLANS

Critical reflection upon the outcomes of the past four years has allowed us to identify key aspects for furthering our redesign efforts. These include addressing time constraints, enhancing efforts to prepare students to design culturally responsive programming, a continued focus on selected client populations, and an increased focus on integrating our curriculum's focus on the scholarship of practice.

The ongoing issue of time constraints will be addressed by shifting the sequence of the curriculum to place these two courses in a nine-week semester. This longer semester will enhance students' opportunities to build relationships with community agency staff and their clientele. The additional four weeks will allow us to introduce both content and learning experiences that will enhance students' understanding of community-based practice. These community internships have often generated cross-cultural challenges that the students have needed to work through. In the past, we have included content intended to engage students in developing cultural knowledge relevant to the populations they would be working with and experiential exercises to help them reflect on their own cultural awareness. Our future plans include upgrading our efforts to overtly portray these community internships as one step in

TABLE 1. Key Adjustments in the Educational Strategy

Activities 1999	Outcomes	Feedback	Reflections
• Life-span Community Assessment • Life-span program development project	• 2 Comprehensive community assessments • 12 Life span focused program proposals • 2 Presentations of assessments	Community Representatives • Cultural naiveté of students • Comprehensiveness of assessments in time frame • Agencies often unaware of other community resources Students • Time constraints • Difficulty addressing needs of segment of population	• Focus on cultural sensitivity • Present results in community forum • Focus on life span too broad • Address needs in a single agency • Formalize methods to measure outcomes
2000	**Outcomes**	**Feedback**	**Reflections**
• Community Agency Profile • Agency Program Dev. Projects • PA Common Grant Application	• 12 Community agency profiles • 12 Program proposals • 12 Grant applications to support program implementation • 1 Networking meeting of agencies	Community Agencies • Programs met need (100%) • Would consider partnership with Duquesne (77%) • Questioned the accuracy of the budget projections (58%) Students • Questioned if agencies would use program (64%) • Increased investment due to real-life application	• Support occupation-based programming • Structure more time in community • Incorporate on-line course components • Allow students to choose agency • Invite broad array of stakeholders to presentations
2001	**Outcomes**	**Feedback**	**Reflections**
• Agency Profiles • Agency Program Dev. Projects • PA Grant • On-line Components	• 9 Agency profiles • 9 Proposals • 9 Grant applications • 1 presentation to agency directors • 1 Networking meeting of agencies, foundation staff, and university administration	Community Agencies • Want intern assigned (100%) • Would consider collaboration on grant writing (87%) • Liked networking with other agencies, funders, & university Students • On-line component helpful • Liked addressing "real" needs • Provide more time, experience in grantsmanship	• Too much diversity in types of agencies • Choose agencies around specific foci • Emphasize the process and products of partnership • Use past products to provide examples • Strengthen grant-writing components
2002	**Outcomes**	**Feedback**	**Reflections**
• PS Agency Profiles • PS Program Dev. Projects • Revised Grant • On-line & grant exercises	• 7 agency profiles • 7 program proposals • 7 grant applications • 1 Capstone poster presentation • 1 Networking meeting of agencies, foundation staff, and university administration	Community Agencies • Students' work integrated into agencies' grant proposals (2) • High interest in all programs • Liked networking with other agencies, funders, & university Students • Feel prepared to develop job in the community (93%) • Assignments provided a significant cross-cultural challenge (93%)	• Continue to focus on PS populations • Enhance the lab & computer exercises • Offer in 9 week term • Use peer review of past projects as learning tool • Support development of creative occupation-based programs

the student's lifelong journey of becoming a more culturally responsive practitioner. Our efforts in this area will be guided by the application of a model of culturally responsive care being developed by the first author, which posits that culturally responsive caring requires a grounding in cultural knowledge, the development of skills for engaging culturally different clients, and a commitment to ongoing development as a multicultural person (Muñoz, 2002).

The other aspects of our redesign efforts involve strengthening the integration of the practice scholar program. The first strategy for achieving this is to continue to focus the students' program creation efforts on populations and community sites within our Practice Scholar Program. Currently, these include homeless, incarcerated, and at-risk youth populations. Additionally, rather than search for new partners each time these courses are delivered, we intend to return to some of our most promising partnerships and assign new interns who can develop a different program proposal or focus on a different segment of the agency's clientele. In this way we hope to deepen the relationships with these partners and increase the potential for community-university collaboration on funding proposals that ultimately lead to new community-based occupational therapy positions.

Our second set of strategies will be focused on helping the students develop their own identity as practice scholars. We intend to place a stronger emphasis on teaching how to integrate outcomes research into the proposals. This will include having the students research the evidence that supports community-based interventions. We also intend to redouble our efforts to teach the students to see the necessity of designing outcome measures that are based upon the proposed mission and objectives of their proposed program. We will create exercises where students critique past proposals, which we hope will enhance the quality and depth of the programs, and grant applications that they ultimately create.

Our final set of strategies will emphasize using the existing practice scholars as role models to demonstrate how an active research component is integrated into their day-to-day practice. Each of the current community-based Duquesne Practice Scholars is involved in outcomes research in partnership with university-based faculty. Students will increase the amount of time they spend in our current practice scholar sites, and practice scholars will provide examples of their own research projects and hold roundtable discussions focused on developing and maintaining the role of a practitioner scholar.

FINAL THOUGHTS AND RECOMMENDATIONS

This paper has provided a description of collaborative educational innovations that have been refined over a four-year span. These innovations were designed to prepare graduates to understand occupation-based service delivery in community settings, to develop community-built programs that are responsive to community needs, and to understand how to both secure funding for and market occupational therapy services in the community. We presented both the process as well as the products of our collaboration in the hopes that other occupational therapy programs might benefit from our successes and our missteps. Our recommendations to other programs are provided below.

- Actively maintain open communication among all members: instructors, students, community agency representatives, and faculty in other courses.
- Create clear mechanisms for collecting outcome data from all who are involved in the process.
- Maintain a regular cycle of critical reflection to use personal experiences and feedback to modify educational strategies.
- Focus on developing depth rather than breadth in the relationships you develop between the university and community partners.
- Integrate content, opportunities for skill development, and experiential and reflective exercises to support students' capacities to provide culturally responsive caring.
- Engage the faculty of your department and build on interests, strengths, and community relationships that already exist.

REFERENCES

Accreditation Council for Occupational Therapy Education. (1998*). Standards for an accredited educational program for the occupational therapist.* Bethesda, MD: American Occupational Therapy Association.

Baum, C. & Law, M. (1997). Nationally speaking–community health: A responsibility, an opportunity, and a fit for occupational therapy. *American Journal of Occupational Therapy, 52*, 1, 7-10.

Cermack, S. A. (1976). Community-based learning in occupational therapy. *American Journal of Occupational Therapy, 30*, 3, 157-161.

Cromwell, F. & Kielhofner, G. (1976). An educational strategy for occupational therapy community service. *American Journal of Occupational Therapy, 30*, 629-633.

Donohue, M. V. (2001). Group co-leadership by occupational therapy students in community centers: Learning transitional roles. *Occupational Therapy in Health Care, 15*, 1-2, 85-98.

Dunbar, S. B., Simhoni, O., & Anderson, L. T. (2002). Classification of fieldwork experiences for the new millennium. *Occupational Therapy in Health Care, 16*, 1, 81-87.

Fidler, G. S. (2000). Beyond the therapy model: Building our future. *American Journal of Occupational Therapy, 54*, 1, 99-101.

Fidler, G. S. (2001). Community practice: It's more than geography. *Occupational Therapy in Health Care, 13,* 3-4, 7-9.

Frank, G., Fishman, M., Crowley, C., Blair, B., Murphy, S. T., Montoya, J. A., Hickey, M. P., Brancaccio, M. V., & Bensimon, E. M. (2001). The New Stories/New Cultures after-school enrichment program: A direct cultural intervention. *American Journal of Occupational Therapy, 55,* 501-508.

Friedland, J., Polatajko, H., & Gage, M. (2001). Expanding the boundaries of occupational therapy practice through student fieldwork experiences: Description of a provincially-funded community development project. *Canadian Journal of Occupational Therapy, 68,* 5, 301-309.

Grossman, J. (1974). Community experience for students. *American Journal of Occupational Therapy, 28,* 589-591.

Heubner, J. & Tryssenaar, J. (1996). Development of an occupational therapy practice perspective in a homeless shelter: A fieldwork experience. *Canadian Journal of Occupational Therapy, 63,* 24-32.

Loukas, K. M. (2000, July 3). Emerging models of innovative community-based occupational practice: The vision continues. *OT Practice,* 9-11.

Mason, L. (1998). Fieldwork education: Collaborative group learning in community settings. *Australian Occupational Therapy Journal, 45,* 4, 124-130.

McColl, M. A. (1998). What do we need to know to practice occupational therapy in the community. *American Journal of Occupational Therapy, 52,* 1, 11-18.

Menks, F., Sittler, S., Weaver, D., & Yanow, B. (1977). A psychogeriatric activity group in a rural community. *American Journal of Occupational Therapy, 31,* 6, 376-384.

Miller, P. A., Hedden, J. L., Argento, L., Vaccaro, M., Murad, V., & Dionne, W. (2001). A team approach to health promotion of community elders: The microwave project. *Occupational Therapy in Health Care, 14,* 17-34.

Muñoz, J. (2002). *Culturally responsive caring in occupational therapy: A grounded theory.* Unpublished doctoral dissertation, University of Pittsburgh, Pittsburgh.

Pennsylvania Common Grant Application. Retrieved January 27, 2003 from http://www.cmu.edu/develop/infoserv/prop/cgaf.html

Perrin, K. & Wittman, P. (2001). Educating for community-based occupational therapy practice: A demonstration project. *Occupational Therapy in Health Care, 13,* 3-4, 11-21.

Rydeen, K., Kautzmann, L., Cowan, M. K., & Benzing, P. (1995). Three faculty facilitated, community-based level 1 fieldwork programs. *American Journal of Occupational Therapy, 49,* 112-118.

Scaffa, M. (2001). *Occupational therapy in community-based practice settings.* Philadelphia, PA: F. A. Davis.

Schaber, P. L. (2001). Qualitative evaluation of a management course project: Creating new job possibilities for occupational therapy. *Occupational Therapy in Health Care, 13,* 1-2, 177-192.

Scott, A. H. (1999). Wellness works: Community service health promotion groups led by occupational therapy students. *American Journal of Occupational Therapy, 53,* 566-572.

Shordike, A. & Howell, D. (2001). The reindeer of hope: An occupational therapy program in a homeless shelter. *Occupational Therapy in Health Care, 15,* 57-68.

Totten, C. & Pratt, J. (2001). Innovation in fieldwork education: Working with members of the homeless population in Glasgow. *British Journal of Occupational Therapy, 64,* 11, 559-563.

Walens, D., Helfrich, C. A., Aviles, A., & Horita, L. (2001). Assessing needs and developing interventions with new populations: A community process of collaboration. *Occupational Therapy in Mental Health, 16,* 3-4, 71-95.

Wittman, P., Conner-Kerr, T., Templeton, M. S., & Velde, B. (1999). The Tillery project: An experience in an interdisciplinary, rural health care service setting. *Physical & Occupational Therapy in Geriatrics, 17,* 17-28.

The Aware Communicator:
Dialogues on Diversity

Jan Froehlich, MS, OTR/L
Susan G. Nesbit, MS, OTR

SUMMARY. Developing cultural competence has taken on increased importance in occupational therapy curriculums. Cultural competency prepares occupational therapy students for emerging practice. This article describes a communication seminar that emphasizes dialogues on diversity as a method for developing cultural awareness, cultural sensitivity, and active listening skills. *[Article copies available for a fee from The Haworth Document Delivery Service: 1-800-HAWORTH. E-mail address: <docdelivery@haworthpress.com> Website: <http://www.HaworthPress.com> © 2004 by The Haworth Press, Inc. All rights reserved.]*

KEYWORDS. Cultural competence, diversity, communication

Occupational therapists interact with clients and colleagues from diverse backgrounds, and relating to persons from unfamiliar cultures can be chal-

Jan Froehlich is Associate Professor, Department of Occupational Therapy, University of New England, 11 Hills Beach Road, Biddeford, ME 04005 (E-mail: *jfroehlich@une.edu*). Susan G. Nesbit is Assistant Professor, Department of Occupational Therapy, University of New England, Biddeford, ME (E-mail: *snesbit@une.edu*).

The authors would like to acknowledge Judith Kimball, PhD, OTR/L, FAOTA, and Louise Dunn, MS, OTR/L, for contributing to the development of this course.

[Haworth co-indexing entry note]: "The Aware Communicator: Dialogues on Diversity." Froehlich, Jan, and Susan G. Nesbit. Co-published simultaneously in *Occupational Therapy in Health Care* (The Haworth Press, Inc.) Vol. 18, No. 1/2, 2004, pp. 171-184; and: *Best Practices in Occupational Therapy Education* (ed: Patricia A. Crist, and Marjorie E. Scaffa) The Haworth Press, Inc., 2004, pp. 171-184. Single or multiple copies of this article are available for a fee from The Haworth Document Delivery Service [1-800-HAWORTH, 9:00 a.m. - 5:00 p.m. (EST). E-mail address: docdelivery@haworthpress.com].

http://www.haworthpress.com/web/OTHC
Digital Object Identifier:10.1300/J003v18n01_16

lenging (Wells & Black, 2000; Schwartzberg, 2002; Townsend, 1997). Individuals from many ethnicities and races live in the United States, Canada, and Australia. In nearly every country of the world, occupational therapists must communicate effectively with clients and colleagues of different ages, sexual orientation, gender, disability status, religion, life circumstance, culture, and class background. Although individuals are more alike than different, the structure of our societies and the processes of socialization currently emphasize the differences (Rothenberg, 1998). Moreover, because complex identities evolve from these differences, understanding others can be difficult (Kreps & Kunimoto, 1994). Communication skills that are culturally sensitive enable the occupational therapy process (Schwartzberg); therefore, the development of culturally competent practitioners is an important solution to the communication difficulties that can occur in today's multicultural health care arena. Occupational therapy curricula can prepare students for emerging practice by promoting cultural competency.

The purpose of this paper is to describe a communication seminar at the University of New England that promotes cultural competency through dialogues on diversity. The dialogues on diversity, called listening partnerships, are structured conversations between two or more students about age, sexual orientation, gender, disability status, religion, life circumstance, culture, and class background. One student speaks for several minutes while the others listen. While learning to be active listeners, students ask questions and provide comments to encourage each speaker to continue with his or her story. Through these dialogues on diversity students begin the lifelong process of becoming culturally competent.

Culturally competent individuals communicate effectively with persons of any culture, and they are able to bridge differences (as cited in Wells & Black, 2000). Furthermore, culturally competent practitioners are responsive to the needs of individuals from populations that are not from the dominant cultures (Wells & Black). The communication seminar is consistent with an educational model of cultural competency developed by Wells and Black. Their model identifies three areas for learning: (a) self-exploration and awareness, (b) knowledge gathering, and (c) skills development. The goal of self-exploration and awareness is to increase students' awareness of their own cultural heritage while learning about diversity in others. This goal is achieved in the communication seminar by having students explore their experiences related to gender, race, class, age, sexual orientation, disability, religion, life circumstance, and culture through listening partnerships, class discussions, and journals. The goal of knowledge gathering is to provide students with specific information about diversity and the effects of discrimination and oppression. This goal is achieved in the communication seminar by sharing knowledge and experiences of diverse cultures through mini-lectures, article presentations, class readings, and class discussions. The goal of skills development is for students to master the ability to interact and communicate in sensitive, appropriate, and relevant ways to clients from different cultures. This goal is achieved in the communication seminar through listening partnerships focusing on diversity and practical exams.

To ensure a successful experience for the students, the communication seminar uses a learning format that includes: (a) why–course objectives, (b) who–the instructors and students, (c) what–the content and structure, (d) when–time parameters, (e) where–the learning environment, and (f) how–evaluating student learning.

WHY–COURSE OBJECTIVES

The overall goal of the communication seminar is to develop aware, sensitive, and skillful occupational therapy communicators, and this goal primarily is accomplished by providing multiple opportunities for students to actively engage in informative dialogues about diversity. This course is designed so the communication seminar students will:

1. Develop the skill of building trust in pairs and groups.
2. Use leadership skills to teach an icebreaker, present an article, and lead discussions related to diversity.
3. Demonstrate active listening skills with attention to verbal and nonverbal communication to help others express thoughts and feelings when sharing life stories related to gender, race, class, culture, age, and ability-disability status.
4. Increase knowledge, awareness, and appreciation of diversity in self and others.
5. Demonstrate sensitivity to gender, race, class, culture, age, and ability-disability status.
6. Understand group process as an important factor in communication and identify the process with the group.
7. Practice strategies for assertiveness and conflict resolution.

WHO–THE STUDENTS AND THE INSTRUCTORS

Ideally, this course is suited for six to 10 learners and one instructor. Although this course can be taught to groups of more than 10 students, the students might receive less individualized attention, possibly leading to slower progress. At the University of New England, one instructor typically teaches a group of eight students. Diversity training (e.g., Brown, 1992) is a prerequisite to teaching this course, and instructors at the University of New England also have a background in communication and group-process skills, including leadership training, and possess basic counseling skills.

WHAT-THE CONTENT AND STRUCTURE

The communication seminar at the University of New England meets once weekly for two hours. Class meetings include: (a) an opening circle–five to 10 minutes, (b) an icebreaker–10 to 15 minutes, (c) article presentations–15 to 30 minutes, (d) review of knowledge related to diversity and effective communication–10 to 20 minutes, (e) dialogues on diversity–30 to 50 minutes, (f) discussion of listening partnerships and groups–optional five to 10 minutes, (g) arranging listening partnerships for the upcoming week–five minutes, and (h) closing circle–five to 10 minutes. The total class time is one hour, 50 minutes, with a 10-minute break. The time frames for each component of class are approximate.

Opening circle. The group is opened with a check-in for the purpose of leaving course-irrelevant thoughts at the door. Students and instructors share new and good events in their lives, and the sharing of challenges also is encouraged. Students have a few moments to focus on positive events, places, ideas, or things and to vent about difficulties. Students report that the check-in process is an invaluable part of the class because it: (a) creates safety for dialoguing, (b) enables students to focus their attention off everyday stressors, e.g., roommate difficulties or car repairs, so they can focus on the class topics, and (c) facilitates group cohesion by giving students the opportunity to learn something new about the other group members. Because the communication seminar is offered first semester in the professional curriculum, for the first few weeks, students share their first and last names before sharing their good news and their challenges, helping to facilitate name recall.

Icebreakers. Icebreakers are short activities or games used to facilitate group members to learn more about each other and to become more comfortable with one another. Students are asked to orient the icebreakers toward cultural diversity. For example, to increase awareness of the experience of gay, lesbian, and bisexual individuals, students have led a guided visualization of attending a dance as a gay, lesbian, or bisexual individual if he or she is heterosexual, or as a heterosexual if he or she is a gay, lesbian, or bisexual individual. In another example, to increase awareness of disability, students have had their classmates assume various disabilities while playing a game.

Icebreakers can be led by students or by instructors; they can be led individually or in pairs. Students individually lead most of the icebreakers done in the communication seminar at the University of New England, giving the students the opportunity to develop leadership skills. To lead the icebreakers, students learn to use resources that provide examples of icebreakers (e.g., Foster-Harrison, 1994).

Article presentations. As the semester progresses, students take turns presenting their interpretations and summaries of articles related to diversity and health and wellness. Most of these articles come from occupational therapy literature. Students develop several questions and lead the group in a discussion. Occasionally, the instructor leads the article presentation and discussion. Knowledge about many contextual and cultural issues is disseminated through these presentations. Contextual and cultural issues include: (a) gender (e.g., Baker & McKay, 2001; Froehlich et al., 1992; Parish et al., 1990), (b) race (e.g., Black, 2002; Cena et al., 2002; Matlala, 1993; Evans, 1992a; McIntosh, 1989), (c) class (e.g., Humphry, 1995; Jongbloed, 1998), (d) religion (e.g., Farrar, 2001; Gibbs & Barnitt, 1999; Low, 1997), (e) culture (e.g., MacDonald, 1998; Evans, 1992b), (f) disability (e.g., Benham, 1988; Eberhardt & Mayberry, 1995; Elliott et al., 1992; Froehlich, 1992; White & Olson, 1998), (g) sexual orientation (e.g.,Williamson, 2000; Kelly, 2000; Jackson, 1995), and (h) age (Letvak, 2002). Through participation in the article presentations, students become more adept leaders by improving their speaking and group-facilitation skills.

Review of knowledge related to diversity and effective communication. Each week, a different aspect of context, e.g., gender or race, is discussed. Before the weekly in-class dialogue begins, the instructor explains and reviews theories related to effective communication and listening (Davis, 1998; Jackins, 1981), relating these communication skills to cultural competence. For example, the importance of taking turns to listen is emphasized as a method for understanding differences and reducing prejudice (Brown & Mazza, 1991). In another example, the concept that listening does not necessarily mean agreement, but can be used to build bridges is shared (Brown & Mazza). Finally, common communication errors such as saying "Merry Christmas" to a group that might include Jews and Muslims or neglecting to use people-first language in reference to a person with a disability (Davis) are reviewed.

Dialogues on diversity. Because dialogues on diversity can be very sensitive, establishing ground rules is important. Ground rules ensure that the process runs smoothly and an atmosphere of respect for diversity is achieved. Ground rules–the social norms or ways of behaving within a partnership or group–can be established on the first day of class. An additional purpose of ground rules is to take unacceptable behaviors away from the personal. For example, if a student exhibits an undesirable behavior (e.g., arriving late to class, interrupting speaker, dominating the class discussion, and participating in side conversations), discussion about this behavior focuses on the related ground rule rather than directly on the person breaking the ground rule. Typically, each group develops its own set of ground rules. Ground rules are dynamic and can be discussed and revised as needed. (See Appendix B for examples of helpful ground rules.)

Once ground rules are established, the instructor provides guided reflections through the dialogue questions. Students practice their listening skills as they dialogue on diversity. They build on the skills learned in previous weeks and continue to answer dialogue questions in their weekly listening partnerships outside of class.

For the first week of the semester, students are asked to use only nonverbal communication, with the awareness that body language can be ambiguous (Zeuschner, 2003), e.g., crossing arms over the chest and how closely you sit to the speaker can have different meanings within and between different cultures. Not making assumptions about nonverbal behavior is emphasized.

Through the forced use of only body language, students learn to use silence to allow for the speaker's reflection. After practicing the effective use of silence, students learn to add open-ended and close-ended questions for clarification. They also learn the importance of paying attention to details so they can summarize the speaker's story. Besides these helpful verbal and nonverbal behaviors, a warm, friendly, and relaxed attitude helps the speaker to stay focused.

Another key ingredient to the success of listening partnerships is equal time for each student to speak. Students set the time limit before the first speaker begins. The listener keeps track of the time and notifies the speaker when his or her time is up. Then the roles are switched. This concept of shared equal time for speaking and listening stems from the basic theory and practice of re-evaluation counseling (Jackins, 1994). Aguilar (1995) described re-evaluation counseling as a culturally competent model because the organization emphasizes the peer nature of helping relationships and the elimination of all forms of oppression. The concept of shared equal time insures that everyone has an equal opportunity to express opinions.

This in-class sharing can occur in pairs, small groups of three or four students, or the entire group. Each student has roughly the same amount of time (two to five minutes) to share, without interruption, his or her thoughts, feelings, and experiences about the weekly class topic (e.g., life stories, gender, race, class, culture, religion, sexual orientation, age, or ability-disability status) while being listened to with respect.

Dialogue questions (see Appendix A) guide each speaker to share identity aspects that are proudly possessed and identity aspects that are challenging.

Students use active listening skills, e.g., clarification (Davis, 1998), to facilitate the speaker's flow of thinking related to the questions. Depending on the available time frame, students choose one or two questions to answer for the contextual or cultural topic being discussed.

Each week outside of class, students practice listening skills in pairs, with each student speaking for 10 minutes. At the University of New England, students change partners weekly, until midterm when they select a partner for the remainder of the semester. This regular pairing enables the students to develop an ongoing relationship for in-depth dialogue.

Discussion of listening partnerships and groups. Each week, a few moments of class time can be spent reviewing how the listening partnerships and groups are progressing, so questions, concerns, and reactions can be addressed.

Arranging listening partnerships for the upcoming week. Students arrange their listening partnership sessions as a reminder that they have important work to do before the next class meeting.

Closing circle. At the end of each class, students do a checkout by sharing one or two highlights from that day's class. Highlights for each student to consider sharing are: (a) an exciting concept from class, (b) a confusing concept from class, (c) a reaction to something heard for the first time, or (d) a reaction to a highlight that he or she is eager to learn about in more depth.

WHEN–TIME PARAMETERS

A communication seminar placed at the beginning of the professional curriculum allows students to acquire and further develop listening skills that can be used in relationships with clients, classmates, professors, and fieldwork coordinators of diverse backgrounds. Additionally, students frequently form support networks with classmates that they otherwise would not have gotten to know, and they report that they use these support networks throughout the curriculum.

The communication seminar requires a weekly two-hour block of time for 13 to 15 weeks, morning, afternoon, or evening. Students tend to be energized by participating, so even end-of-the-day hours are manageable.

WHERE–THE LEARNING ENVIRONMENT

This seminar can meet in a small classroom or conference room. Chairs can be arranged in a circle or around a conference table; however, a table or desks might be physical barriers to communication. Students can arrange private spaces for the listening partnerships outside of class.

HOW–EVALUATING STUDENT LEARNING: THE PROCESS

In addition to attendance and class participation, students are evaluated through: (a) leadership of icebreakers, (b) article presentations, (c) biweekly journals, (d) midterm and final practical exams on active listening, and (e) a learning summary at the conclusion of the semester.

Leadership of icebreakers is evaluated through the ability to be inclusive of all members of the group during the icebreaker itself and to facilitate a discussion at the conclusion of the icebreaker. Article presentations on diversity are evaluated for comprehension and awareness, clarity of presentation, ability to discuss the article in the students' own words, and ability to facilitate a group discussion. The journals are evaluated for written-communication skills and expansion of the cultural-diversity and communication themes addressed in class, the readings, and the listening partnerships. Students reveal both emotional discomfort and genuine excitement about the content and process of the dialogues on diversity. Students can use their journals to express thoughts and feelings and ask questions that they were not comfortable expressing in class, with the understanding that journal content remains confidential. Students do not name their listening partner in the journal and the instructor does not share journal content with the class. The students who use the journals in this manner, i.e., the students who analyze the listening partnerships with depth in exploration and attention to detail, make the most gains in awareness and appreciation of diversity in self and others. Students report that the icebreakers, article presentations, and journal writing promote self-confidence and further development of speaking skills. Many students are surprised by the content of the article presentations that highlight health disparities, discrimination, and inequities in occupational therapy.

For the practical exams, students randomly are assigned partners. At the time of the exam, they decide who will speak first and who will listen first. The first speaker randomly selects three questions and narrows that selection down to one choice. Examples of questions are: (a) describe some high and low points in your life, (b) describe accomplishments that make you proud, (c) discuss discrimination you personally experienced or witnessed and your reaction, (d) describe stressors that you currently are facing, (e) clarify your values as related to your cultural heritage and describe how you developed these values, (f) describe your support system, (g) describe your assertiveness style, and (h) discuss current sociopolitical issues that touch you. When the first speaker has finished and the listener has been given feedback regarding his or her active-listening skills, the students change roles and the second speaker selects three questions before narrowing the selection down to one choice. The students exchange seven to 10 minutes of speaking and listening each way.

In the practical exams, the listener is the student being observed and graded for active listening. He or she is evaluated on the use of helpful nonverbal communication, including: (a) allowing for silence when appropriate and (b) adequate use of body language, facial gestures, and vocal tones that indicate interest. He or she also is evaluated on the use of helpful verbal communication, including: (a) the ability to appropriately use open-ended and close-ended questions, (b) not interrupting or changing the subject, (c) the ability to use clarification, restatement, reflection, empathy, humor, and encouragement as needed, and (d) the ability to summarize the key issues and emotions. The listener also is evaluated for the ability to suspend judgment, create rapport, and arrange the environment to make it conducive for speaking. The environment includes arrangement of the furniture, clothes and jewelry worn by the listener, and actions done by the listener.

Before the instructor provides feedback, the speaker reflects on what went well and what could have been done better, followed by the speaker providing feedback to the listener. The speaker is encouraged to take a risk and disagree if appropriate.

Although the students report that they feel a great deal of anxiety around the practical exams, they are very excited by the gains they make as listeners. Many students felt they were good listeners until they received feedback during the practical exams. Using the feedback from the midterm practical exam, students make significant gains in their communication skills, as observed in their performance during the final practical exam. Students progress in several areas of performance, including: (a) allowing for silence, (b) not interrupting, (c) not changing the subject, especially when someone is emotional, (d) not giving false assurance, (e) giving advice without being asked, (f) not inappropriately sharing their own life story, (g) not asking curiosity questions, and (h) not mentally preparing irrelevant things to say next. Students also become more at ease when interviewing and they learn to ask helpful questions. Moreover, students become more aware of diversity and more capable of listening to people from diverse backgrounds.

The learning summary at the conclusion of the semester is evaluated for written-communication skills, growth in cultural awareness, and ability to self-analyze strengths and weaknesses in verbal and nonverbal communication skills, including active listening and presenting to a group. Students comment on the socialization process. For example, they report significant gains and awareness related to diversity when members of oppressed groups, e.g., homosexuals, blacks, Asians, Jews, immigrants, working-class persons, and persons with disabilities, speak about their experiences. In turn, students from oppressed groups feel relieved by speaking out in a safe environment. Students also report that the dialogue on gender is informative and can be cathartic. Prejudices between different groups are reduced as students share their stories. Students also comment on how the semester-long process socializes them to be effective listeners in their professional and personal lives. Professionally, students report that the listening skills they have gained are invaluable during level-one fieldwork. Personally, students report that as they become better listeners, they begin to notice that many of their friends and family members exhibit poor listening skills. Some students attempt to teach their friends and family the science and art of listening. Other students are excited by the questions for the dialoguing on diversity, so they pose these questions to friends and family members, and they listen to the answers and continue to make gains in cultural awareness. Although the gains outside of class continue, many students report disappointment that the class has ended, because the dialogues in class have been rich.

CONCLUSIONS

Ultimately, client care is greatly enhanced when occupational therapists communicate effectively with diverse clients and colleagues. For more than 10 years, faculty at the University of New England have received extremely positive feedback from our students about the communication seminar. Students grow as listeners and as speakers. Moreover, by examining their own experiences and listening to the experiences of their peers related to gender, race, class, age, disability, sexual orientation, and life circumstance, students increase their awareness and appreciation of diversity in themselves and others. They learn to bridge differences through listening. Students also gain cultural sensitivity. As Wells and Black (2000) state, cultural competence is an evolving process. Our students leave this class eager for more knowledge of diverse peoples and opportunities to offer culturally competent occupational therapy services.

REFERENCES

Aguilar, E. (1995.) *Re-evaluation counseling: A "culturally competent" model for social liberation.* Seattle, WA: Rational Island Publishers.
Baker, S. & McKay, E. A. (2001). Occupational therapists' perspectives of the needs of women in medium secure units. *British Journal of Occupational Therapy, 64,* 441-8.
Benham, P. K. (1988). Attitudes of occupational therapy personnel toward persons with disabilities. *American Journal of Occupational Therapy, 42,* 305-11.

Black, R. M. (2002). Occupational therapy's dance with diversity. *American Journal of Occupational Therapy, 56,* 140-147.

Brown, C. R. & Mazza, G. J. (1991). Peer training strategies for welcoming diversity. In J. Dalton (Ed.), *Racism on campus: Confronting racial bias through peer interventions* (pp. 39-51). San Francisco, CA: Jossey-Bass.

Brown, C. R. (1992, August). National Coalition Building Institute Leadership Training Institute, Washington, DC.

Cena, L., McGruder, J. & Tomlin G. (2002). Representations of race, ethnicity, and social class in case examples in the *American Journal of Occupational Therapy*. *American Journal of Occupational Therapy, 56,* 130-9.

Davis, C. M. (1988). *Patient practitioner interaction: An experiential manual for developing the art of health care.* Thorofare, NJ: SLACK.

Eberhardt, K. & Mayberry, W. (1995). Factors influencing entry-level occupational therapists' attitudes toward persons with disabilities. *American Journal of Occupational Therapy, 49,* 629-36.

Elliott, D. L., Hanzlik, J. R. & Gliner, J. A. (1992). Attitudes of occupational therapy personnel toward therapists with disabilities. *Occupational Therapy Journal of Research, 12,* 259-77.

Evans, J. (1992a). What occupational therapists can do to eliminate racial barriers to health care access. *American Journal of Occupational Therapy, 46,* 679-83.

Evans, J. (Ed.) (1992b). Special issue on cross-cultural perspectives in occupational therapy. *American Journal of Occupational Therapy, 46,* 676-766.

Farrar, J. E. (2001). Addressing spirituality and religious life in occupational therapy practice. *Physical & Occupational Therapy in Geriatrics, 18,* 65-85.

Foster-Harrison, E. S. (1994). *More energizers and icebreakers.* Minneapolis, MN: Educational Media.

Froehlich, J., Hamlin, R. B., Loukas, K. M. & MacRae, N. (Ed.). (1992). Special issue on feminism as an inclusive perspective. *American Journal of Occupational Therapy, 4,* 967-1044.

Froehlich, J. (1992). The issue is: Proud and visible as occupational therapists. *American Journal of Occupational Therapy, 4,* 1042-1044.

Gibbs, K. E. & Barnitt, R. (1999). Occupational therapy and the self-care needs of Hindu elders. *British Journal of Occupational Therapy, 62,* 100-6.

Humphry, R. (1995). Families who live in chronic poverty: Meeting the challenge of family-centered services. *American Journal of Occupational Therapy, 49,* 687-93.

Jackins, H. (1981). *The art of listening.* Seattle, WA: Rational Island Publications.

Jackins, H. (1994). *The human side of human beings.* Seattle, WA: Rational Island Publications.

Jackson, J. (1995). Sexual orientation: Its relevance to occupational science and the practice of occupational therapy. *American Journal of Occupational Therapy, 49,* 669-79.

Jongbloed, L. (1998). Disability income: The experiences of women with multiple sclerosis. *Canadian Journal of Occupational Therapy, 65,* 193-201.

Kelly, J. (2000). Sexual orientation and occupational behavior. *British Journal of Occupational Therapy, 63,* 505.

Kreps, G. L. & Kunimoto, E. N. (1994). *Effective communication in multicultural health care settings.* Thousand Oaks, CA: Sage Publications.

Letvak, S. (2002). Myths and realities of ageism and nursing. *Association of Operating Room Nurses, 75,* 1101-1107.

Low, J. F. (1997). Religious orientation and pain management. *American Journal of Occupational Therapy, 51,* 215-9.

MacDonald, J. (1998). What is cultural competency? *British Journal of Occupational Therapy, 61,* 325-328.

Matlala, M. R. (1993). Race relations at work: A challenge to occupational therapy. *British Journal of Occupational Therapy, 56,* 434-6.

McIntosh, P. (1989, July/August). White privilege: Unpacking the invisible knapsack. *Peace and Freedom,* 10-12.

Parish, J., Carr, D., Suwinski, M. & Rees, C. (1990). Undressing the facts: The problems encountered by male occupational therapists. *British Journal of Occupational Therapy, 53,* 67-70.

Rothenberg, P. S. (Ed.) (1998). *Race, class and gender in the United States: An integrated study* (4th ed.). New York: St. Martin's Press.

Schwartzberg, S. (2002). *Interactive reasoning in the practice of occupational therapy.* Upper Saddle River, NJ: Prentice Hall.

Townsend, E. (Ed.) (1997). *Enabling occupation: An occupational therapy perspective.* Ottawa, Ontario: Canadian Association of Occupational Therapists.

Wells, S. A. & Black, R. M. (2000). *Cultural competency for health professionals.* Bethesda, MD: The American Occupational Therapy Association.

White, M. J. & Olson, R. S. (1998). Attitudes toward people with disabilities: A comparison of rehabilitation nurses, occupational therapists, and physical therapists. *Rehabilitation Nursing, 23,* 126-31.

Williamson, P. (2000). Football and tin cans: A model of identity formation based on sexual orientation expressed through engagement in occupations. *British Journal of Occupational Therapy, 63,* 432-9.

Zeuschner, R. (2003). *Communicating today: The essentials.* Boston: Pearson Education.

APPENDIX A
QUESTIONS TO FACILITATE DIALOGUES ON DIVERSITY

Questions to Facilitate Sharing Life Stories

1. What are some pleasant childhood memories?
2. What are some pleasant adolescent memories?
3. What are some pleasant memories from young adulthood?
4. What are some pleasant memories from middle-aged adulthood (for the nontraditional learner)?
5. Tell me (us) about something that was challenging in your past.
6. Tell me (us) about something that currently is challenging.

Questions for Dialogue on Gender

1. What do you like about being female or male?
2. What is difficult about being female or male?
3. Describe for me something that you do not like about your gender.
4. How can people of the other gender be better allies to you?

Questions for Dialogue on Sexual Orientation

1. What attitudes about sex were communicated to you in your family?
2. What attitudes about sex were communicated to you in grade school?
3. What attitudes about sex were communicated to you in your church, synagogue, or mosque?
4. What attitudes about sex were communicated to you on the streets in your neighborhood?
5. Share your experiences with persons who are gay, lesbian, bisexual, or transgendered. (Occasionally, a student uses the communication seminar as an opportunity to come out. Remind the group that a minimum of 10% of the population is gay, lesbian, bisexual, or transgendered [Brown, 1992] and to avoid making assumptions about persons they meet.)
6. Describe the reasons you feel comfortable being someone of your sexual orientation.
7. Describe the challenges in being someone of your sexual orientation.

Questions for Dialogues on Disability

1. Talk about a disability you currently may have or one that you had in the past, describing positive and challenging aspects of having that disability.
2. Talk about your experiences, both positive and challenging, interacting with persons with disabilities.
3. What disability would be the most challenging for you to have and why?

Questions for Dialogues on Ageism

1. Have you ever felt mistreated for being a particular age? If yes, describe the experience and how you handled the situation.
2. Think about your experiences with elders and answer:
   a. What are your concerns about growing older?
   b. How would you like to be treated when you are an elder?

Questions for Dialogues on Religion

1. Describe your religious heritage and current practices.
2. What are the strengths of your religious background?
3. Tell me (us) about current or past hardships or challenges in your religious background.
4. What do you want to know about religions different than your own?

Questions for Dialogues on Ethnicity and Culture

1. Share about an object from your culture.
2. What is your ethnic or cultural background?
3. What is important to you about your ethnic or cultural background?
4. What are some challenges of belonging to your ethnic or cultural background?
5. Why did you or your ancestors come to the United States?
6. What makes you proud to be an American?
7. How would you like the United States to be different?

Questions for Dialogues on Class Background

1. Describe your thoughts about discussing the socioeconomic status of your family. E.g., are you comfortable discussing this topic?
2. Describe your class background, including the educational level of your parents and grandparents and what type of work they did.
3. Did your family have enough, more than enough, or less than enough financial resources?
4. Did your family's financial resources fluctuate?
5. What is positive about belonging to your class background?
6. What is challenging about belonging to your class background?

Questions for Dialogues on Race

Listening partnerships can assist white persons and persons of color to reevaluate their experiences with persons of the same race and of a different race. A helpful technique is to cluster white students together and students of color together to address the following questions before reporting back to the group. If only one person is white or one person is of color (from one particular race), partner that person with someone of his or her choice.

1. What are your earliest memories of noticing people of different races?
2. Describe your relationships with persons of different races.
3. Describe how has racism affected you.
4. How would you like the world to be different in terms of race?

This sampling of dialogue questions has been useful in fostering communication about diversity. Dialogue questions can be supplemented with a variety of communication exercises related to verbal and nonverbal communication skills, active listening, self-awareness, values exploration, assertiveness, and conflict resolution.

APPENDIX B
GROUND RULES

1. Each student avoids speaking twice before others have had the opportunity to speak once; students are free to pass on taking their turn to speak, however.
2. No one speaker monopolizes the time; the goal is shared equal time.
3. Only one person speaks at a time.
4. Take risks when speaking.
5. Take risks when actively listening.
6. Each person takes responsibility for ensuring that the group runs smoothly.
7. If someone says something of interest in a listening partnership or group, and you want to know more at a later time, ask this person if reopening the discussion is something he or she would be comfortable doing.
8. Honor confidentiality. Two rules of confidentiality are useful. First, the information shared during listening partnerships and group discussions must be kept confidential when outside that pair or group. Second, group members can explain the content of conversations without using names; however, when referring to something someone shared in a listening partnership or group, permission to do so must be gotten first.

How Does One Develop and Document the Skills Needed to Assume a Deanship in Higher Education?

Senior leadership positions in higher education generally require evidence of demonstrated success in mid-level academic administration, a knowledge of the principal issues influencing governance in universities, a working knowledge of public relations and fundraising, and the ability to transcend one's current discipline and look objectively at the needs of an academic unit serving many disciplines in relation to the institution at large. It is useful to elaborate on each of these requirements in more detail.

First, a viable candidate for a deanship must generally show evidence of demonstrated ability at the administrative level just below the position being sought. For a dean, this would most often mean serving as a successful academic unit head, either as a chairperson of an academic department or as a director of a program. Success would be measured by such factors as years of experience (usually completing at least one typical term of service, 3-5 years) and other measures of administrative effectiveness, such as meeting enroll-

[Haworth co-indexing entry note]: "How Does One Develop and Document the Skills Needed to Assume a Deanship in Higher Education?" Christiansen, Charles et al. Co-published simultaneously in *Occupational Therapy in Health Care* (The Haworth Press, Inc.) Vol. 18, No. 1/2, 2004, pp. 185-197; and: *Best Practices in Occupational Therapy Education* (ed: Patricia A. Crist, and Marjorie E. Scaffa) The Haworth Press, Inc., 2004, pp. 185-197. Single or multiple copies of this article are available for a fee from The Haworth Document Delivery Service [1-800-HAWORTH, 9:00 a.m. - 5:00 p.m. (EST). E-mail address: docdelivery@haworthpress.com].

Digital Object Identifier:10.1300/J003v18n01_17   *185*

ment targets, maintaining accreditation standards, demonstrating prudent fiscal stewardship by identifying sources of revenue and staying within budget, and maintaining good relationships with students, faculty and members of the academic and surrounding community. Universities hate negative publicity, and for this reason avoidance of conflict and controversy are necessary for building a reputation as a credible administrator.

A second important qualification is having and demonstrating a working knowledge of the principal issues influencing governance and higher education in one's region. Authority is typically delegated from boards of trustees or regents, who are usually prominent non-academic people charged with giving strategic direction to a university. Student groups, faculty unions and associations and/or university senates are other important governance groups. Each advocates for a different population and agenda. In public universities, other key groups who influence decision-making include the legislature and its higher education committees and, often, agencies charged to coordinate or oversee higher education. A skillful university administrator will recognize the current interests and positions of these groups and plan strategically with this information in mind. For example, there is not much point in proposing certain new programs if an agency or group with power is known to be opposed to expansion generally or in the specific areas being advocated. Effectiveness requires good political timing when proposing change and new initiatives.

Another essential qualification for a dean (or other senior academic administrator) is having a working knowledge of public relations and fundraising. Every university, public or private, depends greatly on philanthropy to secure its future and permit it to have the operating reserves necessary for new program development and maintaining excellence. Fund-raising is a time and labor-intensive undertaking and potential gifts from donors are always at various stages of evolution. Universities cultivate friends (whether prominent members of the community and/or alumni) through sustained involvement, interaction, and careful solicitation. While academic unit heads should involve themselves in these activities, it is essential for deans, vice-presidents and presidents to make advancement (as fundraising is called) one of their most important activities. Every interaction with a student, alumni or member of the community represents a potential investment in cultivating goodwill and later gift-giving. These gifts often constitute the resources necessary for creating programs of excellence such as scholarships, endowed faculty positions, and gifts for capital (building) expansion.

Finally, the ability to transcend one's current discipline and academic allegiance is critical to success at senior administrative levels. Deans typically become part of the senior management team, and as such they are expected to grant their allegiance to the overall missions of the institution. This is where team play and win-win attitudes are tested. The successful dean must often put aside parochial interests and recognize that a rising tide lifts all ships. Thus, if the institution benefits, each of its components will also benefit, since the greater reputation of the university is shared by all of its units. In a similar way, a dean cannot effectively lead without putting aside her or his disciplinary affiliations. Failure to do this will lead to perceptions of favoritism and diminish organizational morale. Leaders are expected to be fair and impartial, making their decisions based on an objective consideration of what's best for the organization and the university. If deans are perceived as biased in their decision-making, their credibility becomes questioned both by the faculty they serve as well as the administrative leadership to whom they report. It is not enough for one to think objectively; an administrator must be *perceived* by the college or school as a person who transcends personal interest.

Certainly, an effective dean is a good communicator and possesses other qualifications and skills not mentioned above. But, the necessary and important competencies described above constitute an important foundation. It is clear that an administrator who aspires to assume greater responsibility in a university must document success over time by gaining credibility with peers, co-workers and university leadership. Setting goals that address important agendas in the institution and region is an important first step; while meeting them year after year is a necessary sequel. Perhaps the most important credential is that of having had effective and cordial working relationships with all constituencies, whether they are faculty, students, the public, or other administrators, since these interactions over time constitute the most effective documentation of readiness for greater responsibility–a reputation that one is competent and trustworthy.

Charles Christiansen, EdD, OTR, OT(C), FAOTA
George T. Bryan Distinguished Professor and Dean
School of Allied Health Sciences
The University of Texas Medical Branch at Galveston
301 University Ave.
Galveston, TX 77551

TRAJECTORY TOWARDS THE STRANGE ATTRACTOR
OF ACADEMIC ADMINISTRATION:
TOP TEN VECTORS FOR PLOTTING

After being invited to submit this short paper, I spent considerable time pondering what to write in response to the editors' request to share recommendations for an occupational therapist interested in academic administration, be it at the level of chairperson or dean. A review of the recent literature in this area was relatively scant, but did provide important information (Wolverton, Gmelch, Montez, & Nies, 2001):

- The majority of deans have been associate or assistant deans prior to becoming deans;
- The culture of deans, overall, is based upon white, middle-aged males, and;
- The majority of deans have a strong track record of scholarship.

Given these findings from the literature, I continued to ponder what would be important to share with those interested in pursuing academic administration. While attending a conference on complexity science,[1] it became clear to me that anyone interested in the journey or trajectory towards academic administration would benefit from knowledge about the vectors or ways to prepare for or direct towards academic administration.

Thus, the remainder of this short paper presents my view of what vectors or forces should be explored by those wishing to embark upon this path, based upon my judgment and personal experience in this trajectory. I call these "ten vectors for plotting" to engage in academic administration, and they follow:

Vector 1.   *Communicate*: Develop a key network of individuals who have influence in your system. Regularly engage in informal communication with them on a personal level and also use the interaction to share your thoughts about directions or actions you would like the system to undertake; this is what good managers do (Kotter, 1990).

Vector 2.   *Develop*: Consider yourself a work in progress, always reaching for more development, but never finished and never perfect. Grow a skill set that all administrators need such as time management, effective business writing, paper and e-mail management and control, and delegation of administrative tasks (Oakley & Krug, 1991).

Vector 3.   *Depersonalize*: Practice the art of taking feedback in a calm and accepting manner, and learn not to take anything personally or emotionally. Without such an ability or filter, no one can survive administration of any sort.

Vector 4. *Enjoy*: Find and discover the joy possible in interacting with or working with every person in your program or school (Ward, 2002). Every interaction with every person has this potential. It is up to you to uncover it!

Vector 5. *Learn*: The new science of complexity is essential for anyone in management and administration. Learn all that you can about it.[1]

Vector 6. *Match*: Always think in terms of matching a person and the job to be done. Do not think in terms of how to remediate areas of concern in an individual. Think in terms of how to match their strengths to whatever task needs to be accomplished.

Vector 7. *Manage*: Learn and master the art of running an efficient meeting (Tropman, 1996).

Vector 8. *Model*: Find a model–be it a chair (not necessarily in occupational therapy) or a dean (not necessarily in health care). Study how they do what they do. Determine what works. Model their ways and methods.

Vector 9. *Scholarship*: Be relentless in your path of scholarship! This is *critical* for your credibility within academia, as well as your own personal salvation from administration. Read about newer forms of scholarship (Glassick, Huber, & Maeroff, 1997).

Vector 10. *Read*: Use Eleanor Clarke Slagle's "habit training" and develop a habit of reading something each day related to your trajectory towards academic administration. Ten readings that I personally recommend are:

1. DeZure, D. (Ed.) (2000). *Learning from change: Landmarks in teaching and learning in higher education from Change Magazine, 1969-1999.* Sterling, VA: AAHE.
2. Gmelch, W. H., & Miskin, V. D. (1995). *Chairing an academic department* (Vol. 15). Thousand Oaks, CA: Sage Publications.
3. Gmelch, W. H. (1993). *Coping with faculty stress* (Vol. 5). Thousand Oaks, CA: Sage Publications.
4. Lucas, A. F., & Associates (2000). *Leading academic change: Essential roles for department chairs.* New York: Jossey-Bass.
5. Knowles, R. N. (2002). *The leadership dance.* Niagara Falls, NY: The Center for Self-Organized Leadership.
6. Eoyang, G. H. (1997). *Coping with chaos: Seven simple principles.* Circle Pines, MN: Lagumo.
7. Wheatley, M. J. (1999). *Leadership and the new science: Discovering order in a chaotic world.* San Francisco: Berret-Koehler Publications.

8. Weick, K. E., & Sutcliff, K. M. (2001). *Managing the unexpected: Assuring high performance in an age of complexity.* San Francisco: Jossey-Bass.
9. Holland, T. (1998). *Emergence: From chaos to order.* Cambridge, MA: Perseus Books.
10. Ward, K. (2002). A vision for tomorrow: Transformational nursing leaders. *Nursing Outlook, 50*(3), 121-126.

Beyond these ten vectors presented to plot your trajectory and your readings, remember the virtues of humor, faith and courage.

Charlotte Brasic Royeen, PhD, OTR, FAOTA
Dean, Margaret and Edward Doisey
School of Allied Health Professions
Saint Louis University
3437 Carolina Street
Saint Louis, MO 63104

NOTE

1. "Complexity Science in Practice: Understanding and Acting to Improve Health and Health Care." Mayo Clinic, Rochester, Minnesota, March 20-22, 2003.

REFERENCES

Glassick, C. E., Huber, M. T., & Maeroff, G. I. (1997). *Scholarship assessed. Evaluation of the professoriate.* San Francisco, CA: Jossey-Bass.
Kotter, J. P. (1990). What leaders really do. *Harvard Business Review, May-June* (No. 3820).
Oakley, E., & Krug, D. (1991). *Enlightened leadership. Getting to the heart of change.* New York, NY: Fireside.
Tropman, J. E. (1996). *Making meetings work. Achieving high quality group decisions.* Thousand Oaks, CA: Sage Publications.
Ward, K. (2002). A vision for tomorrow: Transformational nursing leaders. *Nursing Outlook, 50* (3), 121-126.
Wolverton, M., Gmelch, W. H., Montez, J., & Nies, C. T. (2001). *The changing nature of the academic deanship* (Vol. 28). San Francisco, CA: Jossey-Bass.

ACADEMIC MANAGEMENT: A PERSONAL PERSPECTIVE

My assumptions about academic administration have changed drastically since 1998 when I was appointed to the role of Dean. I had been a Chair for 12 years serving in two different institutions and had an affinity for the role. I often described my responsibilities as a delicate balancing act, where you "led among peers" (Tucker, 1986). Others use the analogy of "herding cats" because of the autonomous and diverse views of faculty. It was the nature of this tension, the conflicting and delicate pull of responsibilities, that interested me. In one day one could be expected to lead, facilitate, coach, mentor and perform faculty tasks like research and teaching. Other chairs shared this excitement at AOTA semi-annual COE Program Director meetings. This group shared information and discussions about Workload, ACOTE scores, ADA, research, tenure and teaching methods. The meetings were lively and crammed with creative ideas that I could implement.

Frankly, I never thought much about being a dean until the opportunity presented. My academic background is deep and varied. When I was asked to serve as Interim Dean, I knew that I was prepared for the role and felt a rush of anticipation but consulted with other deans to make sure that the role would suit my background and personality. Reference materials helped clarify what I was getting into. The most succinct starting point was a series of four questions formulated for individuals who think that they want to become a dean (Tucker and Bryan, 1991):

1. What is your experience in academic administration? Do you know the way that universities and colleges operate? Does this excite and interest you? (p. 8)
2. Do you have the patience to work through issues in a slow-moving hierarchy to achieve your goals? (p. 9)
3. Are you able to receive "raw and unfiltered, occasionally even mean-spirited and vicious" criticism? (Ibid.)
4. Can you make decisions–hard ones regarding people, space and resources–based on the needs of the organization?

I answered these questions and determined that my years of academic experiences, visits to other universities, national and state leadership all provided a background to take on this new role. These questions were also useful when thinking about the similarities and differences between the role of chair and dean. The biggest change for most is the move from a specialized area of teaching and research into the amorphous world of administration where decisions must benefit the university rather than a single individual or profession. To me, this is analogous to a family vs. an organizational perspective.

The second biggest change is the loss of control over scheduling your time. Where a faculty member balances teaching, research and service, a chair adds management to all of the former tasks, and a dean manages these tasks and considers how all the pieces fit together. The dean links the college and department missions and goals to the needs of the entire university and community. Instead of learning more about a focused area of research and teaching, one learns about other professions and majors, budgets, credit hour costs, policies and procedures, legal issues, and external demands on the university.

As a chair, I could garner my dean's support and determine when I would teach, do research, and perform service. I remember taking several days a week to finish a grant application or attend an important AOTA event. In contrast, deans' time-use is determined externally by university, college and community commitments. What does that mean? There is little discretionary time in the calendar. For example, in our institution, deans have a minimum of 8-10 hours of standing meetings per week. This is not true in all institutions but as part of a management team, participation and thoughtful input are essential. Most deans have other demands such as evening events and community organization meetings where they represent the College or University.

Which brings us to the third change, separation from one's professional colleagues. After a few years, one can feel estranged from one's profession. Research in one's area of interest is trumped by management literature on topics such as documentation for problem employees, regulations and legal issues, strategic planning methods and ideas for development and alumnae relations.

Why do I love the dean role now? It requires small-group and one-on-one teaching with faculty, students, staff, deans, administrators, vice-presidents and trustees. There are periodic meetings with the President and service on taskforces, strategic planning and follow-up committees. Short-term feedback is usually absent and one must seek internal and external benchmarks to measure achievements. It is rare to get overt feedback from busy faculty who have more immediate issues on their minds.

The tools deans use to reach long-term gains are effective listening and objective decision-making. Both tools must be grounded in university rather than individual, department, profession or a major's needs. At times, one can creatively combine several needs to satisfy more than one request. On the other hand, there are times when no compromise is possible, and a choice must be made. The choice may not be well-received by faculty and students.

This is why deans think about the political ramifications of their decisions and the interrelationships among departments and colleges. Where the chair voice is personal and family-like, the dean perspective is best when objective and managerial. This means there is a distance between faculty and administration. Faculty may wonder why the academy needs any academic administrators–with the exception of payroll (Fish, 2003).

Digging deeper, my clinical training, knowledge of occupation and task performance have informed my behavior as a dean. Group dynamics, interpretation of verbal and non-verbal communication, and the ability to articulate hope and a vision of future growth and development are helpful skills. Listening, understanding a problem in context, using qualitative and quantitative data to analyze information, designing small, manageable steps to attain successful outcomes, and judging when to push for a dramatic shift in direction are important also.

Finally, I also would like to mention the importance of managing stress because a talented dean should not react to emotion but encourage thought about why the emotion is present. Seasoned administrators think about when and how to communicate information even if unpleasant. The goal of interaction is to listen, learn and promote reflection in the person or group. I have learned to ask a lot more questions. These questions are not pointed and antagonistic but reflective and quizzical. For example, if a faculty member comes in to complain about his or her supervisor, a dean might ask for background information. This simple question might take the individual more than an hour to describe. After listening and jotting down notes, one might check to make sure if one's understanding is complete and then ask, "why do you think you are in the present situation?" "How would you resolve the situation?" I have seen individuals thoughtfully ponder their situation and offer creative solutions. If not, it is the dean's responsibility to foster a resolution that works for both parties. Guiding positive interaction rather than negative stances is a teaching method.

On the other hand, there are times when a direct approach is required. This type of active management may be welcomed or condoned. Thus, there are tacit smiles around dean groups when someone mentions that this or that action will not be applauded. The ability to be flexible but strong in the face of adversity is another facet of the position. All part of a day's work. I find comfort in the adage that it is the journey that is important, not just getting there.

SUGGESTED READINGS

Austin, MJ, Ahearn, FA, and English, RA (1997) *The professional school dean: Meeting leadership challenges.* San Francisco: Jossey-Bass Publisher.

Bergquest, WH (1992) *The four cultures of the academy: Insights and strategies for improving leadership in collegiate organizations.* San Francisco: Jossey-Bass Publisher.

Fish, S (April 4. 2003) Point of view: First, kill all the administrators. *The Chronicle of Higher Education*, p. B20.

Tucker, A and Bryan, RA (1991) *The academic dean: Dove, dragon, and diplomat.* New York: American Council on Education, Macmillan Publishing Company.

The Journal of Higher Education (ISSN 0022-1546) published bimonthly by Ohio State University Press, 1070 Carmack Road, Columbus, OH 43210-1002.

Ruth L. Schemm, EdD, OTR/L, FAOTA
Dean, College of Health Sciences
University of the Sciences in Philadelphia

THE OCCUPATIONAL THERAPIST AS ACADEMIC DEAN

Becoming a dean has not been a common career aspiration for occupational therapists, who primarily choose the profession for its clinical service-related aspects, or even for occupational therapy educators who invest so powerfully in the education of future occupational therapists. However, the philosophy, content areas, and skill-base of occupational therapy are elements that fit well with the requirements of the dean role as this role is one that has a key focus on maximizing occupational performance in others. The dean is responsible for a multitude of activities that maximize occupational performance via supporting faculty, staff, and student development and learning.

In addition to the expertise in facilitating occupational performance that occupational therapists bring to a dean position, many occupational therapy skills and areas of knowledge are valuable in the day-to-day roles of a dean. The ability to analyze tasks and processes is used in problem-solving and development of new initiatives as well as in completing tasks while attending to process, but not allowing process to unnecessarily interfere with task completion. Knowledge of group dynamics is an excellent foundation for leadership of a college, leadership of and membership on committees, and mentoring of others regarding group dynamic issues within committees or departments.

Knowledge of human development, including occupation across the life span, is very helpful in understanding why certain student, faculty, and staff issues arise. The occupational therapist's view about the physical environment and its impact on human functioning also can be a valuable perspective to share with others in selection of environments for specific activities and modification/renovation of environments to enhance human performance. In addition, the occupational therapist's knowledge base in issues associated with disabilities and health care in general are valued resources in representing the college to other groups on and off campus.

For most occupational therapists, becoming an educator and certainly becoming a dean have been more of a matter of circumstances in which there is a fit between knowledge/skills/experiences acquired and the opportunity arising to use one's knowledge/skills/experiences in an academic administrative role, rather than a specific life plan. However, if an occupational therapist aspires to become a dean, especially in the area of health professions, several types of experiences provide an excellent foundation. In applying for a dean position, these experiences can be framed to illustrate the fit with various components of the dean role. These include:

1. *Strong clinical experiences in a variety of practice settings.* Client/patient experiences provide the basis for deeply understanding why we are invested in assuring a high-quality education for students who will be future professionals and colleagues. These experiences serve as a reference point for understanding what students need to learn in content, in skills, and in professionalism. They also support an understanding of the culture and values of health care organizations, which may differ from academic institutions. Appreciating the culture of these organizations provides a foundation for discussions of academic-clinical collaborative arrangements.

2. *Experiences working with interdisciplinary teams in which all team members are valued for their important contributions in addressing client needs.* These experiences allow the prospective dean to become familiar with the values, perspectives, knowledge and skills of other disciplines that are likely to be in a college of health professions. The experience with teamwork is crucial for leading, supporting the leadership of, and being a member of a variety of committees and work groups made up of individuals from different disciplinary backgrounds.

3. *Experiences as a clinical educator.* These are valuable in appreciating the perspective of the clinical educator–and why good academic performance does not always predict good clinical performance. Such experiences insure a clinical perspective in handling issues with students who do not display the clinical skills necessary for program completion, despite success in the classroom. They also are valuable in understanding

the clinical contract process and institutional review board issues from the viewpoint of those in the clinical setting.

4. *Substantial and varied academic teaching experiences.* These provide the prospective dean with a foundation to draw upon to illustrate a powerful investment in high-quality teaching. Such experiences must be sufficiently broad in variety and sustained enough to engender the credibility necessary for the dean role. Such variety could be achieved through a mix of the following options: part-time and full-time teaching; undergraduate and graduate teaching; didactic, laboratory, and clinical teaching; undergraduate and graduate research and supervision; student advising at different academic levels. These experiences allow the dean to appreciate the lived experiences of the faculty member with course preparation, classroom facility challenges, technology applications in the teaching-learning process, grading issues, academic integrity issues, and student performance variability.

5. *Attainment of the rank of Professor.* This rank is often required and always desirable. It indicates to others a record of outstanding teaching and advising, sustained high-quality involvement in scholarship (with peer recognition of one's work), and service internal to the University as well as externally in the community and/or within the profession. Scholarship activities allow for definition of problems, development of plans for qualitative and quantitative data collection, analysis of various types of data, and development of recommendations; all of these skills are needed by deans in a host of administrative projects and in the evaluation of faculty scholarship. Service activities increase the understanding of various units on the campus and the role of shared governance in curriculum, faculty development, and academic policies. Variety in these types of activities allows for different leadership opportunities and contributions to projects that affect the academic environment. Demonstrating the ability to conceive an innovative project and see the project through to completion, including working with others in the process and despite obstacles, is a valuable skill for a prospective dean. Such projects are excellent examples of one's leadership skills and can be highlighted in the application and interview process.

6. *A role in academic administration.* This is vital for almost all dean positions; it provides evidence of academic administrative credibility. An administrative role should include program-specific or department-specific activities and have faculty and staff evaluation components as well as budgetary responsibility. In addition, it should allow for assumption of responsibilities outside the department that illustrate the ability to take on a broader perspective than one's own discipline. These activities provide the opportunity to demonstrate leadership to others, many of whom can become excellent references when seeking a dean position.

For the occupational therapist educator who wishes to consider a dean position, recognizing the professional impact of the shift in perspective from being an occupational therapist to being a dean who represents multiple disciplines is very important in the decision-making process. As an occupational therapy educator, one focuses primarily on the importance and value of occupational therapy and advocates for the profession via a high level of professional activity and direct involvement in the education of occupational therapists. In contrast, the dean typically does not have ongoing, sustained involvement with specific students, faculty, or the profession. The dean's involvement is broader and more policy-related, rather than focused on a single discipline. Connections with the profession are possible, but are more difficult to sustain at a high level.

However, while a shift in perspective may be the greatest challenge for the occupational therapist considering a dean position, this shift in perspective must occur for a dean to be a powerful advocate for all disciplines in the college. This shift is more easily accomplished if one has been involved in meaningful interdisciplinary work. It cannot occur unless one can sincerely take on the perspective that disciplines other than occupational therapy are absolutely vital to the highest quality of health care possible, and thus, the education of future professionals in these disciplines is as important as the education of future occupational therapists.

If the occupational therapist holds this perspective, the dean position becomes an outstanding way to contribute to the quality of health care delivered in two key ways: (1) via education of students and (2) via faculty scholarship in support of high-quality health care and health care education. The dean position inherently enhances access to resources and people and provides abundant opportunities to facilitate key initiatives. The interdisciplinary nature of the position is exciting; valuing the diversity of professions allows the dean to create opportunities that support interdisciplinary education of students and scholarship-service projects and activities that enhance the community and meet health care needs. The dean has the opportunity to personify the values of the health professions in representing the college to the university, to the community, and beyond. In this process, the occupational therapist as dean has the opportunity to use her/his grounding in occupational therapy principles to affect the university in innovative and important ways and to influence the quality of education for a broad range of students. The dean position can be an outstanding vehicle for implementing the values of occupational therapy in a university setting to benefit a large number of individuals and systems on the campus, in the community, and through work in the various professional organizations.

Charlotte E. Exner, PhD, OTR/L, FAOTA
Dean, College of Health Professions
Towson University

What Does the Move
to Master's Level Education
for the Occupational Therapist
Mean for Occupational Therapy Assistant
Education?

By 2007, all students entering the professional level of occupational therapy practice will have earned a Master's Degree. This, combined with other initiatives guiding health care and occupational therapy (OT) are aligning to guide us into a promising future:

- The Accreditation Council for Occupational Therapy Education Standards, which were implemented in July 2000, demand a higher level of information literacy, critical thinking, research competency, and management skills than were the requisite under the Essentials. The Standards are grounded with concepts of occupation that were absent from the previous Essentials for OT and OTA (Occupational Therapy Assistant) Education. As curricula at both levels thread these concepts and professional ideals throughout their designs, they will educate professionals who can lead significant change and proactively redirect the recycled errors of our past.
- The profession has now established the *Framework for Occupational Therapy: Domain and Process* as a guide for education and practice.

[Haworth co-indexing entry note]: "What Does the Move to Master's Level Education for the Occupational Therapist Mean for Occupational Therapy Assistant Education ?" Natell, Barbara J. et al. Co-published simultaneously in *Occupational Therapy in Health Care* (The Haworth Press, Inc.) Vol. 18, No. 1/2, 2004, pp. 199-205; and: *Best Practices in Occupational Therapy Education* (ed: Patricia A. Crist, and Marjorie E. Scaffa) The Haworth Press, Inc., 2004, pp. 199-205. Single or multiple copies of this article are available for a fee from The Haworth Document Delivery Service [1-800-HAWORTH, 9:00 a.m. - 5:00 p.m. (EST). E-mail address: docdelivery@haworthpress.com].

http://www.haworthpress.com/web/OTHC
Digital Object Identifier:10.1300/J003v18n01_18

This is a tool that offers a clear foundation in the tenets and application of occupation and client-centered care.

- Language recently adopted by the World Health Organization examines participation in roles and activity as a determiner of health and wellness. This can act as a catalyst for our promotion of OT philosophies and tenets. The alignment of this language with the terminology in the Framework will allow parties of interest to more readily understand the constructs of occupation-based practice.

The synergy of these recent developments can be a catalyst for a shift in paradigm in health care from a focus on disease and a reductionistic model of health care, to a model that will promote the more holistic perspectives of health and wellness that are the paradigm of occupational therapy. It seems to me that the stars are in alignment! It is time for occupational therapy to shine! With a shared vision of a continuum of education for future practitioners, it is possible for all levels of education to support the future of practice that will finally step out of the adolescent identity crisis we have been in for decades. Rather than be led reactively by values inherent in the medical model, we can proactively establish our rightful place as contributors to best practice in a collaborative model of health care delivery.

A Position Paper published by the Commission on Education in March 2002 was titled, "The Viability of Occupational Therapy Assistant Education." (1) This paper was generated by the expressed concern that technical level education was somehow at risk in the climate of change transitioning to the Master's Level. The definition of "viability" in the American Heritage Dictionary offers three variant perspectives of the word. The first states, "capable of success or continuing effectiveness." (2) I agree that Occupational Therapy Assistants, educated at the technical level, can continue to thrive and be effective contributors to the profession. ACOTE Standards do not dictate the degree earned from institutions. This is regulated by individual institutional prerogative. Rather, the Standards reflect criteria and outcomes that are the requisite for entry-level practice. Most OTA Programs currently offer a degree at the associate level. It matters not with what degree–Certificate, AAS, or AS, these accredited programs are successfully educating individuals who demonstrate competencies defined by Standards. The qualitative revisions required of curricula to comply with the 1998 Standards were successfully managed without significant quantitative changes in credit loads. It is unfortunate that these credits are often not recognized by transferability to professional level programs.

When examined side by side, the OTA Standards are more parallel and identical to the OT Standards than they are different. OTA Education is guided by ACOTE Standards that are parallel to those guiding professional level education.

Section B.2.0, *Basic Tenets of OT,* guides a greater breadth and depth of applied theory for OT education, however, the Standards that guide the paradigm of occupation-based practice are identical. The Standards demand identical processes for program evaluation and strategic planning. This ensures quality and development of curricula reflective of the current dynamics in practice. The variance in Standards is primarily the scope and breadth of identical criteria. Technical level education has been successful at meeting and exceeding their Standards. OTA practitioners are, therefore, excellent ambassadors of occupational therapy tenets and philosophy. In curricula, a primary objective is to guide students to "think and act like an OT." Success in this objective is inherent at all levels of OT education. At both levels, we have a shared vision and identity.

The second perspective on the dictionary definition of viability states "capable of living outside the uterus." (2) Sometimes, as an OTA educator, I have felt outside of the womb of the OT community. I have observed or been confronted with beliefs from individuals who speak and act as though the profession could only grow by nurturing practitioners who make contributions to its scholarly base. Technical education, viewed in this light, is considered "outside of the uterus." Although viable, the contributions of OTA Education would be more valuable if they could share a more symbiotic relationship with professional level practice and education. OTA Education, to truly thrive and productively contribute to the community of occupational therapy, does not need more credits of study. It needs to be accepted and valued as an integral part of the educational process. The fact that enough concern was raised to establish a Position Paper in regards to its viability, is evidence that we may not be operating from a shared vision that respects technical level education as a valued and effective part of the continuum of learning.

A third dictionary definition offers us keys to success for continued viability of OTA education: "capable of living, developing, or germinating under favorable conditions." (2) I do not believe it is in the best interest of the profession to question the viability of OTA education at the technical level. This is not evidence that conditions are favorable. As the AOTA Position paper articulates, technical programs attract a diverse student body to occupational tenets that may not otherwise be recruited to the community. Practitioners educated at the technical level can provide heath care systems a cost-effective and broader application of occupation-based service. (1) In the early 1950s, training of Assistants was initiated to allow the profession to grow into markets that were demanding service when the supply of OT practitioners was inefficient to support our growth. These individuals continue to assist the growth of the profession in this time of expansion into emerging areas that are inherent in the dynamics of current challenges and health care reform.

Enrichment of our scholarly base is certainly one factor that will ensure occupational therapy's viability in health care of the future. It is not, however, the best model for all valued practitioners to begin their educational process. The 1998 Standards outline a developmentally appropriate continuum that articulates outcomes that are the core concepts of all practitioners. These are the majority of Standards that are identical. They then articulate a progressively enhanced breadth and scope that are the requirements for practitioners who will assume supervisory roles, managerial roles, and offer service that is insightful to the needs for an enhanced scholarly base for the profession. The "favorable condition" required for viability of all levels of education, and for the future growth of occupational therapy, is a shared vision and mission, together with the acceptance of the value provided to the academy and to practice from those who meet technical level Standards in OT education.

Barbara J. Natell, MS, Ed, OTR/L
Director of Occupational Therapy Program
Pennsylvania College of Technology
One College Avenue
Williamsport, PA 17701

REFERENCES

AOTA Commission on Education. "Position Paper: The Viability of Occupational Therapy Assistant Education." *OT Practice,* April 10, 2000. Adopted by the Representative Assembly 2002M113.

The American Heritage Dictionary of the English Language. 4th Edition. Houghton Mifflin Company, New York, 2000.

OTA-OT PARTNERSHIPS: OFFERING EDUCATIONAL OPTIONS AND OPPORTUNITIES

We see the change to post-baccalaureate degree entry level for the occupational therapist as a renaissance for occupational therapy assistant (OTA) education. Although an OTA curriculum is typically not found in a comprehensive university that offers 55 undergraduate majors and 10 master's degrees, the University of Southern Indiana (USI) has an educational program for the occupational therapy assistant (initially accredited in 1998) as well as a program for the occupational therapist (initially accredited in 1993). As program directors, we have determined that the change in professional entry level has had a positive impact, which has effected a clearer demarcation between the types of practitioners, resulting in new options and opportunities for people who wish to enter the occupational therapy field.

The new demarcation between types of practitioner education is primarily a timing issue. Before the change in entry level for occupational therapists, USI offered a 4-year baccalaureate degree for people who wanted to be occupational therapists and a 2.5-year associate degree for those who desired to be occupational therapy assistants. (At USI, the OTA curriculum is approximately six months longer than expected because of the university's 25-credit general education requirement for all associate degrees.) Although OTA majors are eligible to begin practicing in less than three years, we found that because USI is a comprehensive university, more than half of the OTA graduates continued taking undergraduate courses to earn a bachelor's degree in health services (BHS), a completion program designed for students holding associate degrees in a professional field. Thus at commencement, OTA grads earning the BHS sat intermingled with occupational therapy majors who also earned a baccalaureate degree. The two types of practitioners earning a seemingly similar degree resulted in confusion in the university and the surrounding geographical area. With the entry-level change, the timing is clearly a 2.5-year versus a 5-year option. Even if OTA students opt for a baccalaureate completion program, there is a clear difference between a bachelor's and a master's degree.

The clear demarcation has resulted in new options and opportunities at all levels. At the student level, faculty who are cross-trained in recruiting and advising for both curricula can offer options that provide an optimal matching of student and program from the first advising session. Students who want to become occupational therapists, but have circumstances that require a faster option, have an opportunity to graduate from the OTA curriculum first, allowing them to enter the field and earn a good living while pursuing courses in the occupational therapist curriculum on a part-time basis. At the program level, these options and opportunities have positively effected improvements in student numbers, particularly in the OTA curriculum. The improved student numbers have in turn positively affected program budgets, which has resulted in additional equipment shared by both curricula. Indeed, the clear degree demarcation has allowed USI to realize the true OTA-OT partnership envisioned when the two educational programs were started. At the university level, the new opportunities offer a more suitable alignment with the university's mission statement of serving traditional and nontraditional students, and the options have improved student retention, especially if students begin as occupational therapy majors, but are more suited for the OTA curriculum.

To experience this rebirth of OTA education, we recommend that OTA curricula form partnerships with area occupational therapy programs. Within the partnership, faculty could become adept at advising and recruiting for both programs. The prospective student who inquires at either curriculum could be matched with the optimal program. Students who wish to enter the field more quickly could complete the OTA curriculum first. Finally, the occupational therapy major who is more suited for the OTA curriculum could easily transfer to a different program.

As occupational therapy educators, at USI, we are afforded the opportunity to continue with our goal of assisting our clients, who are our students, in achieving maximal occupational role performance by fitting the program to the individual.

Susan G. Ahmad, MS, OTR
OTA Program Director & Assistant Professor

Aimee J. Luebben, EdD, OTR, FAOTA
Program Director & Associate Professor of OT
University of Southern Indiana
8600 University Blvd.
Evansville, IN 47712

IMPLICATIONS OF THE MOVE TO MASTER'S LEVEL EDUCATION FOR THE OCCUPATIONAL THERAPIST AND FOR OCCUPATIONAL THERAPY ASSISTANT EDUCATION

The Occupational Therapy Assistant (OTA) educational process has progressed just as the Occupational Therapist (OT) educational process has advanced. If anything, the move to a master's level education for the OT has increased the content value and necessity of the two-year technical education for the OTA. Also, when considering the costs of education, occupational therapy education is enticing.

The two-year associate degree has also grown and developed with a greater depth of the education required to practice. This technical education focuses mainly on direct care skill development leading to excellent patient care. An OTA has good clinical reasoning and critical thinking skills, technical skills, and strong interpersonal relationship abilities for working with patients or clients of all ages, with a wide diversity of diagnosis. Additionally, they have the skills to participate collaboratively in innovative practice. Many community colleges have smaller class sizes and more direct student faculty contact than the larger colleges and universities, thus allowing high-quality practice skill development.

It takes more years and more educational funding to earn a master's degree. How many people can afford this greater educational cost? Meanwhile, the Certified Occupational Therapy Assistant (COTA) can earn an associate degree in a two-year community college, probably living at home, at a significantly lower cost.

In conclusion, from my observations of the COTAs currently in practice, there appears to be a new and increased demand for them. Therefore, just as the educational preparation for OTs extends, it behooves those of us in OTA education to continue to set high standards and goals for our students to meet the needs of the work environment today. Clearly, this change in entry for the OTs will ripple into opportunity for OTAs.

Martha Branson Banks, OTR
OTA Program Director
Bertrand Crossing
1905 Foundation Drive
Niles, MI 49120

Index

BOOK ORDER FORM!

Order a copy of this book with this form or online at:
http://www.haworthpress.com/store/product.asp?sku=5225

Best Practices in Occupational Therapy Education

___ in softbound at $24.95 (ISBN: 0-7890-2176-5)
___ in hardbound at $39.95 (ISBN: 0-7890-2175-7)

COST OF BOOKS _____

POSTAGE & HANDLING ....
US: $4.00 for first book & $1.50
for each additional book
Outside US: $5.00 for first book
& $2.00 for each additional book.

SUBTOTAL _____

In Canada: add 7% GST. _____

STATE TAX _____
CA, IL, IN, MN, NY, OH & SD residents
please add appropriate local sales tax.

FINAL TOTAL _____
If paying in Canadian funds, convert
using the current exchange rate,
UNESCO coupons welcome.

❑ **BILL ME LATER:**
Bill-me option is good on US/Canada/
Mexico orders only: not good to jobbers,
wholesalers, or subscription agencies.

❑ **Signature** _____

❑ **Payment Enclosed: $** _____

❑ **PLEASE CHARGE TO MY CREDIT CARD:**
❑ Visa ❑ MasterCard ❑ AmEx ❑ Discover
❑ Diner's Club ❑ Eurocard ❑ JCB

Account # _____

Exp Date _____

Signature _____
(Prices in US dollars and subject to change without notice.)

PLEASE PRINT ALL INFORMATION OR ATTACH YOUR BUSINESS CARD

Name

Address

City   State/Province   Zip/Postal Code

Country

Tel   Fax

E-Mail

May we use your e-mail address for confirmations and other types of information? ❑ Yes ❑ No We appreciate receiving
your e-mail address. Haworth would like to e-mail special discount offers to you, as a preferred customer.
We will never share, rent, or exchange your e-mail address. We regard such actions as an invasion of your privacy.

Order From Your **Local Bookstore** or Directly From
The Haworth Press, Inc. 10 Alice Street, Binghamton, New York 13904-1580 • USA
Call Our toll-free number (1-800-429-6784) / Outside US/Canada: (607) 722-5857
Fax: 1-800-895-0582 / Outside US/Canada: (607) 771-0012
E-mail your order to us: orders@haworthpress.com

For orders outside US and Canada, you may wish to order through your local
sales representative, distributor, or bookseller.
For information, see http://haworthpress.com/distributors

(Discounts are available for individual orders in US and Canada only, not booksellers/distributors.)

Please photocopy this form for your personal use.
www.HaworthPress.com

BOF04